Pleasing Myself

FRANK KERMODE

Pleasing Myself

FROM BEOWULF TO PHILIP ROTH

ALLEN LANE
THE PENGUIN PRESS

ALLEN LANE
THE PENGUIN PRESS
Published by the Penguin Group
Penguin Books Ltd, 27 Wrights Lane, London w8 5TZ, England
Penguin Putnam Inc., 375 Hudson Street, New York, New York 10014, USA
Penguin Books Australia Ltd, Ringwood, Victoria, Australia
Penguin Books Canada Ltd, 10 Alcorn Avenue, Toronto, Ontario, Canada M4V 3B2
Penguin Books India (P) Ltd, 11, Community Centre, Panchsheel Park, New Delhi – 110 017, India
Penguin Books (NZ) Ltd, Private Bag 102902, NSMC, Auckland, New Zealand
Penguin Books (South Africa) (Pty) Ltd, 5 Watkins Street, Denver Ext 4, Johannesburg 2094, South Africa

Penguin Books Ltd, Registered Offices: Harmondsworth, Middlesex, England

First published 2001
3

Typeset in 10.75/14.5 pt PostScript Linotype Sabon
Typeset by Rowland Phototypesetting Ltd, Bury St Edmunds, Suffolk

Printed and bound in Great Britain by The Bath Press, Bath

Cover repro and printing by Concise Cover Printers

A CIP catalogue record for this book is available from the British Library

ISBN 0-713-99518-1

Contents

Introduction

This collection of essays is a successor to *The Uses of Error*, published in 1990, and contains a selection of the pieces I wrote in the course of the next decade. Most of them were written for the *London Review of Books*, but some were *New York Review* commissions, and one appeared in *The New Republic*. What these journals have in common, besides their generosity in asking me to write for them, is an interest in the review-essay, anything from 2,500 to 4,500 words. Newspapers commonly want briefer notices, and lectures call for anything up to double the length of the review-essay, which occupies a comfortable middle ground.

It is in my view a satisfactory genre, for the writer can be moderately expansive and please himself, as well as modestly explanatory and willing to please, with due amenity, the sort of reader who reads these journals. It is almost true to say that this middle ground between the barbarous jargons and swollen books of the modern academy and the quick satisfactions of the newspaper review is nowadays cultivated only by a few journals like these, and it is just as well for our intellectual well-being that they should exist. The understanding between writer and reader is that the former will perform as an educated audience has a right to expect, and that the latter will, under those conditions, take pleasure in what may from time to time be a mildly strenuous bit of reading, justified by a faith that authors who write for these papers on the whole know what they are talking about, but are not so proud of that accomplishment that they cannot refrain from vainglorious displays of their professional prowess.

Fortunately it sometimes happens that one is asked to write about matters outside one's usual beat, so that the task becomes, gratifyingly, part of the reviewer's education. I daresay I am not alone in finding this kind of work especially enjoyable. James Buchan, for example, gave me a reason to meditate about money, an interesting topic on which I was entirely ignorant; I have to say I remain so, but can now associate my dullness with the pleasure of reading and expounding Buchan's book. Both Alain Corbin and Jonathan Raban revived ancient memories of the sea, for which, despite some fairly alarming maritime experiences in my youth, I still have the remnants of an infantile romantic attachment. Then again I have included some as it were extra-curricular pieces about painting, philosophy, and, in one instance (the notice of James Kugel's book), Judaica. So I educate myself in public, which I take to be the reviewer's privilege.

I thought it right and pious to put poets first, and, because to treat them in chronological order seemed as sensible as any other arrangement, the collection starts off with a recent piece about *Beowulf* and what the translators, who include the Nobel laureate Seamus Heaney, have made of it. After that come certain divagations, for example John Jones and Zachary Leader on poets' revisions, to me a deeply interesting subject. In one case hereabouts I have included a review which, though respectful, as one always tries to be, condemns practices I want condemned. After the paintings and the philosophies and so forth, a few novelists bring up the rear: the curious case of Sylvia Townsend Warner, William Golding, whose posthumous novel – even more a victim of changing fashion than the rest of his work – seems to have been generally ignored, and finally Philip Roth and the novel which introduced the latest and finest phase of this great novelist's work.

Most of my working life has been spent in universities, and most of my work has been addressed primarily to academic audiences; that sort of thing is not represented here, though I think I have occasionally allowed academic prejudices to intrude into these lighter exercises. It is true that for forty or more years I have had a second career outside the academy as a literary journalist and editor, so leading a double life which was, at its best, made possible, made fruitful, during my years at University College London. I have never had an extensive acquaintance in what Dr Leavis used to excoriate as 'the London literary world'; nevertheless I have sometimes written about people I happened to know and like – Henry Reed, for instance, and Roy Fuller. I knew William Empson at least as well as either of us wanted, and Adam Phillips is a friend, though I don't think I'd have written about him differently if he hadn't been. The piece on Ern Malley contains a bit of autobiography, for it is virtually certain that no other living English critic was as close as I was to the wicked plots of literary Sydney in 1945, and, while that may not be thought much of an occasion for boasting, the temptation to cry 'I was there!' was simply too strong. As I remarked above, one virtue of the review-essay is that it offers writers opportunities for such self-indulgence, surely permissible so long as they don't break their tacit contracts with the author under consideration and the readers of the review: both of which require that they provide a fair account of the book and write decently about it.

As usual, I now feel sorry about the exclusions and uncertain as to the reasons I found for them. This could have been a very different book. But out of so many fugitives only a few souls can be saved, and we all know better than to think we understand the operations of grace. Of course it is to be remembered that in these cases election is not only intermittent but also impermanent. The afterlife in these circumstances is to be sought only in the pleasure, necessarily transient, of readers. And, if I may repeat the remark of Lord Chesterfield I quoted in the Introduction to *The Uses of Error*, that result will best be achieved by reviewers, especially donnish reviewers, who attend to this admonition: 'Speak the language of the company you are in: and speak it purely, and unlarded with any other.' This advice I have tried to follow throughout.

Acknowledgements

All the essays in this book appeared first in the *London Review of Books*, except 'The Modern Beowulf', 'On a New Way of Doing History', 'The Bible as it Was', 'The Search for a Perfect Language' and 'Philip Roth', which appeared in the *New York Review of Books*; and 'Ern Malley', which appeared in *The New Republic*.

The Modern Beowulf

The Old English poem *Beowulf* tells, in a little over 3,000 lines of verse, the story of a great hero of the Geat tribe, which long ago inhabited what is now part of Sweden. Beowulf hears of the protracted sufferings of the neighbouring Danes at the hands of a monster called Grendel, a wildly destructive and cannibalistic ogre who bursts, night after night, into the great hall of Hrothgar, the Danish king, and tears both the place and its defenders apart. Beowulf, seeing an opportunity for heroism, resolves to go to the aid of Hrothgar and crosses the sea with the intention of taking on Grendel singlehanded. On arrival at the Danish court he does the required amount of boasting and feasting, and when Grendel arrives that night Beowulf, scorning to use a weapon, wrestles with the intruder and tears off his arm. Grendel dies, but a greater ordeal lies ahead, for his mother, a monster even more frightening to ordinary mortals though not to Beowulf, sets out to avenge him. She and Beowulf have a phantasmagorical struggle in her underwater lair, which ends when he happens to find a sword in her cave and uses it to kill her. Loaded with gifts and praise, he returns home and tells his story to his own king, Hygelac. There follows a fifty-year gap in the story, and when we meet Beowulf again he is an old man and has himself long been the king of the Geats. Now his own kingdom is threatened by a terrible firebreathing dragon who guards a hoard, quite in the manner of Wagner's Fafner. Beowulf fights the dragon; all but one of his supporters flee, but the King, with this single helper, prevails, though at the cost of his own life. The dragon's hoard is appropriated, and

Beowulf is given a ceremonial burial, along with the treasure, in a conspicuous barrow on a headland. So the basic structure of the poem consists of three episodes – Grendel, Grendel's mother and the dragon – though with a good deal of ancillary information concerning Danes, Geats and other Scandinavian tribes and customs.

If you are prepared to admit that it was written in English, *Beowulf* is by far the oldest poem of its length in our language. When struggling through it as a student I preferred to call its language Anglo-Saxon, regarding the official description, Old English, as a trick, a means of getting into an English Literature course a work in a remote Germanic dialect. My instructors could be thought to have a vested interest in the poem and the language; they had gone to a lot of trouble to learn a lot about them and, since teaching it was to be their chief means of support, they were clearly in favour of making their study compulsory. Or so it seemed, no doubt unfairly; the poem is, after all, in the language spoken in England for centuries, and the greatest poem in that language must be a legitimate object of historical and philological inquiry.

The interests of the teachers were indeed exclusively philological and antiquarian. *Beowulf* provided them with a great variety of complicated scholarly problems, and it was in these that they wanted to involve their students. They rarely found it necessary or desirable to speak of *Beowulf* as a poem, and when they did so they were quite likely to say it was not a particularly good one. Moving house a while ago I found an essay of mine, some sixty years old, on 'The Fight at Finsburgh'. This is a poetic fragment, preserved by chance, of some forty-odd lines, some baffling, from a lost longer work, not a part of *Beowulf* though obscurely related to it. Somebody must have believed that an attempt, however callow, to understand the problems of that relationship would somehow sharpen my wits. Of course I was not required to do any literary criticism.

Nobody knows, for sure, the date of *Beowulf*. Conjectures range from the early eighth to the late tenth century. Possibly it was composed in Northumbria but written down by monks in the south, perhaps long afterwards. The culture of the time of writing was

Christian, but the poem, though it includes some pious Christian sentiments, looks back to a pagan past, to heroic deeds performed in another country by men who could perhaps be thought of as remote ancestors. *Wyrd*, which is untranslatable but means something like 'fate', is a stronger idea in the poem than Christian providence. During much of the period when the poem was written down and read, Danes of a later vintage were persistent and successful enemies of the Anglo-Saxons, which suggests that it was possible to distinguish, in poems, between dangerous, ugly modern Danes and old-time Danes whose antique heroic virtues belonged at least as much to the tradition of the inhabitants of England as to that of the modern raiders. There is a question as to whether the Christian material in the poem was there from the start or intruded into it later, which is not impossible, considering that the practice of writing came in with Christianity. And of course, as R. M. Liuzza suggests,* the poem may have undergone changes during its life of oral performance – changes of which we can know nothing – before it reached the hands of the final author.

At that time it presumably took its place along with many other writings of the same sort, but the extant body of Anglo-Saxon literature is quite small; we can say that such poems as 'The Battle of Maldon' and 'The Seafarer' have a good deal in common with *Beowulf*, but it remains historically rather isolated. For a long time so little was known about the culture that produced such a poem that it must have seemed that all its talk of splendid gold ornaments, rings, cups and swords and the like was mere fantasy, until the discovery, just before the outbreak of war in 1939, of the rich seventh-century ship-burial treasure at Sutton Hoo; the effect on our sense of the civilization that produced it might be thought comparable to that of Sir Arthur Evans's excavations at Knossos on the understanding of the Homeric world. We may even think the rich trappings of Beowulf's burial chime with those of the Sutton Hoo

---

* *Beowulf: A New Verse Translation* (Peterborough, Ontario: Broadview Press, 2000).

treasure, but the experts warn us not to make too much of such parallels.

The unique manuscript of the poem dates from the tenth century. It is written out continuously, with no break between the verse lines, and it survived centuries of almost total neglect until Sir Robert Cotton acquired it early in the seventeenth century. In 1731 it was damaged by fire, but it is now in the British Library, legible except for a few charred lines. Interest in it was slight until early-nineteenth-century Romantic nationalists claimed the work as an early English epic, comparable to Homer, the *Nibelungenlied* and the *Chanson de Roland*, and gratifyingly older than the last two. Scholars – by no means just the English but learned men and women of many nations, German, Danish, Icelandic, British and American – have worked on it ever since. It has often been translated into modern English, in the nineteenth century by Longfellow and William Morris among others. But on the whole the versions made in recent years are better, a development that may be explained, at any rate in part, by a rather striking scholarly event that occurred in 1936.

This was the publication of J. R. R. Tolkien's lecture '*Beowulf*: The Monsters and the Critics'. It would not be easy to think of a parallel to this occasion, a professorial lecture that changed a generation's attitude to a document of national and historical importance. Tolkien noted that previous scholarship had treated *Beowulf* less as a poem than as matter for archaeological and historical inquiry. 'The shadow of research has lain upon criticism,' says Tolkien; the current of interest had been antiquarian rather than critical. An unhappy consequence had been the erroneous assumption that the poem was 'primitive' when in fact it looks back, from a much later civilized period, on to a primitive heroic age long past. More important, the experts, obsessed with the idea of its primitiveness, had simply neglected the poem as a poem, or criticized it for its 'thin and poor' story: Beowulf sees off the ogre Grendel, then he defeats Grendel's ogre mother, and then, after fifty years have elapsed in a few lines, he kills a fiery dragon and dies of injuries sustained in the fight. Apart from anything else, the structure of the tale, looked at in this way, looked weak, 'primitive'.

Tolkien, however, has no difficulty with the episodic structure and finds in the poetry a high seriousness, a grim understanding that monsters are evidence of what cannot be denied, the potential of evil in the world; they are the enemies of men and gods (and God). The poem is a celebration of the necessary defeat of even the greatest human valour, of the tragic truth of mortality – a theme always valid, though in the poem set in a pagan past by an author whose Christianity is attested by the scriptural references, to Cain (ancestor of the monsters who like him, bore the wrath of God, *godes yrre*) and to the war of the giants against heaven.

Tolkien commends the metre of the poem (the lines 'more like masonry than music') but particularly loves those monsters, 'the evil side of heroic life'. Beowulf himself can be seen as a hero in a more general and more impressive way, not merely as a Germanic adventurer: 'he is a man, and that for him is sufficient tragedy'. And Tolkien endorses W. P. Ker's resonant account: these heroes of the north offer 'absolute resistance, perfect because without hope'. The mood is that of the lines, better remembered than most Anglo-Saxon verses, in the tenth-century poem 'The Battle of Maldon', originally in the same manuscript as *Beowulf* but destroyed in the fire, though fortunately somebody had made a copy of it: in a version of the lines by W. H. Auden, 'Heart and head shall be keener, mood the more/ As our might lessens.'

Beowulf, on this view, is to be described not as an epic or a lay but as 'an heroic-elegiac poem', its climax the death and funeral of the hero in the last lines. Somebody else had said *Beowulf* was 'small beer', but Tolkien, in what became a famous phrase, described it as 'a drink dark and bitter, a solemn funeral ale with the taste of death'. And after this the poem, we were counselled, should never be treated as it had been hitherto; it was henceforth to be studied as great literature: 'There is not much poetry in the world like this.'

Naturally some of Tolkien's views have been called into question over the years since 1936, but we can assume that translators coming after him will have his work and his estimate of the poem, or at least some resonance of them, in mind. He offered his own views on the problems of translation. First he ruled out prose translation, except when legitimately used by a student as a crib, and that is surely right; without the strange, strong, halting movement of the verse, its ceremonial, archaic quality, the solemnity of the boasts and promises, the rituals of the mead hall so stiffly recalled, there may be very little left to interest us, only a fairy story of ogres and dragons, of repetitive boasting and drinking and gift-giving.

So the translators must use verse; but here there are fearful obstacles, such that Seamus Heaney tells us that for a while he gave up the attempt.* Anglo-Saxon verse resembles nothing in modern English prosody, and attempts to imitate it with any exactness may seem barbaric, unless managed with the virtuosity of Auden in *The Age of Anxiety*. Each verse is divided by a caesura, and each half-line has two stresses. Alliteration, or what Tolkien prefers to call 'head-rhyme', is an agreement between stressed elements beginning with the same consonant or lacking consonants. Tolkien provides a few lines of an English version that obey these rules, marking principal and subordinate stresses, showing that the half-lines are themselves divided, and stressing the head-rhymes. The lines are from a passage early in the poem which describes Beowulf and his men setting forth on their mission of mercy to the Danes:

> Time pássed a | wáy. On the tíde | flóated
> under bánk | their bóat. In her bóws | móunted
> bráve mèn | blíthely. Bréakers | túrning
> spúrned the | shíngle. Spléndid | ármour
> they bóre | abóard . . .

Probably 3,000 lines of this would be too tiring, but it still seems clear that a translation ignoring the rules altogether and converting everything into modern iambic pentameters, for instance, would

---

* *Beowulf* (London: Faber, 1999).

fail, if only because it would be constantly proclaiming its own anachronistic character. Liuzza, in an appendix, gives twenty versions of another passage (ll. 229–57, the Danish watchman's challenge to Beowulf's arrival as he and his men disembark on the shore of Denmark). Some have the alliteration but not the break; others try for both but are unfaithfully wordy. The earliest example that sounds a bit like the original is Charles W. Kennedy's of 1940, but Ruth P. M. Lehmann's of 1988 and Frederick Rebsamen's of 1991 are more ambitious and more successful.

On the whole the versions now under review would seem to be better than their predecessors. Seamus Heaney in an elegant introduction pays his tribute to Tolkien, who would certainly have enjoyed his account of the monsters, especially his description of Grendel's mother, 'a creature of sea-slouch and lunge on land if seal-swift in the water', and of the dragon defeated by Beowulf in that terminal encounter: 'there is something glorious in the way he manifests himself, a Fourth of July effulgence fireworking its path across the night sky; and yet, because of the centuries he has spent dormant in the tumulus, there is a foundedness as well as a lambency about him'. Heaney needs no prompting to represent *Beowulf* as a poem, a great one that demanded considerable technical resource of its author, and something similar of its translator: 'Often . . . the whole attempt to turn it into modern English seemed to me like trying to bring down a megalith with a toy hammer.' But he eventually persuaded himself that he had the means, reflecting that the first poem in his first published collection was made, unconsciously, to comply with the requirements of Anglo-Saxon metrics: 'the spade sinks into gravelly ground:/ My father, digging. I look down . . .' The conceit upon which the effect of that poem partly depends (the poet himself digs not with a spade but with the pen in his hand, 'snug as a gun') sounds, for a moment, remote from Anglo-Saxon poetry, but then one remembers that Anglo-Saxon poetry has its own conceits, even its own jokes and puzzles, such as the riddles, sometimes obscene, found in the *Exeter Book*, a tenth-century collection preserved in Exeter Cathedral; and also in the kennings ('whale-road' or 'swan's path' for the sea, 'sky-candle' for the sun, etc.) that are frequent in *Beowulf* and sometimes set more problems to its translator. As for alliteration, Heaney knew something about the trick of it, having started out as an imitator of Gerard Manley Hopkins. He claims a further advantage: the Irish-English of his Northern Irish youth, in which certain words survive that have died in English-English: for example the verb 'thole' meaning 'suffer', which is found in *Beowulf* (and in a poem of John Crowe Ransom's) as well as in Irish dialect. Heaney felt that this historical accident justified his use of other Anglo-Irish words and locutions in his translation. The first word of *Beowulf* is 'Hwaet!', a call to attention, usually translated as 'Lo!' or 'Listen!' But Heaney's version begins 'So', which 'in Hiberno-English Scullionspeak' is an idiomatic way of inaugurating a new topic. He says he knows a little Anglo-Saxon, but not much; his qualifications as translator were quite different: he is an exceptionally good Hiberno-English poet.

His version of the lines given above in Tolkien's translation is as follows:

> Time went by, the boat was on water,
> in close under the cliffs.
> Men climbed eagerly up the gangplank,
> sand churned in surf, warriors loaded
> a cargo of weapons . . .

The second line has a bit missing – 'in her bows mounted', the sense being loosely included in the line that follows. The third line, newly arranged, does not alliterate. 'Sand churned in surf' is as good as Tolkien's 'Breakers . . . spurned the shingle', but the adjective that should go with the armour is missing. Liuzza gives us

> The time came – the craft was on the waves,
> moored under the cliffs. Eager men
> climbed on the prow – the currents eddied,
> sea against sand – the soldiers bore
> into the bosom of the ship their bright gear . . .

This has more of the original substance, and more of the alliteration, but at the cost of some diffuseness. And 'sea against sand' is surely weaker than the rival versions. It could be said that the Liuzza lines explain more, but lack the brusqueness, of the original.

Heaney admits in his Introduction that

in one area my own labours have been less than thoroughgoing. I have not followed the strict metrical rules that bound the Anglo-Saxon *scop*. I have been guided by the fundamental pattern of four stresses to the line, but I allow myself several transgressions. For example, I don't always employ alliteration, and sometimes I alliterate only in half of the line. When these breaches occur, it is because I prefer to let the natural 'sound of sense' prevail over the demands of the convention. I have been reluctant to force an artificial shape or an unusual word choice just for the sake of correctness.

This means he grants himself a fair amount of licence and relies on a poet's apprehension of the 'sound of sense'. In other words, we are required to trust him as a poet; fortunately he has given us cause to do so.

Liuzza's book is in some respects more useful than Heaney's. Understandably he doesn't demand unqualified confidence in his own powers as a poet; he is not a Nobel laureate, and in any case his attention is modestly concentrated on the object poem. He takes account of recent scholarly research and provides a commentary, a collection of supporting texts, and an excellent introduction to this 'Christian poet's bittersweet elegy for the doomed heroic life'. His account of the peculiarities of Old English poetic style is particularly helpful. Here he discusses the difficulties for the translator of the 'profusion of synonyms':

Alliterative poetry required a number of different ways of saying the same thing in different lines: depending on the meter, context, and the necessity of making an alliterative link, a king might be called a *cyning*, *dryhten*, *hyrde*, *raeswa*, *sigedryhten*, *eodcyning*, *weard*, or *wine*. Of course these words are not quite synonyms, any more than their nearest equivalents in Modern English ('king', 'lord', 'shepherd', 'prince', 'victorious lord', 'king of the people', 'guardian', 'friend'), but it is hard to avoid the suspicion that their use in Old English is only partly determined by the nuances of their connotations. At times metrical necessity must have played a decisive role. The aged and ineffectual king Hrothgar, for example, is called *helm Scyldinga* 'protector of the Scyldings' (Danes) in lines 371, 456, and 1321, presumably not because he is such a great protector of his people – under the circumstances the title could at best be regarded as a courtesy – but because *helm* alliterates with *Hrothgar*. But the elaboration of synonyms is part of what gives the poem its notable formality, another instance of the recurrence-with-variation that is the essence of its art.

It might be added that there is a Homeric flavour about this epithet for Hrothgar, as when Achilles is 'brilliant' or 'swift-footed' because at a particular point the metre, though not necessarily the sense, requires it. As Milman Parry demonstrated, these formulaic epithets have a mnemonic function and belong to the tradition of oral poetry, still practised, at any rate in his day, by illiterate Yugoslavian bards.

Few prospective readers will ignore the obvious appeal of the Heaney translation, knowing from his own poetry that the Nobel laureate has the resources to do the job and has by now won the vote of the public, which has made his book a slightly surprising best-seller. Here is part of his version of Beowulf's wrestling match with Grendel:

> And now the timbers trembled and sang,
> a hall-session that harrowed every Dane
> inside the stockade; stumbling in fury,
> the two contenders crashed through the building.
> The hall clattered and hammered, but somehow
> survived the onslaught and kept standing:
> it was handsomely structured, a sturdy frame
> braced with the best of blacksmith's work
> inside and out. The story goes
> that as the pair struggled, mead-benches were smashed
> and sprung off the floor, gold fittings and all.
> Before then no Shielding elder would believe
> there was any power or person on earth

capable of wrecking their horn-rigged hall
unless the burning embrace of a fire
engulf it in flame.

Liuzza translates *ealu-scerwen* literally as 'ale-sharing' and explains that it probably meant 'panic' or 'terror', though he cannot explain why the word for such an innocent-sounding activity should come to mean those things. Heaney avoids the difficulty by simply saying the Danes were 'harrowed'. Liuzza continues:

> It was a great wonder that the wine-hall
> withstood their fighting and did not fall to the ground.
> That fair building – but it was fastened
> inside and out with iron bands,
> forged with skill. From the floor there flew
> many a mead-bench, as men have told me,
> gold-adorned, where those grim foes fought.
> The Scylding elders had never expected
> that any man, by any ordinary means
> could break it apart, beautiful, bone-adorned,
> or destroy it with guile, unless the embrace of fire
> might swallow it in flames.

You could compare these passages line by line and say that Heaney wins some and loses some. On the whole he is neater ('the story goes' for the more literal and literary 'as men have told me'). And perhaps Liuzza is more confident in the strangeness of the literal: 'bone-adorned', which is more literal, for 'horn-rigged', though they are perhaps equally odd. Heaney's 'Any power or person upon earth', though rather free, is better than Liuzza's equivalent, 'any man, by any ordinary means'.

The point of these comparisons, however, is simply that the less celebrated translator can be matched with the famous one; which of the two is Beowulf and which Grendel is not easily decided. Given that Liuzza's book contains a perfectly good and well-informed translation as well as much valuable ancillary material, and that Heaney has long since earned the right to be carefully attended to whatever he chooses to do, the answer to the problem of choice is simple enough: since each book in its way enriches the pleasure to be had from the poem, the best plan is to buy them both. The edition of Heaney's book here reviewed has the Old English and modern versions on facing pages, which gives him an additional advantage, since anybody with a smattering of the language can at least play at checking the new against the old.

World-Famous Irishman

F. S. L. Lyons, who first undertook this large-scale biography of Yeats, died in 1983, and after some vicissitudes the task devolved on Roy Foster,* the professor of Irish history at Oxford. He has had access to Lyons's notes and transcripts, invaluable to a successor confronted, as he says, with 'a vast and unfamiliar subject'. Vast it remains, but the unfamiliarity has clearly evaporated. Foster insists that his business is history, not literary criticism: Yeats, he remarks, was a poet but he was 'both serially and simultaneously, a playwright, journalist, occultist, apprentice politician, revolutionary, stage-manager, diner-out, dedicated friend, confidant and lover of some of the most interesting people of his day'. Foster therefore offers not a study of the poetry from a biographical angle but a chronological account of the life during which the poetry was written – the packed and laborious life of an extraordinary man, a genius, if the word is still allowed to mean anything; a great though sometimes rather absurd figure whose career is inextricably involved in the history of his country (and with much else) from the 1880s to the 1930s. 'Most biographical studies of WBY are principally about what he wrote; this one is principally about what he did.'

Foster has had the benefit of John Kelly's magnificent, though all too slowly emerging, Oxford edition of the correspondence, and has himself done Herculean work in the archives. Among his chief sources

* R. F. Foster, *W. B. Yeats, Vol. 1: The Apprentice Mage* (Oxford: Oxford University Press, 1997).

is of course Yeats's own 'disingenuous' prose masterpiece, the *Autobiographies*. For this work, as for his subject generally, Foster feels a mixture of deep respect and exasperation, understandable in a historian who has undertaken to sort out the facts from these carefully crafted, much revised, beautifully unreliable texts, and set them out in the right order. Here, as everywhere, Foster's skill and unforced pertinacity are beyond praise; he really does give a coherent account of the serial and simultaneous lives of his huge subject. It is not easy to see how this book could have been improved, or how lovers of Yeats's poetry (despite the historian's modest disclaimers) could have been better served.

The greatness of Yeats, and his position among twentieth-century poets, is of a kind not natural in an age like this. Searching the history of English poetry for a writer of comparable national stature one is driven back to Milton, another apocalyptic revolutionary – at times the justifying voice of revolution, the apologist of a new republic, the commentator, sometimes eloquently bitter, on the great affairs of the day. Both writers had their potent fallible heroes, such as Cromwell and Parnell; each flaunted heretical opinions (for example, both publicized unpopular convictions about divorce law). Yeats's *A Vision*, a private theology, is in a way comparable to Milton's *De Doctrina Christiana*. And in the course of their lives both men strenuously remade themselves as poets.

Sooner or later, of course, such comparisons cease to be illuminating; though Milton could boast of a work that made his name famous throughout Europe, and earned a reputation even more controversial than that of Yeats, he was not what Yeats became, an emblem, for some, of nationhood, the victor in all the necessary struggles to establish a modern Irish literature, and at the same time, to use a word he came to fancy in old age, 'world-famous'.

Milton had been educated for greatness; Yeats was virtually an autodidact. His father – a wit, a good writer, and a gifted painter who rarely finished a picture – was perpetually broke and shamelessly improvident. He wanted his son to be a poet, but seemed not to care much about the boy's schooling; and, however grim the financial prospect, he disliked the notion that his son, being an Irish gentleman, should ever have to take a job, especially in England. He regarded the English as very inferior company; this disdain for the lower orders was one of many traits his son inherited.

Yeats's school record would have dismayed most middle-class parents – in a class of thirteen boys he was twelfth in classics, twelfth in modern languages, and thirteenth in maths and English. So for academic as well as financial reasons there was no hope of his following the family tradition and going to Trinity. He was an atrocious speller throughout his life (Foster leaves all the mistakes uncorrected). He never learned a language other than English, even though to have no Irish was an embarrassment, and to fail to acquire French a great disappointment. His friendships with such as Lady Gregory and Arthur Symons offered him only limited access to either language.

Despite his wretched start and these persistent incapacities, he became a remarkably well-read intellectual, with a passion for Nietz-sche, for Plato and Neoplatonism, for learned Italian things, obscure histories, and occult treatises. Like some other poets, including Shakespeare, he gives one the impression that what he read was more or less exactly what he needed for purposes of his own. He acquired much knowledge of Irish myth and folklore, which he contrived to amalgamate with his theories about that universal store of images the Great Memory, and with other occult notions. 'If I had gone to a university, and learned all the classical foundations of English literature and English culture, all that great erudition which once accepted frees the mind from restlessness, I should have had to give up my Irish subject matter . . .' But he had a practitioner's hands-on acquaintance with the English poetic tradition, and not only with Blake, whom he edited, and Spenser and Shakespeare, whom he greatly admired. (For example, seeking a stanza form suitable for his elegy on Robert Gregory, he silently adopted that used by Cowley 300 years earlier in his verses on the death of William Harvey.)

On the whole it was probably just as well that Trinity, the Ascend-ancy college, was barred to him. He often complained of the Trinity culture, and had mixed feelings about Edward Dowden, TCD's celebrated professor of English, a friend of his father's whom he had known well in his youth; Dowden was too lukewarm, too English, as he himself might have become had he gone to the College. Later there was a time when Yeats implausibly, dubiously, fancied he might succeed to the chair of this learned man, his fame as a poet compensating for his lack of orthodox scholarship; but fortunately it came to nothing. He already had enough to explain to his Anglophobe Dublin critics.

Foster minutely records underachievements and achievements, with ample documentation of Yeats's unstable social and political attitudes. Given the complexity of such matters, the potential tediousness of some of the detail, it is just as well that he is an excellent writer, with an Irish edge to his prose, a teasing, sardonic manner that is at certain moments reminiscent of the Yeatses', both father and son. There is in *Autobiographies* a description of a visit to Verlaine, who had invited Yeats to 'coffee and cigarettes plentifully'. Verlaine's leg was heavily bandaged, and looking in a dictionary for the correct description of his disease, he 'selected . . . with, as I understood, only comparative accuracy, "Erisypelas"'. Such adverbial qualifications are also a feature of Foster's style, and are used to mock 'the mage of Woburn Buildings' in a rather similar way. Yet Yeats respected Verlaine, and Foster by no means underestimates the importance of the mage business to Yeats. His tone blends respect and amusement. When Yeats writes a poem ('The New Faces') to Lady Gregory speculating as to whether she will die before him, Foster notes that, although she was, at sixty, fourteen years older than the poet, she received the poem just as she was setting off to New York to join her lover John Quinn – one of Yeats's many 'moments of superb tactlessness'.

Yeats's ambition to be a mage as well as a poet was proclaimed very early, and it never faded. Magic is one of those serial and simultaneous careers that challenge the biographer's organizing skills in the writing as much as they did the poet's in the living of them. In youth beguiled by Mme Blavatsky, Yeats soon developed an intense, even domineering, interest in the hermetic Order of the Golden Dawn. For a man who frequently expressed a need for solitude he was an inveterate joiner of hermetic, political and poetical clubs and societies, and so were many of his friends. Most of them emerge from this biography as slightly absurd – for instance, the hysterically misogynistic Edward Martyn ('moon-faced, obese, epicene, frantically Catholic'), the impostor poet 'Fiona Macleod', the manic McGregor Mathers, Scots Jacobite romantic ('the comte de Glenstrae'), and Florence Farr, the actress for whose favours Yeats competed with Shaw and others, and for whom he had Dolmetsch make psalteries to accompany the chanting of verse. Foster has much quiet fun with the psalteries, and for good measure reproduces Jack Yeats's satirical drawing of his brother explaining 'speaking to the psaltery' to an audience in the American Wild West. Nobody seemed to like what Shaw called the 'nerve-destroying crooning' this practice entailed, except of course the poet, who was tone-deaf, and Miss Farr, who liked performing and had a sense of humour.

Considering the amount of time Yeats devoted to hermetic philosophies, Indian sages, seances, psalteries, and so forth, it is astonishing how much else he managed to do. In his twenties he was already a force in the London literary world. Later long years were devoted to Dublin theatre business – directing plays; sorting out or causing squabbles with patrons, including the difficult but rich Annie Horniman, and with the actors, led by the Fay brothers, who had good reason to resent his frequent high-handedness.

Throughout these years he also suffered continually from the many wounding disappointments inflicted on him by Maud Gonne, whose intransigence he rewarded with the best love poetry of the century. Eventually he found complicated reasons to be grateful for her unrelenting refusal to understand or accept him: 'What matter? – How much of the best I have done and still do is but the attempt to explain myself to her? If she understood I should lack a reason for writing, and one can never have too many reasons for doing what is so laborious.' But that was a later mood. Earlier she caused him much anguish. He survived, drawing energy from seances or from dreams and astral encounters with his inaccessible mistress, or seeking further consolation from hashish pills.

Even more essential was the support he had in almost everything he did from Augusta Gregory, who also provided him with solitude and the freedom of her 'great' house at Coole. He many times gracefully expressed his gratitude, though he did manage, not irreparably, to offend even her. She had her reward in some good poems but also in the enrichment of her life; under Yeats's influence she became a considerable writer herself and a force in the nascent Irish theatre.

Yeats too wrote a great many plays, sometimes with collaborators, including Lady Gregory. Not all were successful, but *Cathleen ni Houlihan* was effective political propaganda (though Yeats denied it was so intended), and there are some strange and brilliant experiments, such as his Noh play *At The Hawk's Well*. For a while all was theatre. He recognized, celebrated and dedicated himself to the genius of Synge. The brawl at the Abbey over Synge's *Playboy of the Western World* affected him so deeply that he bracketed it in importance with the death of Parnell. This was the occasion when his father, J. B. Yeats, outraged an angry audience by calling Ireland 'this land of saints – of plaster saints'. The objection of the trouble-makers was the usual one: that Synge had traduced pure Irish womanhood, not least by the speaking out loud of the word 'shift'. Yeats himself, as a famous epigram demonstrates, saw the demonstration as evidence of the intellectual and emotional sterility induced in the urban Irish by sexual abstinence – something he himself knew a lot about, though apparently not suffering the same effects.

As time went by he talked more and more about his distaste for the Dublin populace, which broke up Synge's play, kept shops or worked for a living, and read gutter newspapers which attacked him and his friends. He had some difficulty in reconciling his role as a nationalist poet with his angry contempt for so significant a part of the nation. By 1914, the date of *Responsibilities*, he was sick of quarrelling with Dubliners about their indifference to Hugh Lane's proposed national gallery and their moralistic objections to *The*

Playboy; he had long before spoken of his 'endless war with Irish stupidity'.

These matters, and his anger over them, are part of the rich mixture of poems in *Responsibilities*, which is generally taken to be the first of his major collections, a remarkable advance even on its notable predecessor, *The Green Helmet*. Strong topical epigrams, anathemata on 'Paudeen',* celebrations of the lost, aristocratic Parnell blend with a series of great love poems, including 'Fallen Majesty' and his finest lyric to date, 'The Cold Heaven', all inspired by Maud Gonne. Here his multiple interests are strongly expressed in the new more colloquial, more direct manner he had been cultivating. 'A Coat' is his defiant defence of this developing manner: 'there's more enterprise/ In walking naked'. The late-Romantic style is transfigured by modernity; the time is now, and the poet an ineradicable presence in its midst.

Meanwhile his increasingly undemocratic postures were more and more warmly resented, especially when, on Lady Gregory's advice, he accepted a British Civil List pension. He had always needed more money than the little he made, and what he made he made mostly in London, where he was published and accepted far more readily than in Dublin. The pension, arranged by powerful London friends, was a deserved godsend, as the Nobel Prize would be later on; nevertheless, he was mocked as 'the pensioner' for taking it. He grew accustomed to satire and calumny, and felt he had become 'Notorious, till all my priceless things/ Are but a post the passing dogs defile'.

With his usual alternations of boldness and caution, he had opposed the party that wanted the new Irish literature to be in Irish; and when one thinks of Yeats himself – and Joyce and Beckett, not to speak of Wilde and Shaw – one can only believe he was right. What he wanted was an Irish cultural renaissance with English as its language. He once entertained the fine thought that a reborn Dublin could be more like sixteenth-century Urbino than like London; or

---

* A variant of 'Patrick' and a contemptuous way of referring to a lower-class Irishman.

that it might match the cultural unity achieved 'by theologian, poet, sculptor, architect, from the eleventh to the thirteenth century'. But he also believed that the world fell apart about the time of the birth of Shakespeare, and that civilization, not least in Dublin, had continued and accelerated that collapse into disunity.

This state of affairs seemed to be reflected in the angry disarray of contemporary Irish political opinion. Yeats may have wished to avoid conflict with the out-and-out separatists, and to preserve literature from politics, but it turned out that this could not be done, at least by him. He wanted self-government for Ireland, but was sure that more than that was needed if the new Ireland were not to be demoralized. This conviction had political implications. 'It may well be that Ireland will have to become irreligious or unpolitical even, before she can change her habits.'

The nation's only defence against middle-class vulgarity was mounted by 'a few educated men and the remnants of an old traditional culture among the poor'. Unlike the fierce Maud Gonne, an incendiary mob orator, he abandoned the idea of appealing directly to the mass of the people. He prided himself on his very remote aristocratic connections, and his notion of a good Ireland was really founded on the image of the great (Ascendancy) house with its contented peasant community around it – a vision already endangered by the redistribution of land to the peasantry. Thus inspired, he could not long keep the peace with all the other brands of nationalism, especially with the intolerant Catholic variety; 'by the end of 1912 he would no longer find it possible to give automatic assent to public statements avowing Protestant trust in the liberality of Catholic opinions'. Nor did he believe that intolerance would be ended by Home Rule. As Foster slyly remarks, he remained committed to Home Rule, 'but its apparent advent [referring to the promise of the British government that it would be made operative after the war] coincided with WBY's own discovery of family tradition, his burying the hatchet with Trinity College culture, his friendships in great houses . . . and his assumption into a kind of artistic establishment in England'.

The young Yeats had known John O'Leary, who despite his long political exile remained a representative of 'a free-thinking Catholic intelligentsia' capable of dialogue with those 'few educated men' of the Protestant Ascendancy. But the decline of Ascendancy power coincided more or less exactly, as Foster remarks, with Yeats's youth; and in any case faith in such an alliance was soon to die. Yeats fell out with O'Leary and did not attend his funeral; but he is one of the heroes celebrated in later poems.

This volume ends at 1914, when Yeats, already famous, might well have imagined that his life had reached some kind of plateau. The terrors of 1919 and the civil war that would follow the achievement of Home Rule were in the future; and he could hardly have predicted his own even greater achievements. *Responsibilities* by itself had already confirmed his status as a major poet, but its 'Introductory Rhymes' (highly praised by T. S. Eliot, who was not usually an admirer) ask the poet's ancestors their pardon

> that for a barren passion's sake,
> Although I have come close on forty-nine,
> I have no child, I have nothing but a book,
> Nothing but that to prove your blood and mine.

And it seemed more proof of his value was needed. Before the decade was out he was married and a father. Although the early days of the marriage produced some eerily disconsolate poems, he had at last, having once again asked Gonne to marry him (and, on her refusal, asked her daughter Iseult), found some relief from that obsessive and barren passion.

There is necessarily a lot about Maud Gonne in Foster's book; she was always at the centre of Yeats's emotional life and was also deeply involved in his occult interests. She often came between the poet and other women with whom he sought distraction or relief. Foster is, as ever, down-to-earth about his subject's erotic life – the long years of abstinence (he didn't share his friend Symons's taste for dancing girls); his first affair in his late twenties with Olivia Shakespear, brief, Gonne-clouded, but the foundation of a long friendship; his more casual relationships with Florence Farr and Mabel Dickinson, who gave him a terrible scare when she claimed she was pregnant. The marriage to George Hyde-Lees and the Wild Old Man's sexual goings-on in his last years have to wait for the next volume.

It is notable that the women who attracted Yeats, and were attracted by him, were nearly all occultists of one sort or another, and many were actively political; yet we know from all he later said about the Gore-Booth sisters and Maud Gonne that he was sure politics ruined women:

> That woman's days were spent
> In ignorant good-will,
> Her nights in argument
> Until her voice grew shrill.
> What voice more sweet than hers
> When, young and beautiful,
> She rode to harriers?

The principal responsibility of women, as he said in many poems, was simply to be beautiful, to think only with their bodies. So much for Constance Markievicz, who fought in the Rising and was sentenced to death but only sent to prison. In her imprisonment she received a compensating tribute in the exquisite lines 'On a Political Prisoner'. Maud Gonne had many similar rebukes and tributes. Foster believes that Yeats's union with her was not, in the end, merely astral: that they were, though briefly, lovers – a reasonable inference made long ago by Virginia Moore and Richard Ellmann, though his publisher seems to think Foster the first to make it securely. In the long run it matters less than the occult union, and less than Yeats's sympathy in her marital misfortunes. There is nobility in his commemoration of John MacBride in 'Easter, 1916', though MacBride had not only married Gonne but abused her. He is named, along with only three others, as a martyr of the Rising – a violent man in a violent manifestation Yeats probably deplored, though he had come to recognize its symbolic power.

Despite all the distractions, and his commitment to a new Ireland,

Yeats somehow managed to get on with his more literary life. In that life, as everywhere, he showed considerable talent for manipulating people, fixing reviews, placing his own work to advantage. Back in the 1890s he was, as of right, the star performer in the Rhymer's Club, those 'companions of the Cheshire Cheese' – ('the one thing certain,' he observed, 'is that we are too many'). A favourite rhymer was Lionel Johnson, whose obscure learning Yeats venerated and exaggerated. He owed a good deal to Arthur Symons, and was a main attraction of Symons's journal the *Savoy*. He came, in his quest for a hard-edged style, to reject the 'decadence', but the 'tragic generation' of Johnson, Dowson, Beardsley and Wilde became part of his mythical world. He had the ability to make all his interests coalesce, and Foster has shadowed him carefully. He wrote incessantly, and 'that extravagant style/He had learnt from Pater' lingered on in the firm prose of the *Autobiographies* and even in *A Vision*, where the famous passage about Byzantium could almost be by the master himself.

Yet he was also capable of harshness; he gave George Moore, once a collaborator but in the main a detractor, at least as good as he got. Even on fellow mystics, like W. T. Horton, he could be editorially severe; and in the end he ran out of tact in dealing with another occultist, rich Miss Horniman, who thought her gifts of money entitled her to interfere with his dramatic programme. And he wrote eloquently against his enemies in Dublin.

He was certainly a proud man, though also a little timid; hence the need for antiselves, and for imaginary representatives like Michael Robartes and Owen Aherne. Pride did not prevent his acknowledging such youthful talents as the disrespectful Ezra Pound, whose critical comments the older man sometimes accepted. When Pound tampered with some poems of Yeats before sending them on to the Chicago journal *Poetry* the poet was cross but only briefly: 'he has, I think, some genius and great good will'. And Pound's brashness did not prevent him seeing Yeats's genius; he got to know him very well and, as Foster puts it, thought him 'magnificent, unworldly, very slightly ridiculous, but . . . unquestionably the real thing'. That is close to

Foster's view of his subject, and one expects his second volume to be magnificent, worldly, perceptive of the ridiculous, and unquestionably the real thing.

Eliot's Missing Lectures

T. S. Eliot's Clark Lectures 'On the Metaphysical Poetry of the Seventeenth Century with Special Reference to Donne, Crashaw and Cowley' were commissioned in 1925 and delivered at Trinity College, Cambridge, in 1926. Since then they have been famous for not being available. Eliot intended to make them into a book called *The School of Donne*, which would be far longer, partly because – on the face of it unexpectedly, given his title – he wanted to write a lot more about Dante. On Dante, as he remarked in a preface, the whole of his argument depended. But this book was itself to be merely part of a larger project, a trilogy of which the other volumes would deal with the Elizabethan drama (on which he had already written a good deal) and the Sons of Ben. The whole would be known as 'The Disintegration of the Intellect', a title suggesting an almost Spenglerian ambition, and a scope beyond the usual range of literary criticism as he himself claimed to understand it.

Eliot never did enlarge the Donne book, though in 1929 he wrote a long essay on Dante, by now much more important to him, the model of the great poet. The other members of the trilogy lost their original titles and became *The Outline of Royalism* and *The Principles of Modern Heresy*, but they too remained unwritten, at any rate in the promised form. By 1931 he had come to think that the occasion for a book on Donne had passed or been seized by others; but, lacking time to write brand new ones, he gave the lectures in a reduced and somewhat altered version as the three Turnbull Lectures at Johns Hopkins University in Baltimore in 1933.

At that time his main reason for being in America was to give the Charles Eliot Norton Lectures at Harvard, duly published as *The Use of Poetry and the Use of Criticism*. In a year that would have seemed laborious even to a writer not suffering from marital disaster and general ill-health, Eliot added to his Harvard commitment the University of Virginia lectures called 'After Strange Gods: A Primer of Modern Heresy', a topic that interested him more than his Harvard theme. These three lectures became a book, published at once but never subsequently reprinted. It is hardly surprising that he chose to meet his obligation at Baltimore by potting the old Clark series. The Turnbull Lectures, entitled 'The Varieties of Metaphysical Poetry', are here printed for the first time.* This was worth doing because they contain some lively new material about himself, especially in the last lecture.

To be a Turnbull lecturer you were supposed to have achieved distinction as a poet, and it is interesting to overhear Eliot instructing his audience on a topic he often meditated, the difference between great poets and non-great poets:

There is no reason why one should not try to write great poetry, except that great poetry is not written in that way: I mean that if one cares enough about poetry, 'greatness' is not the aim or the criterion. The aim is not to emulate Shakespeare or Homer or Dante or anybody else; for if and so far as one is a poet these criteria and ambitions are nonsense. Poetry is in this respect like science: the aim of the true poet is not to be a 'great poet', but to make a contribution to poetry: merely to say the true thing at one's time; to say the thing to be said in the circumstances, in the right way . . . Greatness is not a state that poets really seek; greatness is a matter, so far as we are concerned, of chance, of what happens afterwards when we are dead; and that depends upon a great many things outside of ourselves.

He concludes that 'the important poets will be those who have taught the people speech', alluding for the first time to the line of Mallarmé remembered years later in 'Little Gidding': 'To purify the dialect of

* *The Varieties of Metaphysical Poetry*, ed. and intro. Ronald Schuchard (London: Faber, 1993).

the tribe'. This act of purification – no less than 'a perpetual return to the real' – is to be achieved by devoted technical effort on the part of poets; and Eliot does not forget that when he insists that literary criticism has to do with the study of that technique, and is only secondarily involved with sociology or psychology or anything else. This principle he tries but, perhaps inevitably, fails fully to honour in his treatment of Donne in these Clark Lectures; there are a few, but too few, instances of close literary criticism, nose to text, brisk, dogmatic, arguable and fun. Nevertheless he insists that the lectures are works of literary criticism, not meant to be anything else, and certainly not professing scholarship; but of course he cannot draw the line firmly, especially since he is persuaded that the decline of poetry is a symptom or consequence of a more general intellectual and cultural collapse that was increasingly preoccupying him.

In 1961, when all intention of publishing *The School of Donne* had vanished, he resigned the title to A. Alvarez, who used it for a book published in that year. The lectures, celebrated but largely unread, remained in two typescript copies, a top copy in the King's College Modern Archive and a carbon in the Houghton Library at Harvard. Now they appear in a scrupulously edited text. The editor conjectures that they will 'have as much impact on our revaluation of [Eliot's] critical mind as did the facsimile edition of *The Waste Land* (1971) on our comprehension of his poetic mind'.

The Clark Lectures are generally thought to be, so far as critical celebrity in this country is concerned, the big ones. The series have in recent years got shorter, but in 1925 there were normally eight lectures, enough for a book – for example, in the following year E. M. Forster gave the lectures that made up *Aspects of the Novel*. Ronald Schuchard, the present editor, is naturally curious as to why a thirty-seven-year-old American, a banker, and, as a critic, practised in the journalistic essay rather than the full-scale academic book, should have been chosen for this high office. The short answer is that he had made a great impression with *The Sacred Wood* and *The Waste Land*, and had achieved a small but choice audience as editor of *The Criterion*. The newly established English Faculty at Cambridge, and especially I. A. Richards, had taken him up, and Middleton Murry, his predecessor in the lectureship and still a powerful name, had suggested Eliot as his successor to its sponsors, the Fellows of Trinity. They had already offered it to A. E. Housman, himself a Fellow of the College, but when he turned it down they called on the youthful banker.

The occasion was formidable enough to make anybody nervous. The Trinity fellowship at that time contained, among other great men, J. G. Frazer and Francis Cornford, whose works had been an inspiration to Eliot, as well as G. E. Moore and Housman, who, we are told, sat in the front row at all the lectures. Also present were Richards and F. R. Leavis, then a keen admirer; some known enemies, especially F. L. Lucas; and many undergraduates, especially women. The undergraduate William Empson, who did not go to lectures on principle, attended the morning-after discussions of them.

They seem not to have been a spectacular success. Some judged them too recondite, and others were unable to hear much of discourses delivered in a low tone and in a cold hall with bad acoustics. The audience, as lecture-series audiences will, dwindled week by week. Eliot's own confidence in the lectures was somewhat shaken by the criticisms of his friend Herbert Read and of the Italian polymath Mario Praz, then teaching at Liverpool, whose work in the same field Eliot greatly admired. In 1937 he pronounced them 'pretentious and immature'. Should one now agree with Schuchard that they contribute to our understanding, if not of Donne, then of Eliot himself?

Eliot had already published some famous brief remarks about Donne and some of his contemporaries; 'The Metaphysical Poets', a review of Herbert Grierson's anthology *Metaphysical Lyrics and Poems of the Seventeenth Century*, is at least as well known as anything else in his critical work, and for many years it set the agenda for discussion of the subject. By 1921 the revival of Donne was well established, and Eliot's essay was in some ways less revolutionary than it later seemed; but nobody had so persuasively suggested that the sort of praise accorded the best of Donne – those poems or moments of poems when thinking and feeling could be said to coexist – might be systematically worked into a theory of cultural decline from the thirteenth century to our own. The inability of later poets to achieve Donne's fusion of thought and feeling was held to be due to a vast spiritual catastrophe which Eliot, unlike any before him but like thousands after him, called a 'dissociation of sensibility'. Never having recovered from it, we are condemned to think and feel by turns, for ever unable to synthesize disparate experience in language. This fall or dissociation occurred in the seventeenth century. In the earlier phase of Eliot's thinking on the subject – we can now see that he was already, in the Clark Lectures, preparing a change of mind – Donne was a prime example of undissociated sensibility, that 'direct sensuous apprehension of thought, or a recreation of thought into feeling' which is not found in later poets. 'A thought to Donne was an experience, it modified his sensibility.' That is what poets can or could do, and ordinary people can't; their experience is 'chaotic, irregular, fragmentary'.

However, the great poet of unified sensibility was not Donne but Dante, who didn't look very like Donne, but was certainly metaphysical; so that it was necessary to explain both their resemblance and their differences. Also to be accounted for was that moment in the nineteenth century when, Eliot believed, the true metaphysical quality emerged in France, announced by Baudelaire and coming to flower in Eliot's model Jules Laforgue. So the historical moments of metaphysical poetry are three: the age of Dante and some contemporaries, the age of Donne and some contemporaries, the age of Laforgue and some contemporaries (Rimbaud, Tristan Corbière). Or rather four, though the lecturer was too modest to say so right out. On the whole, however, the damage done by the seventeenth-century dissociation, despite isolated efforts to mend it, was as good as irreparable. In terms of poetry it can be fixed at the time when the world of Donne gave way to that of Milton and Dryden.

This idea evidently implied or required some larger theory of the 'disintegration of intellect', but for the most part the job of working it out was left to the care of compliant academic disciples. Meanwhile there were those who found the whole set of notions, at first rather cursorily and dogmatically proposed, and later elaborated by unthrilling epigoni, to be vague and ill-formulated. The meanings given to such terms as feeling, emotion, sensibility, intellect, fusion and dissociation were not made clear. Given the chance to write a book explaining them on his own account, Eliot wrote these Clark Lectures and planned even fuller development in the unwritten trilogy, which was to provide the full-blown historical theory of poetry, culture and religion he thought necessary.

He was not happy with the first steps, confessing to Grierson that the lectures were 'full of hasty generalisations and unsubstantiated statements'. And he progressively lost confidence, not in the fact of cultural decline, but in the way he had once dealt with it; in the British Academy Milton Lecture of 1947 he said that, although he still thought there really was something in the idea of a 'dissociation of sensibility', he now regarded its causes as 'too complex and too profound to justify our accounting for the change in terms of literary criticism'.

However, that is roughly what he set out to do in these lectures. And they do provide a clearer idea of his efforts to give body to his thinking about poetry. The statement at the beginning of the first lecture, that 'it is valuable to understand the poetry of the seventeenth century, in order that we may understand that of our own time and understand ourselves', was one for which in 1926 there was a fit audience, even though few. But how to go about understanding it in just this way – that is, with a view to understanding ourselves (sc., the mess we'd got into)? That called for long bold views, and in particular for an acceptance of the central importance of Dante.

Accepting that pre-eminence, he was now free to do some comparison and analysis, and offer some limiting judgements on Donne. Dante, he allows, is not a poet one would normally think of under the more usual trade definitions of 'metaphysical', derived largely from Dryden and Johnson, who had in mind not Dante but Donne,

Cowley, Cleveland, etc. We have to take account of poetry that is metaphysical in the less specialized sense – Lucretius, Dante, Goethe – philosophical poetry possessing the means to make us feel thought and think feeling. We need not insist on the presence in such poetry of whole systems of thought, but an interaction of thought and feeling we must have. We are looking for poetry in which 'what is ordinarily apprehensible as an intellectual statement is translated in sensible form'.

This 'translation' is what Eliot found in Dante. We know from the essay of 1929 to what degree of subtlety he developed his taste for that poet. He did so in a manner best described by himself: first one surrenders oneself to a line or a stanza, then, possessed by it, seeks a way of saying something relevant about this impassioned moment, showing how it might be related to all else that one thinks about the poet, and about oneself. Eliot did this so well that for many English readers the most familiar, even the most valued, passages of Dante are the ones he chose to comment on. They are, in a sense that would not perhaps have pleased him, touchstones. But what are the resemblances between these Dantesque 'bewildering minutes' and the poems of the conceited Donne? To see them we have to remember and explain that, although Dante is 'metaphysical' in a much larger sense, the limited sense of 'metaphysical' ('fantastic, elaborated') is not irrelevant to him. Having done that we may speak of those three phases of metaphysical poetry, and the inexplicit fourth. Eliot was evidently well aware that Dante had somehow to be given a cardinal position in his scheme, and of some difficulty in doing so. Such a position it might not have occurred to others to claim for him. In so far as Eliot manages to do so his success is due less to the hair-splitting about the meaning of 'philosophical' and 'metaphysical' as applied to poetry than to the splendour and certainty of his passion for Dante.

When he turns directly to Donne the results are, not unexpectedly, less satisfactory. He is keen to dismiss the arguments of M. P. Ramsay in her important book *Les doctrines mediévales chez Donne* (1917), for he does not want a Donne too closely allied to scholastic philosophy, a medieval Donne with a system of doctrine rather like Dante's.

Admittedly Donne did a lot of reading in that area, but his real interest was in the big (and disastrous) theological controversies of his own time; in any case it was not in his nature to have the sort of relation to a body of belief that is to be found in Dante. This is broadly true, and it prompts Eliot to describe Donne as modern, and also as Jesuitical, a modern thing to be at the time.

To be modern in this way is to belong to an inferior civilization. The Church splits into quarrelling factions; polemic replaces serious theology – these are symptoms of dissociation, like the impending philosophical disaster of Descartes. One consequence of his living at the dawn of dissociation is that Donne, who read so much, never sounds wholly serious. He arrests ideas rather than pursuing them into their larger intellectual contexts, so the result is often a scrappy assemblage. Bits of thought are detained for witty enquiry, grilled as to what emotion they can produce. In this he is, of course, quite unlike Dante.

Accordingly Dante and his times here get more devoted attention than the seventeenth century. Praz gently ticked Eliot off for depending too much on secondary sources, especially Rémy de Gourmont, but as an earnest of earnestness the lecturer, to the recorded discomfort of some in his audience, quotes a great chunk of Richard of St Victor in Latin (impressively apologizing for his Italianate Latin accent). He does this because he wishes to contrast the intellectual purity of medieval mystical practices with the 'spiritual haschisch' of Ignatius Loyola, whose sixteenth-century *Exercises* were more familiar to Donne. Having done so he can give 'The Extasie' an examination minute enough to make you think that, in spite of applauding some things in it, he doesn't like it much. The critique is detailed, lively and contestable, but it turns out that what is really wrong with the poem is that it accepts what is called the crude 'modern' separation of body and soul, a recent vulgarity impossible to St Thomas Aquinas. I daresay it might be possible to prove this wrong.

Eventually, in the fourth lecture, Eliot tackles the question of the English 'metaphysical conceit', and finds that Donne's similes and metaphors lack the 'rational necessity' of Dante's. Here there is room for argument. For instance, in explaining 'rational necessity' he turns his attention for a moment to Shakespeare. He quotes Dante's passage about Brunetto Latini (famous with us because of Eliot's admiration):

> *Poi si rivolse, e parve di coloro*
> *che coronno a Verona il drappo verde*
> *per la campagna; e parve di costoro*
> *quegli che vince e non colui che perde.*

(Then he turned back, and seemed like one of those who run for the green cloth at Verona through the open field; and of them he seemed to be like him who wins, and not like him who loses.)

That is, Brunetto is damned, a loser, though he surprisingly looks more like a winner. Eliot, in the later essay on Dante, talks of being hit by these lines, but, as in the case of Francesca, also in hell and lamenting the good times, seems to attribute their force to the salutary way they emphasize the severity of the sinner's punishment. Here his immediate purpose is to compare the Brunetto passage with what Octavius Caesar says about Cleopatra's body at the end of Shakespeare's play:

> But she looks like sleep,
> As she would catch another Antony
> In her strong toil of grace.

Shakespeare's lines have not the 'rational necessity' of Dante's, but they are admitted to have a different, even a superior, necessity, offering 'an image absolutely woven into the fabric of the thought'. It is true that Dante is in syntax and vocabulary expansive (*parve di coloro* – *parve di costoro*, *quegli–colui*, the apparently inessential *per la campagna*), whereas Shakespeare is extremely intensive. But both depend on paradox. On the one hand there is the loser/winner simile, spelled out with fleeting details of the race and the prize; on the other the 'strong toil of grace', a compressed figure, a sort of oxymoron, with scriptural antecedents. There is an apparent impropriety of sense in both the green cloth and the toil (nets or traps); both are surprising, both hit you. As Octavius remarks, Cleopatra should have some post-mortem symptoms but hasn't, so he is surprised; but our surprise comes rather from the sudden emergence of the great paradox from a less powerful similitude, 'she looks like sleep'. Thus once more we are hit, and strangeness has much to do with the violent success of either passage. The comparison remains interesting, but the passages hardly have that generic differentiation here posited. It may be right to remark that the Shakespeare lines would be 'impossible for Dante', and the Dante passage could as well be said to be impossible for Shakespeare. It doesn't sound much like Donne, either. But it would be hard to agree that the difference is about 'rational necessity'.

The close readings of Donne are ostensibly based on the dictum – correct I think – that 'you must construe [Donne] analytically and enjoy [him] synthetically'; but in fact the analyses are a shade disappointing. You feel that Eliot can always surrender to a particular line – 'A Bracelet of bright hair about the bone' – but external considerations then induce him to include it in a hostile analysis of its context, regarded as over-conceited, so that the promise of a true union of thought and feeling is not long kept. Such failures are explained by the contention that Donne really doesn't believe anything; instead he isolates a thought and makes it 'an object of sense'. 'A conceit is the extreme limit of the simile and metaphor which is pursued for its own sake, and not to make clearer an idea or more definite an emotion.' Here we are moving rapidly towards Eliot's later and lower estimate of Donne. Rather surprisingly, he argues for the long poems as the best, though one would have thought the *Anniversaries* offered hundreds of examples of thoughts briefly entertained for whatever emotional surprises they can be induced to provide.

Crashaw gets a lecture, and is much admired, though found, not surprisingly, to be 'on the side of feeling rather than thought' – unlike Dante, for whom feeling and thought are 'reverse sides of the same thing'. There follows a lecture centred on the 'mediocre' but not unimportant Cowley; and the last is devoted to that brief rebirth of metaphysical poetry in nineteenth-century France. Otherwise all is disintegration, the disintegration of verse following on a greater one, the disintegration of intellect, of which we were to hear more later, though not in the form promised here.

The lectures have occasionally a rather severe jauntiness, as in certain rude remarks about the likes of Middleton Murry and Frank Harris, and some sly digs at Richards in the audience. And Eliot has prefixed a fascinating double epigraph, which couples an exalted passage from the *Vita Nuova* – 'Ladies, the end and aim of my love was but the salutation of that lady of whom I conceive that you are speaking' – with a fragment of some lost 'popular song':

> I want someone to treat me rough.
> Give me a cabman.

The assiduous editor has found no source for this, and perhaps it needs none. It makes a calculated bathos of a kind Eliot always enjoyed. This is a rare failure on the part of Mr Schuchard, who offers a great deal of very well-judged annotation. And he dutifully corrects the volleys of misquotation in the lectures. Eliot's inaccuracies in this respect have been commented on before and found interesting. The most striking in the present volume is in a passage said to be from Chapman's *The Revenge of Bussy D'Ambois*:

> fly, where men feel
> The cunning axletree, and those that suffer
> Under the chariot of the snowy Bear.
> And tell them all that D'Ambois now is hasting
> To the eternal dwellers . . .

Chapman wrote 'The burning axletree', and he wrote it in *Bussy D'Ambois*, not in its sequel. When, seven or so years earlier, Eliot remembered this passage in 'Gerontion' he wrote 'Beyond the circuit of the shuddering Bear'. Referring, in his Harvard lectures of 1933, to Chapman's original in Seneca, he further remarked that what the imagery meant to Seneca, Chapman or himself, was 'too obscure to understand'. Certainly, as in other instances, elements of the dying speech of Bussy mingled in his head with other apparently irrelevant associations; but how the axletree became 'cunning' certainly seems too obscure to understand.

It is probably true to say that if Eliot had published this book in the 1920s the course of later critical writing about Donne and the Metaphysicals would have been different. As to his own 'critical mind', it is illuminated by the book, as Schuchard claims, but also by his rejection of the positions taken in it. The scope of his 'dissociation of sensibility' is much enlarged. And it becomes even more clear that Dante, used here as a model, was the end and aim of his love. Donne faded, Dante didn't; possibly it was, for him, the measure of that difference, repeatedly pondered, between a great and a lesser poet. As to where he stands himself, we can only agree with him that this is a matter for decision elsewhere and at another time.

Marianne Moore

We are told by the editors* that some 30,000 letters of Marianne Moore survive, many of them extremely long, and that she sometimes wrote fifty letters a day. When she was young and not famous her family saved her letters; later on people kept some because she had become rather famous, and then kept a great many because she had become very famous. Correspondents, some as famous as she was, treasured every word she wrote them. There survive 100 letters to Ezra Pound and another 100 to T. S. Eliot; 500 to the historical novelist Bryher (Winifred Ellerman) and 60 to Hilda Doolittle (H. D.), who was Bryher's lover. Elizabeth Bishop, a favourite in later years, received over 200, over a period of almost forty years.

Faced with such abundance the editors have had to make severe choices, and have occasionally and understandably made cuts in letters they did include. On the whole they seem to have done their work well. Their interchapters on the life of the poet are relevant and informative, and there are useful glossaries. Their annotations, however, are irritatingly scanty. It would be too much to expect annotation on the scale of the Oxford edition of the Yeats correspondence; that is quite another world. But even on this humbler scale much more could have been done; and notes so modest in scope might be expected to avoid inaccuracy. On p. 300, for instance, there is a translation of an Italian book title that could only have been made

* *The Selected Letters of Marianne Moore*, ed. Bonnie Costello, Celeste Goodridge and Cristanne Miller (London: Faber, 1998).

by somebody under the not uncommon but incorrect impression that Italian is a transparently simple language, understandable without effort. Avoidable slips of that kind would have irritated Marianne Moore, who repeatedly insists on the virtue of accuracy, whether in Wallace Stevens's poems or in Ralph Kirkpatrick's harpsichord playing ('gossamer precision') or, indeed, in translation, at which she showed herself to be exceptionally good. Still, her editors have, as they claim, fulfilled Eliot's prediction (1959) that 'one of the books which obviously must in the fullness of time be published . . . will be the *Letters* of Marianne Moore'.

One aspect of American modernism, baffling at first sight, is the diversity of means by which its principal figures developed their gifts, and the variety of manners and modes they eventually exploited. Exigencies of occupation and location did something to prevent the formation of influential metropolitan cliques, though groups of that sort did exist in New York and also in Chicago. But the great ones, though they may have occasionally frequented these *foyers*, were usually about their business elsewhere. Think, for example, of Charles Ives and Wallace Stevens, both New England insurance executives, living in the same town, and both doing the entirely unexpected things they chose to do, while remaining unknown even to one another, and quite out of the public eye. W. C. Williams was a hard-working New Jersey physician. They were all originals but all in the American grain, declining the European alternatives chosen by Eliot and Pound, and all engaged in discovering idiosyncratic but American ways of being modern. Marianne Moore, emigrating from Kirkwood, Missouri, to Carlisle, Pennsylvania, and only a good deal later to Brooklyn, looks at first glance like a sheltered spinster who inexplicably devised complex stanzas of syllabic verse quite unlike anything that was being done elsewhere. It is an indication of her independence of mind that among the influences she admitted we find Thomas Hardy, whose poetry, on the face of it, belonged to another world; she took what she wanted wherever it came from. Yet she very well understood the modern American virtues of Williams,

Stevens, Cummings, Eliot, Pound, Kenneth Burke and Yvor Winters; and, in return, they were remarkably quick to see hers.

Poets did come together in powerful little magazines such as *Poetry* (Chicago), *The Egoist* and *The Dial*, which Moore came to prefer, and which she herself edited with conscience and discernment for several years in the 1920s. And they might, in time, sample the bohemian life of Greenwich Village. Yet their voices remained distinct and their inventiveness very personal, so that modernism had from the beginning this dispersity; it was to be defined partly in terms of its not being English, but more largely in terms of individuals rather than of a concerted movement – of individuals who nevertheless saw the point of other individuals, and supported them. The chorus of praise for Moore's strange poetry, led by Eliot but sustained by Williams, Stevens and others, is virtually without a discordant voice. She herself understood her worth; when she came across a dissentient view she carefully recorded it in her correspondence, but with no suggestion that such dissent was very wounding. She had decided early and irrevocably to have success as her own kind of writer.

She left a considerable volume of prose writings as well as all these letters, and they also testify to her modest but firm confidence in her powers. Above all there are the poems, so accurately written, and with such disciplined pleasure, yet so inexplicably and repeatedly revised. Anything could get into them, including all the chosen pleasures of her life, the ball games and prize fights, the paintings and the exotic animals. To an extraordinary degree she did, though with great labour, exactly as she liked.

Moore began life in a highly literate family, who communicated with one another in a 'special language' – her brother understood her poems to be instruments for making this language intelligible to 'aliens'. She went to Bryn Mawr in 1905, which was two years after the poet Yeats paid that college a memorable visit. He was very pleased with the education on offer at 'the chief woman's college of America', where, as he remarked, the rich sent their daughters. He was delighted to hear from one of the professors that 'we prepare the girls to live their lives but in England they are making them all teachers', for this fitted in well with Yeats's idea that girls should be taught to think less with their heads than with their bodies. For Bryn Mawr graduates, he said, 'were as charming, as well-educated in all necessary things, as if they had spent their youth in the impulsive laborious ignorance of the studio'. In so far as this remark suggests a cult of high-minded feminine unknowing it is false, for Bryn Mawr students are famous for being workers. Moore, who enjoyed her time at the College, years later gave a less extravagant version of the matter: 'My experience there gave me security in my determination to have what I want . . . At Bryn Mawr the students are allowed to develop with as little interference as is compatible with any kind of academic order and the more I see of other women's colleges the more I feel that Bryn Mawr was peculiarly adapted to my special requirements.'

This makes more sense than the grand Yeatsian perception that Bryn Mawr had hit on a method of endowing girls with the means to achieve something like Unity of Being; Moore, accurate, quietly self-assertive as usual, merely says it enabled her to have what she wanted. The vague shape of what she wanted was already present in her mind and habits, and the college years allowed it to become more definite. She was already writing poetry, but it is in her letters rather than in the juvenile poems that one sees how early her interests were formed. A trip to New York elicits a minute and critical description of the goods at Tiffany's, meals and clothes are described with the usual accurate elegance, and so are people: 'Mr Z. is an easy, tall man, with flat long shoes, very clever fair sized hands and smooth, straight gray hair, very quiet hair, rather old fashioned.'

Meanwhile her programme of reading, though partly prescribed by the College, bore the marks of individuality as well as an interest in fashion: Pater, Sappho, Stevenson, Thackeray, Whistler, 'a book on Wagner's operas'. Later she celebrated Trollope at a time when nobody read him. Against the current of opinion she admired George Saintsbury, and when she became editor of *The Dial* commissioned work from this writer, already over eighty and hardly to be thought of as belonging to any avant-garde. Indeed her notion of what was worth having, whether avant-garde or not, was based on confidence in her own independent judgement.

She was capable of severity in comment, speaking, for instance, of Yeats's 'cheap brainless fakirism'. She found the later work of Joyce inferior to *Dubliners*, which she described as 'pretty nearly a manual . . . of the fundamentals of composition', admiring 'the unaccountable effect of finality despite tentativeness, in the closing sentences of every one of the stories'. (Even at the expense of annoying Eliot she declined to join the protest against the piracy of *Ulysses*.) As editor of *The Dial* she was politely sure of her judgements, turning down poems by Hart Crane, suggesting cuts in Conrad Aitken, and boldly improving other people's poems, not always to their satisfaction. But when she was taken by a poem she was full of praise, not least for the early work of Elizabeth Bishop.

Bishop went to Vassar – the next best thing, Moore might have thought, to Bryn Mawr. She was a generation younger, but both women seem to have recognized an unusual affinity, and almost at once they went to the circus together, an important threshold-crossing. Bishop is the poet closest to Moore in temperament, her rival as a letter-writer, and also as a devotee of the accurate. She took harpsichord lessons from Ralph Kirkpatrick, and, like Moore, admired the intricate little boxes of Joseph Cornell, some of which she owned and liked to show to guests. Early in their acquaintance Bishop, twenty-three at the time, published an essay on Gerard Manley Hopkins which Moore admired so much that she quoted it in a letter to Pound. It spoke of 'the way in which the rhythm of a poem keeps up with itself like an acrobat catching his partner's ankles while affording, in safety, an extra turn and flourish within the fall'. Probably she liked this because it struck her as applying to her own poems, as indeed it does.

Moore once remarked that 'prose is a step beyond poetry . . . and then there is another poetry that is a step beyond that'; you had to go through prose to come out on the other side purged of that disposable prior poetry, with its irrelevant inversions and its subjection to conventional rhythms. The posterior poetry would have built into it the virtues of good prose. In the syllabic poems, where 'each stanza [is] a duplicate of every other stanza' (much as Donne set himself argumentative problems by exactly replicating an arbitrarily complicated opening stanza), the sentences could, indeed must, be capable of being written straight out as prose; what is lost in the process of doing that is precisely the machine-like precision of the repetitions of line length and covert rhyme. If the effect seems mechanical, so be it. In 1922, on the brink of celebrity, she remarked that 'a thing so mechanically perfect as a battleship is always a pleasure to me'.

One can see something of what this means by looking at the 'The Steeple-Jack', the poem which, though not an early work, having been first published in 1932, stands first in both the *Collected Poems* of 1981 and the *Selected Poems* of 1941. It was much admired by both Eliot, who arranged the order of the poems for Moore, putting this one at the head, and by Wallace Stevens, who analysed it at some length, commending, among other things, the poet's attachment to truth. The opening six-line stanza sets the arbitrary pattern of line length and rhyme, and has a full close:

> Dürer would have seen a reason for living
> > in a town like this, with eight stranded whales
> to look at, with the sweet sea air coming into your house
> on a fine day, from water etched
> > with waves as formal as the scales
> > on a fish.

(Dürer because he travelled far and fruitlessly to inspect a beached whale, but also because of the etched scales; and, more generally, because he is deeply in the thought of the poem.) The second and third stanzas repeat the stanza pattern but form a continuous sentence which flows over the scheme without disturbing it, stopping at the last line of the third stanza. The fourth stanza strictly observes the pattern and the rhymes, one of which, 'the' and 'sea-', is virtually not there. At that point the two texts diverge, the *Collected* offering the original thirteen perfectly regular stanzas, the *Selected* only eight, with the fourth torn and deformed. 'Omissions are not accidents,' says the epigraph of the *Collected Poems*, and it is hard to think of any of Moore's strangenesses as accidental, whether she is describing a seaside town or an exotic bird, playing her sense across the machine-like stanza, or simply abandoning that game and many fine things along with it. She cuts her own poem as ruthlessly as when editing *The Dial* she cut Archibald MacLeish's. Either version enables one to see why Auden admired her so much that he later took up the syllabic cause. Moore herself, having abandoned it in favour of free verse, returned to it about the time of 'The Steeple-Jack'. She did as she pleased, though she was ruthlessly hard to please.

Moore became a cult figure, the old lady in the tricorne hat who threw the first pitch of the baseball season, went to prize fights with George Plimpton, dined with Cassius Clay, as he then was, and was hired, unavailingly, to give a name to a new Ford car. On the whole people think rather little of the poems she wrote after about 1936, although she published many more before her death in 1972.

What the letters tell about her is that however one divides her long life into periods there is from the outset the sense of a presiding personality, and a pretty self-assured one. With the family, especially the mother with whom she lived until she was over sixty, and her brother, a parson who rose high in the Navy, she was always easy and private, sure of their intelligently sharing her avocations. They all had what she called 'unconscious fastidiousness', though it wasn't always unconscious. Reading her poems about animals – 'The Jerboa', 'The Plumet Basilisk', 'The Fish' – one is struck by the fact that her bestiary is given jewelled settings, so that the vicinity of animals is made as strange and gorgeous as they are. The letters contain dozens of minute descriptions of exotic insects and lizards, the fruit of many visits to the Natural History Museum and of enquiries to experts; all are reported at length to her brother.

Poetry, the arts and the natural world in its more brilliant and detailed manifestations were what mattered most. Politics do not figure largely in these letters, though when young she was a suffragette, later a Republican and a Hoover supporter. Whether seriously or for fun, she remarked during the presidential campaign of 1932 that 'America is pestered at present by a man named Franklin D. Roosevelt, as Germany has been with Hitler'. She was *echt* American, but saw herself as having begun life under a form of civilization now superseded by a new one that was turning out badly; hence one's illusion that in a charmingly old-fashioned way she was, in that new world, an isolated figure. Yet she clearly had the power to assemble around her, if only in correspondence, a group of friends and fellow practitioners who certainly constituted a civilized elite. To be finely tuned to poems, while remaining obstinately herself, was her purpose in life. It is agreeable to think of her as a young woman impressed by the civilization of Bryn Mawr, impressed even by the dreadful Deanery (now happily pulled down to make room for a library extension) in which visiting lecturers sweltered amid masses of Indian furniture before making their offerings to the brilliant, self-motivating students who followed in her footsteps. It seems to have been a place that played its part in that old superseded culture which provided so fertile a soil for American modernism.

Empson the Poet

Empson has been dead these sixteen years, and although his voice was quite often recorded it now seems quite difficult to describe it. John Haffenden* says he had one voice for poetry and another for prose. Empson himself thought 'the reader should throw himself into the verse, and not do it with "reserved" English good taste'. The best idea was to ham it 'like a provincial Shakespeare actor a hundred years ago'. According to Naomi Lewis this effort resulted in his 'presenting his love poems in the sardonic tones of a seventeenth-century New England elder directing the trial of a witch'. Haffenden describes Empson's as 'a patrician voice, with a slightly sardonic timbre', which seems a fair description of his everyday tones, and so is G. S. Fraser's – 'an odd, sad, snarly voice'. Of his poetry reading John Wain said he rendered some passages 'like a Neapolitan steve-dore, laryngitically croaking others'. In private sitting rooms he used a quieter tone, 'though the curious angularity of rhythm', which some like and some do not, was still present.

The first time I ever heard him read was in a private sitting room, about 1953, and I recall my astonishment when he read 'Note on Local Flora'. He began sedately, but at the last two lines – 'So Semele desired her deity/As this in Kew thirsts for the Red Dawn' – he slowly rose up from his chair and delivered them in a sort of strangled apocalyptic whisper. Kathleen Raine once observed that it was just

* *William Empson: The Complete Poems*, ed. John Haffenden (London: Allen Lane, 2000).

like Empson to visit Kew and read the botanical labels rather than look at the trees. There seems to be some learned dispute as to whether there is or ever was a tree that 'will ripen only in a forest fire' in Kew Gardens. The Tree of Heaven, said in the poem to have been nearby, was blown down in the gale of 1987, and possibly the Turkestani pine suffered the same fate. Nevertheless it seems that Kew still has specimens of which it may be possible to say that their cones cannot disperse their seeds without help from a forest fire. In any case the idea struck the poet as worthy of remark both as calling to mind the fate of Semele, impregnated with Bacchus by Zeus in his full and fatal splendour, all thunder and lightning, and an image of apocalypse, the fire that must burn this world. The tree thirsts for the Red Dawn, which is, as Empson himself noted, 'the Communist victory'. So it was thoughts of the glorious fate of Semele, and of the coming revolution, as well as the imminence of his own splendid epiphonema, that forced the poet out of his chair. They called for a voice different from that used in a recording mentioned by Haffenden in the line immediately preceding the pair I've quoted: 'I knew the Phoenix was a vegetable.' This was delivered, we are told, humorously as if deprecating the erudite mythology of the opening lines, but was in fact a craftily deceptive lull before the final conflagration.

A poem of ten lines demanded all this variety of tone, these ways of emphasizing its plot. The plot is also an argument; most of the poems are both narrative and argument. When either or both are obscure the reason is that the terms in which each is expounded are abruptly metaphorical, and the metaphors are so far-fetched that they seem to divert the reader from the immediate sense, and the personal import of the poems. So despite the passion at the heart of the enterprise there is in the product a certain bleakness. Empson described the influence of Eliot as being 'perhaps not unlike an east wind', and the expression may be applied to many of his own poems.

These we can now study in Haffenden's almost wantonly magnificent edition. The poetry itself, complete except for one manuscript poem the editor wanted but the Estate withheld, occupies hardly more than 100 pages, the commentary close to three times as many. A highly informative introduction adds another ninety or so. Haffenden's easy, expansive manner cannot quite disguise the quantity, care and detail of his work. Reading such an elaborate edition one has an uncharitable keenness to find mistakes, however slight, and editors often profess to be glad to have them pointed out. So: I think there is a mistranscription in line 10 of the interesting verses quoted on pp. xliii–xliv ('to do so' rather than 'you do so') and another in an unpublished letter on p. xlvii, where it seems likely that Empson wrote 'And I should not apologize for notes on such a scale' rather than saying he *should* apologize, since on a good many other occasions he firmly declined to do so. Another slip may be explained by the editor's relative youth: he does not know what 'degaussing' means or meant. It is used in a nice little poem not by Empson but by a friend of his, to accompany a wedding present. In 1942, when the poem was written, everybody had known for a year or so that degaussing involved the fitting of a demagnetizing cable round the hulls of ships to frustrate German magnetic mines; indeed the OED dates the word from 1940, which is when the device was introduced. This sense, missed in Haffenden's note, is necessary to the understanding of the friend's poem and to the poet's rather beautiful response. Finally, *Ulysses* is misspelt on p. 328.

Empson believed in notes. *Poems* (1935) and *The Gathering Storm* (1940) both contain defences of his practice. 'There is no longer a reasonably small field which may be taken as general knowledge. It is impertinent to suggest that the reader ought to possess already any odd bit of information one may have picked up in a field where one is oneself ignorant; . . . and it does not require much fortitude to endure seeing what you already know in a note.' And notes are 'meant to be like answers to a crossword puzzle . . . There would be no point in publishing a puzzle in a newspaper, if it were admittedly so simple that there was no need to publish the answer.' He remarked that the craze for obscurity in poems came in about the same time as the fashion for crosswords. (Like Auden, who also wrote lots of notes if he felt like it, Empson was devoted to crossword puzzles.)

However, a poem should have more than this crossword kind of interest.

Empson was always sure that the interest of a poem arose from its representation of what passed in the mind of the poet, and the piling up of information about what the poem means is in the end an investigation of the mind that produced it. Here there is certainly a piling up of information: Empson's own notes, as included in his books of verse; further notes provided by him on records, at readings and interviews, in letters; and the thick top layer of Haffenden's elucidations. Of course the notes can't always help much. Empson told Christopher Ricks in an interview that his poem 'The Teasers' developed in such a way that he began to dislike it; he 'cut it down to rags so that it doesn't make sense, you can't find out what it is about . . . But it's a beautiful metrical invention, I do say.' Elsewhere he remarked that 'The Teasers' was 'nearly very good, above my level altogether', though with a final moral he felt the poem hadn't earned. He liked the novel effect of making a quatrain by breaking the second line of the three-line stanzas in two. As it stands it has that half-awake dreamlike quality Empson achieved in other late poems, notably 'Let it go', said by Empson to reflect a decision to give up writing poetry:

> It is this deep blankness is the real thing strange.
> The more things happen to you the more you can't
> Tell or remember even what they were.

> The contradictions cover such a range.
> The talk would talk and go so far aslant.
> You don't want madhouse and the whole thing there.

This poem is printed on the back of the jacket of this edition, and it does work as jacket copy, though Empson once said it was 'hopelessly bad'. It is worth attending to his self-judgements; he is often hard on his own work, but if he thought it deserved praise he gave it unstintedly and perceptively, as when he celebrated *The Structure of Complex Words* as his masterpiece. His condemnation of 'Let it go' seems to have been caused by its supposed resistance to the reader's understanding, but readers of his work are accustomed to that problem and anyway in this instance we have a kind of mumbling between sleep and wake from which simple sense is not to be expected. The last line vaguely threatens a madness brought on simply enough by the constant effort to understand, and to remain steady in the midst of, the vast system of contradictions life obliges one to contend with (a theme of earlier poems), and the deep blankness seems premonitory of that feared ending.

Yet the poem is still a kind of muttered song, as it were composed for performance by that strange voice. Empson admired what he called 'the singing line', especially if it also had some clarity of thought. One of his most beautiful poems is 'Chinese Ballad', based on a poem by Li Chi: 'It's not by me at all, you see, but I always feel it clears the palate after a reading of my stuff.' Ricks called the poem 'Empson's *nunc dimittis* as a poet', an assurance that, 'though life may be essentially inadequate to the human spirit, the human spirit is essentially adequate to life'. The parting lovers entrust their faith to two dolls, made of mud; the dolls will be smashed and reconstituted, 'grain by grain',

> 'So your flesh shall be part of mine
> And part of mine be yours.
> Brother and sister we shall be
> Whose unity endures.
>
> 'Always the sister doll will cry,
> Made in these careful ways,
> Cry on and on, Come back to me,
> Come back, in a few days.'

The conceit is worthy of Donne, Empson's own chosen master, and the tone is genuinely ballad-like (as Donne's sometimes was). It is an allegory of the pain of a parting that seems perpetual, of a resistance (supported by art, by the making and mixing of the dolls) to the dreadful sense of the contradictions involved in living and thinking about it, that seems to underlie much of Empson's work, as indeed it does that of his admired Milton. The radical contradiction is between the hope of human happiness, for which, at least at certain moments, we feel ourselves so wonderfully suited, and the power of the world as it inescapably is to frustrate or even ridicule that feeling. Hence Empson's endorsement of the Buddhist position that 'no sort of temporal life whatever can satisfy the human spirit'. Yet Buddhism also takes account of the fact that 'birth as a human being is an opportunity of inestimable value. He who is so born has at least a chance of hearing the truth and acquiring merit.'

It would be too crude to argue that tensions such as those touched on in 'Let it go', between the threat of madness and the requirement of sanity, can by themselves fully define the stresses within the verse, or explain why Empson felt he must give it up; but the effort to handle the contradictions, which attracted him to Buddhism and perhaps shaped him as a poet, may be heard even in the vagaries of that voice.

Empson certainly thought of himself as a poet, it was his vocation; and he had a strong, I suppose ultimately a Romantic, sense of the necessary estrangement or outsidedness of poets, who may have a more urgent apprehension than others of the mismatch between desire and reality, or, simply, of the tragedy of being in the world. Graham Hough, in an obituary published in the *London Review of Books*, remarked that 'It is often the case that what comes across to most readers as an intricate intellectual puzzle was experienced as a painful knot of feeling', and the poet's friend G. S. Fraser spoke of 'puzzling form being imposed on a massive and almost unbearable personal unhappiness'. If that is the right way to talk about it, the burden on the poet who wants to communicate a full sense of what others just feel in their disordered way and, at a lower level, just put up with is enormous. And these differences cannot be ignored; they may declare themselves not only in poems but in a manner of talking so different from other people's that admirers, not only aspiring poets but aspiring critics, are in danger of unconsciously and ridiculously imitating it. That patrician voice, colloquial, even chatty in prose, transformed for verse, highly intellectual but with none of the poses or shortcuts of ordinary intellectual talk, is an image of the spirit in which Empson could say that 'whether or not the values open to us are measurable, we cannot measure them, and it is of much value merely to stand up between the forces to which we are exposed'. These remarks were made in the 1930s, but Haffenden says that Empson never lost his high regard for Buddhist teaching, which he often contrasted with the hateful doctrines of Christianity. The intensity with which he contemplated what might be called spiritual issues, as well as problems of personal behaviour, make it clear that, although he could not easily be called a religious man or poet, he thought painfully about matters that the religious think important.

A much-quoted remark occurs in Empson's notes to the poem 'Bacchus': 'life involves maintaining oneself between contradictions that can't be solved by analysis'. They can only be presented with due regard for their virtually insoluble complexity. In personal life, this may call for old-fashioned virtues such as courage and honour. Honour can be forced on one; in the very obscure early poem 'High Dive' the point seems to be made that a person having got on to the high board would lose face by climbing down without diving. The poem wraps this point in more or less occult references, explained in the poet's notes, to Northern mythology, a heretical Egyptian sun-god, the fact that green coats are worn by hare hunters, Cornford's theory that the order of nature was thought of as the lifeblood of a tribe, the mathematics of water, the clotting of blood, Lucifer, Jezebel, Jonah, and much else. You need to know what words like 'irrotational' mean. There is a calmly elaborate and authoritative interpretation by Veronica Forrest-Thompson in an essay quoted by the assiduous Haffenden but worth reading through in the *Yearbook of English Studies* for 1974. It gives one some idea of what was going on in the poet's head when he was about twenty-two. Courage and honour may not come up in the notes, but they are there in the poem.

The early poems are somewhat ostentatiously crammed with ideas that belong to Empson's Cambridge youth, but some are still vigorously alive: 'To an Old Lady', for instance, and 'Camping Out' and 'Arachne', 'Legal Fiction', and the beautiful 'Villanelle', which begins, 'It is the pain, it is the pain, endures.' (Empson remarks with customary generosity on the technical superiority over his own villanelles of the one Auden wrote for Miranda in *The Sea and the Mirror*, which, he said, 'wipes the eye of everyone who tries to revive' the form.) One should add to this list 'Homage to the British Museum' and 'Note on Local Flora'.

But although the cognoscenti often find a falling off after *Poems*, Empson's finest are, I think, later: 'Aubade', 'Courage means Running', 'Missing Dates' and 'Success'. He has been with some justice accused of sometimes being arrogantly awkward, of making matters more difficult than they need to be, but these faults, if faults they are, belong mostly to earlier poems. There are, of course, problems even in the more lucid later work. I remember John Wain, who adored Empson, joking about the evident difficulty the poet had in keeping up the rhymes in 'Missing Dates':

> Slowly the poison the whole blood stream fills,
> It is not the effort nor the failure tires.
> The waste remains, the waste remains and kills.

All is well, the rhyming holds up till we get to 'They bled an old dog dry yet the exchange rills/Of young dog blood gave but a month's desires', and later there is 'a skin that shrills'; but the villanelle is still beautiful. So with 'Success': the opening is certainly arresting: 'I have mislaid the torment and the fear./You should be praised for taking them away', but a few lines later 'Verse likes despair. Blame it upon the beer' sounds a bit desperate. Still, it may catch the mood of its writing as Empson describes it: 'It's recovering from a love affair and saying it did you good.' His view of love was that it saves you from madness.

Wain says of 'Aubade' that it 'really happened', the poet and a Japanese girl (apparently a nursemaid) are caught in bed by an earthquake. '"The heart of standing is you cannot fly", one of Empson's great reverberating lines . . . covers a wide range: the whole point of turning to fight is that running away will not save them and is in any case contrary to their code.' That seems right – the last line changes 'you' to 'we' – even when balanced against 'It seemed the best thing to be up and go.' The poem enshrines contradiction, and even that reverberant line, with its patrician sentiment, has a patrician deviance from ordinary ways of speaking. What makes it reverberant is the voice, an excitement proper to the speaker. When Empson rose slowly from his seat to match the expectations of the tree in Kew he was still, after more than twenty years, thrilled by the prospect of the poem's climax. It celebrated a victory, you rose to meet it, as you took the high dive and dealt with the earthquake in a structured, moody form that was itself a challenge issued by poetry to the poet.

Empson as Critic

William Empson maintained that there was a right and a wrong moment to bring theory into the business of intelligent reading, and that the professionals chose the wrong one. But he could not do without theory altogether, and his book *The Structure of Complex Words* (1951) contains quite a lot of it; so it is not surprising that a generation of literary theorists, having sensibly decided not to remain totally out of touch with the best critic of his time, has decided to appropriate *Complex Words*, a work hitherto much less influential than the very early (and prodigious) *Seven Types of Ambiguity*. Christopher Norris* comes right out and calls it 'a work of deconstruction'.

Norris's collection is meant to demonstrate that Empson can be accommodated in modern Theory. It can now be shown that he was in many ways anticipating the interests and procedures of a newer criticism, though Norris in his preface cautiously denies any intention to annex Empson's criticism to some prevailing trend; 'it is a hopeful sign', he remarks, 'that "theory" is coming of age when it manages to find room for a strong but problematical figure like Empson, a critic whose thinking goes so markedly against some of its basic precepts and principles'.

As a rhetorical concession this is prudent and ingenious, but it gives some measure of the size of the task. Norris knows very well

* *William Empson: The Critical Achievement*, ed. Christopher Norris and Nigel Mapp (Cambridge: Cambridge University Press, 1993).

what Empson thought of these precepts and principles. He once sent the great man some essays from the new French school, including Derrida's famous lecture 'Structure, Sign and Play', later treated as a manifesto by his American followers. Empson wrote back to say he found all these papers, including the one by Derrida – or 'Nerrida' as he preferred to call him – 'very disgusting'. Norris – or Dorris, as Empson might have called him in his later career as a theorist – laments, not without reason, that his correspondent showed no signs of having understood what he had found disgusting. On the whole the current tendency is to compare and contrast him not with Derrida but with de Man – Norris spends time on this comparison, and Neil Hertz has a whole essay about it. One can only imagine what Empson would have said about that, or what names he would have found for these in so many respects unlikely mates. True, Empson and de Man shared a certain hauteur, and a certain iconoclasm, but the political adhesions were different, and so were the critical dialects – one conscientiously bluff, the other rarefied and prone to Gallicism.

That *Complex Words* is what Norris calls it, 'Empson's great theoretical summa', is the view also of his contributors William Righter, Alan Durant and Colin MacCabe, and Jean Lecercle, whose lively piece includes a remark to the effect that the poem 'Camping Out' mentions a girlfriend cleaning her teeth into the lake; Empson, so keen on biography, would have liked him to know that this was not a girlfriend but a sister – or so he himself once alleged.

Norris's own essay takes up a good third of the whole and best explains what is going on. There are, as he rightly remarks, more misunderstandings of Empson's critical positions than are defensible – for example, his loose association with the American New Critics of long ago has given rise to the notion that he agreed with their anti-intentionalism, although for forty years he went on explaining with increasing force and irritation that the purpose of criticism was to follow the movement of the author's mind. He saved some of his more brutal insults for W. K. Wimsatt, co-author of a famous article about 'The Intentional Fallacy'. In the end, I think, this particular bogey distracted him from what he did best, and in *Using Biography*

(1984) he seems to have given up movements of mind in favour of fancies and speculations he wouldn't at earlier dates have thought relevant.

However, you would expect that this strain in his thought, alien not only to the old New Criticism but to the new New Criticism, might give Norris some trouble. He gets out of it by what I take to be a change in his own position, so that theory, now come of age, can henceforth permit some attention to what was intended. Again, it is a congenial consideration that Empson thought the New Critics had adapted his methods in a sneaky way in order to import Christianity into the argument; indeed he believed that the decay of criticism was directly due to this intrusion of what Norris calls 'surrogate or ersatz theology'. This accounts for his habit, sometimes baffling to the agnostic opponent, of condemning criticism he disagreed with as 'neo-Christian'. The prefix suggests that indignant denials of Christian faith were merely evasive and would do you no good; you could be neo-Christian without being Christian. I think that historically this has something to do with a certain fashion for Christian criticism, and a more general worry about poetry and belief, at the time of Empson's return from China in the early 1950s; led by such as C. S. Lewis and practised by such as Fr Martin Jarrett-Kerr, it seemed interesting to others, who may then have seemed, willy-nilly, to be crypto-Christians.

One point of importance in this, as usual good, but as usual digressive, essay concerns Empson's refusal to distinguish between the truth of poetry and the truth of science. He rejected the 'pseudo-statement' theory of his mentor I. A. Richards, and as time went on had many tussles with the problem of figurative language, which often apparently says the thing that is not. He came to think of most contemporary literary criticism as a dreary professional attempt to avoid decisions about truth-statements made in poems. And of course he suspected a Christian plot. Norris is quite right to say that 'what comes through most strongly is his deep-laid conviction that the best – indeed the only – way to make sense of complex or problematical novels or poems is to read them with a mind unburdened by the self-denying ordinances of modern critical dogma'. But of course there are other forms of prejudice. Problems arising from arguments about truth and prejudice were to lead to noisy arguments about Donne.

I believe firmly that Empson was a great critic, but have to regard as wasteful his advocacy, over many years, of an eccentric view of Donne. To understand that view, now documented in full and supported by John Haffenden's conscientious and adulatory commentary,* one point at least is essential. Empson found it all but impossible to believe that any intelligent and honest person could possibly be a Christian. A lot of his work is devoted to showing that even writers who would have been amazed to hear it nevertheless did at some level of sensibility or intellect see through the horrors of the religion; Milton is the most obvious example (*Milton's God*, 1961), but the very devout Herbert is another.

Donne he had early taken as his model, regarding him, he says, with awe and love, and trying to write poems like his. That Donne became a famous parson was not too grave a problem, since he took orders against his will, because no other way of making a living was open to him; he wrote most of his poetry, and all of his erotic poetry, before he did so. (Empson doesn't show much interest in the sermons and devotional writings.) He cannot have accepted such absurd doctrines as the Trinity, and such horrible notions as Atonement, or believed in a religion that permitted you to torture your theological adversaries and burn them alive.

A minor instance of Empson's reflex of disgust at Christian thinking comes up in Norris's introduction, worth mentioning only because it shows how that reflex could block understanding. I had remarked, in a book he reviewed, that in Mark 4: 11–12, a famous crux, Jesus is plainly reported as saying that he uses parables to ensure that the people will miss his point: in order that 'hearing they

---

* William Empson, *Essays on Renaissance Poetry, Vol. 1: Donne and the New Philosophy*, ed. John Haffenden (Cambridge: Cambridge University Press, 1993).

may hear, and not understand'. Empson professed to think that I, in his peculiar view a palpable neo-Christian, was reverently offering this as a piece of divine wisdom; as Norris puts it, he 'was quick to discern the hints of a quasi-theological dimension'. My supposed misrepresentation of the bearing of the passage is dismissed in the interests of 'a forthright appeal to common-sense' and Empson is applauded by Norris for what in any lesser figure would be dismissed as a mere failure of attention.

Critics who disagreed with Empson about Donne got specially harsh treatment. The poet came from a devout Catholic family which was all too familiar with the penalties of recusancy; and it cannot be denied that he was very well read in theology, which Empson regarded as doubletalk, a means of hiding from good men the insane wickedness of the God they were obliged, under state penalties, to worship. It cannot be argued that Donne was indifferent to religion. However, it can be maintained that he saw through Christianity and made up a religion of his own, the tenets of which can be reconstructed from some clues in the poems, and involve the idea of woman as a rival and superior Logos. This religion of love transcended Christianity, and was very modern in that it more or less secretly accepted the doctrine of plurality of worlds and the possibility of life on other planets. So it depended heavily on the New Philosophy of the time. Empson believed that Donne often imagined lovers rejoicing in a liberty unknown under the political circumstances of the time, but available in America, and conceivably on some inhabitable planet in the newly opened-up universe.

Though nobody had taken quite this line before, Donne and the New Philosophy has long been a stock literary-history problem. Empson went carefully into the question of Elizabethan Copernicanism. In 1576 Thomas Digges published a book by his father with an addition accepting Copernicus; it was often reprinted, though without alteration or further addition. Since Digges went on doing advanced astronomy Empson took this continual reprinting of an unchanged text as evidence of censorship. This is possible, but mere conjecture without positive support. But in any case it is probable that Donne, a well-connected young man, with an immoderate thirst for learning, would know quite a bit about Digges, and about the novae which, after 1572, upset the traditional idea of the incorruptible heavens. Moreover Giordano Bruno, the main proponent of the idea that there were other inhabited planets (it gave rise to awkward theological problems, especially concerning Incarnation and Redemption), had made a stir in England and was well known to Sidney, for example, and doubtless to London groups of freethinkers, like those around Ralegh and the 'wizard' Earl of Northumberland.

Haffenden talks about the 'School of Night', dominated by such figures as Thomas Harriot, magician and atheist. The School of Night is conjectured to have been an organization devoted to this kind of modern study; here this focus is offered as undoubted historical fact. The term derives from a dubious reading in *Love's Labour's Lost*, and good authorities treat it sceptically; Haffenden says nothing of this in his text, consigning evidence against it to the backnotes. But even if there was no group called the School of Night there were certainly people who behaved as its members are thought by some to have done. Harriot had a special reputation as an original thinker; not as much is known about his thought, but one has a rough idea of the kind of thing he would go in for. At that time the patterns of learning were not as they later became, and an interest in scientific cosmology was perfectly consistent with astrology, alchemy, scrying and magic in general. Marlowe, it was reported, thought Harriot a better magician than Moses.

Wanting to make Donne as like himself as possible, Empson argues that he would have been very interested indeed in the work of these groups, though he seems to take little account of their interests other than in the new astronomy. The great mage John Dee, a central figure, was a scholar and had one of the great libraries of the age; he was famous not only for editing Euclid but for extraordinary feats of magic, alchemy and fortune-telling. So one ought not to think of these people simply as intellectual revolutionaries dedicated to the advancement of modern science in its early phase. And Donne's poetry uses far more alchemy, angelology and scholastic philosophy in general than up-to-date astronomy. He would be aware that there were exciting new ideas around, but that would not be a reason to give up all the old and more familiar ones; and on any unembattled view he was far from doing so.

In this respect his position is indeed somewhat like the young Empson's, for the study of Donne in the 1920s was conditioned by the mistaken idea that he strongly resembled the Symbolist poets, an idea given up when people, with the help of Grierson's edition, perceived that the poems, although difficult because of their extraordinary intellectual ingenuity, normally had perfectly clear arguments one could follow if one could come to terms with the unfamiliar allusions. These, as I say, were more often to scholastic philosophy, angelology and indeed the old Ptolemaic cosmology than to Copernicus. When Donne talks about spheres he is quite naturally thinking of the Ptolemaic ones, one to each planet including the moon, with the earth at the centre; round these spheres an angel or intelligence drove the planet, rather, as the contemptuous Scaliger was later to remark, like horses in a pound. This sense of 'sphere' was not altogether suitable, so Empson has to insist that Donne also habitually used the word to mean 'planet'.

Empson wants badly to keep hold of the belief of his youth, that the ideas of the New Philosophy were central to Donne's poetry, and Haffenden's collection contains repeated affirmations of that belief. I have to say that, however ingenious and entertaining the arguments, nothing here persuades me to alter the opinion tersely expressed and supported by citation in 1951 by J. C. Maxwell, a scholar whose name is absent from the index of Haffenden's book: namely that the impact on Donne of the New Philosophy has been much exaggerated. He was needed, at a time of worrying cultural crisis, to represent an earlier worrying cultural crisis – the earth was no longer at the centre of the creation, there was a general ferment of religious and philosophical ideas, and so on. The truth seems to be that Donne was interested in Copernican theory exactly as he was interested in other forms of learning; exciting as they may have been, there were other considerations that limited their force. In *The Second Anniversary* he gives a list of baffling intellectual problems and closes it with a dismissive couplet:

> In heaven thou straight know'st all concerning it,
> And what concerns it not shalt straight forget.

Empson, I think, abhorred the notion that somebody could be quite passionately interested in learning, yet at the same time remain somehow uncommitted to it. And well he might be, for it is an old Christian idea, and Donne had a severe Christian education. The sin of *curiositas* was a desire for human learning strong enough to impair performance of the higher duty of saving one's soul. It was possible for very learned men such as Augustine and Milton to condemn it. This condemnation was sometimes stated in very repressive forms, as indeed it is in *Paradise Regained*. That Donne should have such an opinion even in a mild form was unacceptable to Empson because he would feel contempt for anybody who held it. So he fights throughout for a Donne who was not only profoundly interested in all this new science, but gave it his real assent and even used it as the foundation of a new religion to supplant disgusting Christianity.

Haffenden backs him up loyally whenever he can, saying, for instance, that Donne might have known Kepler's *Somnium* long before it was published in Prague, because Kepler corresponded with Harriot and Donne may have known Harriot. The possibility is admittedly slight, especially since nobody outside Prague, according to Kepler himself, saw the *Somnium* until 1611, a year after Donne's skit *Ignatius his Conclave*, which could otherwise have been indebted to it. Oh well, says Haffenden, 'it is not unimaginable that Kepler got the date wrong'. This is a way of introducing supporting evidence even when you know it to be false, a practice now common in our courts of justice but still not admirable. There is more of this kind of 'not impossible' argument – it is even suggested that when Donne wrote the *Conclave* he might well have included an allusion to Bruno's *De Immenso*; as it isn't there now he must have discreetly crossed it out later.

The real point is not, I think, affected by arguments as to whether Donne knew or read this author or that. It is to decide how, if he knew quite a bit about these matters, which is plausible, he responded to them. One answer is that they mostly got into his poems as witty and conceited arguments or illustrations, demonstrating the same degree of commitment as the repeated allusions to the conduct of angels and alchemists. Haffenden, taking his tone from the master, would condemn this position as an instance of 'superficialism' – or, worse, as implying that Donne was a liar. This is a curious objection from a poet often himself given to conceits and to a wide range of allusions which are not themselves to be taken as simple statements of truth ('All those large dreams by which men long live well/ Are magic-lanterned on the smoke of hell').

This difficulty about belief and figuration in poetry is central to the problems posed in this book; it is as if Empson, with Haffenden in attendance, had devised a special philosophy of rhetoric for this poet, the favourite of his youth. However, to make it clearer how this arrangement affects the reading of the poems I had better give a sample or two, explaining first that Empson, who hated what Helen Gardner made of the texts, and often attacked her with asperity and justice, also wanted readings that suited his view of the matter best, just as he rightly says she did. The quarrel extends to many poems, but I must select, and the best place to begin is probably the Elegy 'To his Mistress going to bed', disagreement about which caused Empson to be remarkably nasty to not one but two Merton Professors, Helen Gardner and John Carey.

The poem is an impatiently erotic series of exhortations to a woman to hurry up and undress:

> Off with that girdle, like heaven's zone glistering
> But a far fairer world encompassing . . .
> License my roving hands and let them go
> Behind, before, above, between, below.
> Oh my America, my new found land . . .

The textual difficulty comes near the end, when he is talking about the last garment:

> cast all, yea this white linen hence.
> Here is no penance, much less innocence.

Such is the version in the belated first printing of the poem in 1669; it was omitted in 1633, presumably on moral grounds. Helen Gardner accepted the reading of 1669, but there is manuscript authority for a different reading:

> There is no penance due to innocence.

Empson wants this to be the true version: the poet is saying that there is no guilt in sex, that the woman represents freedom, like America; he also compares her to an angel, and a good angel; bad ones

> set our hairs, but these the flesh upright.

Moreover he says, in a theological figure, that women are the source of grace to the elect. In short, he could not have written a line saying the woman wasn't innocent. Empson supposed it had been altered, at first carelessly, by somebody who substituted 'much less' for 'due to', whereupon somebody else changed 'Here' to 'There', to make sense. The reading given by Helen Gardner he can't accept, since it is out of key with the rest, which can be fitted into Empson's general view that the young Donne was serious about sex; in any case it would be a blunder for the lover in these circumstances to tell the girl she wasn't innocent, while on the whole claiming that in going to bed with him she would indeed be behaving very correctly. Critics who favour the Gardner reading, he thought, are likely to be the sort that deplore young people doing such things.

In short, Empson needs the manuscript version. He could be right, though it is not very likely. This is, for all its undoubted erotic force, an odd poem; as Barbara Everett once pointed out, it might be thought a record of failure, since the only participant who is undressed at the end of the poem is the man ('To teach thee I am naked first'). What Empson seems to have left out of consideration is that there is quite a lot of Donne that takes a Juanish view of women; for instance, the question of what women are to be loved for is taken up in a witty macho way in the next elegy, 'Love's Progress', and since virtue is specifically named among the qualities for which we are told they should not be loved we can be sure that innocence was not, in the warmth of pursuit, thought essential or relevant. 'Innocence' might well be read as an ironic citation from the lexicon of conventional attitudes to sex; as in 'The Dream', 'shame' and 'honour' are said to have no place in the play of love.

My point is the simple one that one could reasonably prefer the reading Empson hates without having any of the reasons for doing so that he always angrily alleges. But he really needed his enemies, and enjoyed working hard to catch them out. One consequence is much textual quibbling, for instance in his studies of 'A Valediction: of weeping'. All will agree that it is a superb poem:

> Let me pour forth
>   My tears before thy face, whilst I stay here,
>   For thy face coins them, and thy stamp they bear,
>   And by this mintage they are something worth,
>   For thus they be
>   Pregnant of thee;
>   Fruits of much grief they are, emblems of more,
>   When a tear falls, that thou falls which it bore,
> So thou and I are nothing then, when on a divers shore.
>
>   On a round ball
>   A workman that hath copies by, can lay
>   An Europe, Afrique, and an Asia,
>   And quickly make that, which was nothing, All,
>   So doth each tear
>   Which thee doth wear,
>   A globe, yea world by that impression grow,
>   Till thy tears mixed with mine do overflow
> This world, by waters sent from thee, my heaven dissolved so.

O more than moon,
Draw not up seas to drown me in thy sphere,
Weep me not dead in thine arms, but forbear
To teach the sea what it may do too soon;
Let not the wind
Example find
To do me more harm than it purposeth;
Since thou and I sigh one another's breath,
Who e'er sighs most is cruellest, and hastes the other's death.
[This is a modernized version of the Gardner text.]

The opening seems straightforward, but the first edition says 'falst' instead of 'falls'. Grierson preferred 'falst' and so does Empson, who says the variant 'raises large issues'. If the correct version is 'falls' the line means 'that image of you that is on the tear falls with it'. In the last couplet of Shakespeare's Sonnet 130, 'My mistress' eyes are nothing like the sun', you make a bad mistake if you take 'she' to be the subject of 'belied' rather than a word for 'woman':

And yet by heaven I swear my love is fair
As any she belied with false compare.

In rather a similar way it might be thought that some copyist mistakenly wrote 'falst' because he thought 'thou' was a pronoun subject, not a noun. Empson will have none of this, regarding 'falls' as dull, perverse and pedantic: 'She [Gardner] is doing what Theobald did to Shakespeare, altering the text to make a duller and simpler kind of poetry.' 'falst' has the backing of Grierson in the original Oxford edition, though his gloss seems to me rather to fit 'falls': 'as your image perishes in each tear that falls . . .' However, Empson argues that 'falst' is essential to the idea that the lady has a 'real presence' in her reflection. I cannot see why you couldn't believe that while reading 'falls', thus avoiding not pedantry or harshness but nonsense. Empson sometimes gets himself into cantankerous fights without necessity; here his argument is as obscure as it is contemptuous.

One final instance: 'The Dream'. Here the poet is dreaming about his mistress when she arrives and wakes him. She joins him in bed and later, to his regret, leaves, presumably out of caution. He consoles himself with the thought that she will return. Empson scolds Gardner for printing

> Thou art so true, that thoughts of thee suffice
> To make dreams truth . . .

when the first edition has 'thou art so truth . . . to make dreams truths', and Empson wants this. Here I agree entirely; the reading has good authority and is much more striking. John Carey and Gardner, I also agree, got this poem as a whole wrong, and are chid for it, but so does Haffenden, when he says the lover chides himself as 'weak'; what he says is that 'love is weak' if it takes any notice of fear, shame or honour.

Empson is right about 'so truth', and about two other disputed readings in this beautiful text; but he feels obliged to argue that getting them and the poem right depends upon one understanding that the lady is really God or rather better than God. At first the man thought his visitor was an angel, but then realized she couldn't be, for she has read his mind and angels, unlike God, are not empowered to do that. So

> I do confess I could not choose but be
> Profane, to think thee anything but thee.

So, concludes Empson, she must be God, or his superior. But this hardly seems a necessary conclusion: the lover is saying that it would be profane to think her God, so he must settle for her being just her. An alternative reading is

> I do confess, it could not choose but be
> Profaneness to think thee anything but thee.

Rather remarkably, Empson likes this; and here, having been right about the drift of the poem, he is wrong on a detail because he wants support for his theory about a new religion. He thinks Donne changed the original reading because he 'got cold feet', and says that on purely textual grounds 'it . . . profaneness' has more authority. The textual argument is indeed very involved, and Empson went into it pretty thoroughly when attacking Gardner's edition; but he could not have claimed that his textual choices were not, like hers, influenced by his coming to the poems with a set of prior assumptions about them and their author.

The battle is fought through these pages, and in finer detail than can possibly be indicated here. But the conclusion has, I think, to be that following one's nose – a practice Empson recommends for critics – can occasionally cheat one into following false scents. It remains impressive that one true poet should so wish to identify with a predecessor, should wish to credit him with the attitudes the new-comer finds most admirable, and wherever possible to clear him of all moral and intellectual blame, even if it means that less important commentators will sometimes be traduced. All Empson's writings about Donne are labours of love, and have their own inwardness. Not many professional critics nowadays love poets in this manner, and Empson's new admirers do not love him for loving a poet, only for having had the prescience or luck to anticipate some of their theories. For on the whole it is for the theoretical elements of *Complex Words*, rather than the individual and devoted study of complex words in poems, that they seek, according to their lights and without necessity, to rescue Empson from critical oblivion.

Henry Reed

Henry Reed was a sad man but a funny man, and his poems are funny or sad – often, as in the celebrated 'Lessons of the War', both at once. I first met him in 1965, in the office of Robert Heilman, then the benevolent but firm head of the English Department at the University of Washington in Seattle. Calling to present my credentials, I walked into a row, Heilman benevolently firm, Reed furious, licensed to be furious. He was in Seattle as a replacement for Theodore Roethke, the regular poet in residence, who had suddenly died. Whether Roethke had contributed to the routine work of the department I don't know, but if he hadn't Heilman did not regard his immunity as a precedent and was requiring Reed to give some lectures on the Brontës. Reed argued that he had been hired exclusively as a poet and furiously declined to speak of these tiresome women. I came in when he was telling Heilman this, and also scolding him for referring to the novelists by the fancy name their father had affected in order to suggest a connection with Lord Nelson. 'How can you ask me to lecture on the O'Pruntys?' he shouted. But he did as he was asked. He and Heilman were, or became, great friends.

The secretary of the department had an affluent businessman husband, and they had taken Henry under their protection, driving him around in one or other of their Thunderbirds, labelled 'His' and 'Hers'. Once we all four went to lunch in the revolving restaurant on top of the Space Needle, and when our hosts left to get on with their work they left us slowly spinning there, with plenty of champagne to get us through the December afternoon. Henry, having been funny, now grew sad, holding up a bottle and contemplating the label, Mumms Extra Dry: 'Poor baby!' he sighed. The conversation sinking into melancholia, I quoted the advice of Thoreau: 'Do not be betrayed into a vulgar sadness', but he rejected it, pointing out that Thoreau's crown of Thoreaus was remembering happier things. (He liked puns; John Stallworthy* points out that the epigraph to 'Lessons of the War' – '*Vixi puellis nuper idoneus/ Et militavi non sine gloria*' – substitutes *puellis*, 'girls', for Horace's *duellis*, 'wars'. This is a better pun than the Seattle ones, especially as it subtly emphasizes the heterosexuality of the Implied Author of 'Lessons of the War'.) Later in that lost day we found ourselves in a deplorable bar, where we were set upon by the resident *puellae*. 'Surely they can tell I'm homosexual,' Reed said as if puzzled, though quite how they could be expected to do so was obscure to me, and anyway there were ample other reasons for abstinence. The girls must have wondered what we were doing there, but so did we.

Back in London I would sometimes get back home after a hard day at the office and find him already there. He would invariably ask for Mozart, and we would listen to one of the piano concertos. And he would invariably be moved as if coming upon a wonder for the first time: 'Exquisite,' he would murmur. 'Who's the pianist?' 'Still Ingrid Haebler, I'm afraid.' Around eleven he would ask to be poured into a taxi, and so the evening would end with a long chilly wait at the rank in Rosslyn Hill.

I don't remember much of his conversation on these occasions, except that he sometimes lamented his association with what had been the Third Programme. Much of his writing had been for radio: it included the successful series of comic programmes, seven in all, about the composeress Hilda Tablet and her associates; an adaptation of *Moby Dick*; and many translations, including some plays of Betti that were very well thought of at the time. The editor has exhumed good verse from *Moby Dick* and from some of the others – verse

* Henry Reed, *Collected Poems*, ed. Jon Stallworthy (Oxford: Oxford University Press, 1991).

remarkable for its fertility and density – but in the 1960s it was hard to imagine a bright future for radio drama. Some of Reed's translations reached the stage, but he was not cut out for television.

He was gentle, amusingly sad, and without conscious effort gave one a strong sense of his unaffected dedication to poetry, not least to Italian poetry; and also, tacitly but powerfully, a sense that his life, though marked by a good deal of idiosyncratic achievement, was radically disappointing. Stallworthy remarks on the frequency with which he laments that he had lost his way, or his way back, to the great good place that makes fairly frequent appearances in his verse; it is there, figured as Verona, in the first poem of his early collection. It is reimagined in a remarkable poem called 'The Changeling', which appeared in *The Listener* early in 1950: after many vicissitudes a man at last reaches the destination he has always thought proper to him:

> And comes, at last, to stand
> On his scented evening lawn
> Under his flowering limes,
> Where dim in the dusk and high,
> His mansion is proudly set,
> And the single light burns
> In the room where his sweet young wife
> Waits in his ancient bed.
> The stable clock chimes.
> And he to his house draws near,
> And on the threshold turns,
> With a silent glance to convey
> Up to his summer sky,
> Where his first pale stars appear:
> 'All this is false. And I
> Am an interloper here.'

In another fine unpublished poem, 'The Château' ('Yet will I fear no evil: not even here'), the theme recurs as it were in the major, and the excluded figure is imagined as finally entering his own domain and discovering that the time of exclusion, properly understood, was part of his total felicity. He approaches his 'own and veritable door':

> I shall open it, enter it, and learn
> That in all this hungry time I have never wanted,
> But have, elsewhere, on honey and milk been fed,
> Have in green pastures somewhere lain, and in the mornings,
> Somewhere beside still waters have
> Mysteriously, ecstatically, been led.

A Map of Verona was published in 1946, when Reed was in his early thirties, and stood alone, though Douglas Cleverdon produced a fine limited edition of 'Lessons of the War', designed and printed by Will and Sebastian Carter, in 1970. Another collection, to be called *The Auction Room and other Poems*, was promised in 1977 but never appeared. Reed left certain pencilled instructions on his manuscripts which suggest that he was expecting or hoping for a *Collected Poems*, and this we now have, thanks to Catherine Carver, who sorted out the heaps of drafts, clippings, and corrections left by the poet, and Jon Stallworthy, who has made this a model edition of a modern poet, with adequate textual and bibliographical annotation, and a useful biographical introduction.

He can justly claim that the result dispels the 'gross misperception' of Reed, author of 'The Naming of Parts', as a one-poem poet. Reed is always refined, calculated, expert, and nearly always alive within his sadnesses. Stallworthy does him a slight injustice by prefixing as an epigraph some very gloomy verses by Leopardi ('l'infinita vanità del tutto'), quite rightly pointing out that Reed had a special attachment to Leopardi – he wrote two plays about him and translated several of his poems; but I find these the least impressive in the volume. Leopardi feeds too directly into Reed's deep reservoir of gloom, and the translations, unlike the original poems, somehow sound rather inert. One of them, 'The Broom', reminds one a little of the Arnold of *Empedocles on Etna*, rejected by its author as altogether too glum.

There was always this danger. On lighter occasions he sometimes sounds more like a less dandyish Clough. But the strongest influence, hardly surprising in a younger poet of his time, was Eliot. Stallworthy reminds us that the celebrated parody of Eliot, 'Chard Whitlow', was written before 'Little Gidding', but the cadences of Eliot, the rhythms of the earlier Quartets, mimicked there with such absurd accuracy, were always in Reed's head:

> Waking to find the room not as I thought it was,
> But the window further away, and the door in another direction

is as close to Eliot, though unparodically, as 'Chard Whitlow'. So, in another mode, is this, from one of Reed's dramatic monologues, 'Philoctetes':

> The noiseless chant has begun in the heart of the wound,
> The heavy procession of pain along the nerve.

It may be worth adding that the influence seems least assimilated when Reed must have been working fast, for the radio; in the verses from *Pytheas* (1947), here printed for the first time, the master too audibly presides over all. And somewhere behind Reed's dream allegories lurk 'Gerontion' and *The Waste Land*. But he was also intimate with Hardy, and worked for a long time on a biography before giving it up; his narrative poem 'The Auction Sale', though very individual, and ending with the characteristic exclusion from delight, is in Hardy's manner. Finally there are, no doubt inevitably, echoes of Auden, too.

Yet he holds his own note. 'Outside and In', a fine early poem, strikes it: intense apprehension at the prospect of a fate one would rather endure than continue to endure the apprehension of it:

> A house so vulnerable and divided, with
> A mutiny already inside its walls,
> Cannot withstand a siege. I have opened the doors
> In sign of surrender. The house is filling with cold.
> Why will you stay out there? I am ready to answer.
> The doors are open. Why will you not come in?

A fine late poem, 'Three Words' (too highly wrought for quotation except in its entirety), has the lexical agility of 'The Naming of Parts', and is as witty, but in a sense excluding laughter. Two others, 'The Town Itself' and 'The Blissful Land', revisit in terminal sadness the lost Verona – 'I had not known that the weather, in what seemed,/ At first, unchangeably sought out by the sun,/ Could be so variable . . . I have come to a place where I have nothing to give . . .' – and its counterpart, that lost blissful land which, once entered, would make all torments and losses the themes of a present delight ('It was not you that we wanted! How dared you to come here alone?'). Finally there is a resigned, elegantly executed signing-off little allegory called 'L'Envoi'. Reed certainly earned his 'Collected'. Stallworthy is right to claim distinction for these poems, and it can be seen the more clearly by his having brought them together.

Roy Fuller

One of Roy Fuller's 'Quatrains of an Elderly Man' is called 'Poetry and Whist':

> How enviable Herrick's
> Fourteen hundred lyrics!
> – Though, as the Scot complained when they dealt him all
> The trumps, a lot of them were small.

The envy seems unjustified, for Fuller must have written far more than 1,400 lyrics – indeed there are more than that in the *Collected Poems* of 1985, with dozens more to come.

Some of Herrick's are small indeed:

> To Print our Poems, the propulsive cause
> Is Fame, (the breath of popular applause.)

Worth printing? Fuller might have thought so if only because 'propulsive' is the sort of unexpectedly posh word he rather enjoyed, either for its own sake or for the sake of a cosy joke, the humour of the Blackpool breakfast table he always fondly remembered. Another Herrick, somewhat more in the elderly Fuller manner:

> When one is past, another care we have,
> *Thus woe succeeds a woe; as wave a wave.*

The only thing missing from this aperçu is any touch of self-critical humour, as in Fuller's 'shopping list of fleshly ills'. What Fuller tends to comment on – though often with equal brevity – is, as a rule, less general, more personal; rueful and wise, but less incontrovertibly and complacently wise than this observation of Herrick's. He made many poetic jottings, and characteristically would start a piece off with 'Odd how' or 'Strange that . . .'

> Feeling my heart about to accelerate,
> I swallow a pill of phenobarbitone.
> Odd how one enjoys the bitterness, knowing
> It will fade . . .

Or, from a poem about being sixty-five:

> Strange that obsessive observation seems
> To be an overture to verse . . .

The habit was deprecated much earlier:

> In this the thirty-ninth year of my age
>
> .   .   .   .   .   .   it seems
> That any old subject fits into my verse . . .

Among the *New Poems* (1968), published when he was still under sixty but already complaining regularly of the ills of old age, there is one that begins thus: 'Rising at dawn to pee . . .' He will note the unavoidable presence, so familiar to the ageing, of the vitreous floater, which your GP tells you not to worry about; annoying though the phenomenon undoubtedly is, it is regarded – unlike flashers – as harmless, one of the lesser human problems, but not too trivial to be noticed here.

The last years of Fuller's life saw an extraordinary outpouring of poems. His son, the poet John Fuller, aware of the great quantity already published in his father's declining years, was surprised to find a posthumous mass of additional typescript. *Last Poems,** selected by John Fuller from this cache, includes an 'Aubade' beginning 'Actions on waking: inserting some upper teeth . . . socks/Achieved with grunting' and going on to this self-perception:

---

* London: Sinclair-Stevenson, 1993.

> To plough through the prosaic to poetry –
> The only way of versing that I know.
> The life so simple, the dreaming so bizarre.

Fifty years or so earlier the poetry was sometimes much more strict, as in the fine opening poem of Fuller's third collection, *A Lost Season* (1944):

> For those who are in love and are exiled
> Can never discover
> How to be happy: looking upon the wild
> They see for ever
>
> The cultivated acre of their pain . . .

The prosaic here was wartime homesickness, commonplace as well as painful, but the poetry has what may now seem a slightly dated exactness and elegance, learned in part from Auden. Fuller was well known in the early 1940s as a war poet, and there was a great demand for war poets. The experiences offered by the Navy were for the most part strictly prosaic, but some of them he turned, with ambitious care, into good poems. I have heard *A Lost Season* called his best book, but that seems rather insulting when you remember a half-century of technical enterprise, a virtually incessant quest for his own voice, and poetry everywhere detected, even when the immediate occasion is picking up a senior citizen's bus pass, or taking a pair of shoes to be mended ('Your welt has gone').

It would be a considerable mistake to think Fuller a careless or merely opportunistic poet. He was always trying something – for example, he was curious about stanza forms, and there are dozens and dozens of sonnets of almost every conceivable kind. Quite late in life he began as it were spontaneously, and rather unexpectedly, to write syllabic verse – a departure which led to his calling on the aged Elizabeth Daryush, then a little known exponent of the method, and to the publication of a volume of hers with his preface.

Yet for all his various skills there is often in his writing, prose and verse, a certain ungainliness. It is to be not wished away, but registered as native to his person or perhaps it would be better to say to his tessitura, in prose and verse. Once while living in Kennington he met two Oxford undergraduates, Jack Clark and Rodney Philips, who were interested in poetry; they 'were in some disbelief that close to the Clark family house could actually reside a contributor to *New Writing*, as, in a way that now seems baffling, had been reported to them'. That sentence, with its contrived inversions, has a very characteristic stagger – Neil Powell* prefers to talk about a style 'slightly skewed'. In the same volume of his autobiography, *Vamp Till Ready* (1982), Fuller discusses a poem in which he had spoken of 'the penis lighthouse . . . Aloof with rolling eye'; he didn't like the neologistic epithet 'penis', partly because George Barker had used it first, partly because penises can only with difficulty be imagined to have *rolling* eyes. 'What the lighthouse was more like (the one at Dungeness) was a vinegar bottle with a perforated ceramic attachment to its cork, enabling the acetic fluid to be sprinkled over a plate or newspaper of fish-and-chips.' This is staggering Fuller – not only does the mandarin periphrasis for vinegar coexist with the demotic meal it sprinkles, but the whole dependent clause has a touch of comic formality that mimics the way in which people, including some solicitors, try to sound impressive. Fuller was glad a reviewer found his autobiography funny; it is, and some of the fun depends on his writing like this.

I once noted, in a review the poet certainly read, that he seemed to be under the impression that 'Hibernian' meant 'Scottish', and Powell's biography provides evidence that he believed this from his earliest days, even when he was in Aberdeen with the Navy. It must have been a childhood error, derived from the Scottish football scores, but there is something rather staunch about his not correcting it; it reminds one of the high valuation he always put upon early experience, the chatter of fellow clerks. And it is of course intended

---

* Neil Powell, *Roy Fuller: Writer and Society* (Manchester: Carcanet, 1995).

to be a rather classy way of saying 'Scottish'. It confirms the stubborn individuality of his gait.

As it happens, the poem of his I like best has to do with gait: it even has a rather limping title, 'Homage to Dr. Arnold Gesell and to my Grand-daughter Sophie'. It is to be found in *Buff* (1965). Incidentally, although the poet was a great believer in non-obscurity, this poem, like many others, requires some collaboration from readers, who won't make much of it if they are completely ignorant of the theories of Dr Arnold Gesell. However, it's worth that trouble, being beautifully balanced and finished, even if here and there, like the little girl, appropriately staggering. It turns out, in the affectionately selfish way of poets, to be more about poetry than about the two-year-old girl. The child's 'jargon' reminds Fuller of his own, and the contest of obscure dream with waking language:

> The best part of my life is bringing out
> Jargon with words – but how minute a part,
> Since ordered language is most loath to admit
> The excited dream-soaked gibberish of its start.

Powell's biography is done with proper affection and respect, though it is far from being uncritical, and even goes in for a certain amount of quite severe close reading. But of course his main business is with the remarkable double life of this writer. It was a topic on which Fuller himself often brooded. First, and most obviously, he was an extremely successful solicitor and man of affairs, in a world away from poetry. But he was also a poet, a novelist, a children's writer and, in verse as well as prose, an autobiographer. There are in fact ten novels, many collections of verse, four volumes of auto-biography and several of criticism, all produced in the spare time of a man who liked to call himself indolent. Perhaps it was his insomnia which, far from driving him to distraction, enabled him to do more reading than normal sleepers can manage, but his industry is still astonishing. Because it was habitual he seemed not to notice it, or get tired; prone to self-reproach but never frenzied, he even supposed he ought to be doing more than he did.

Within the doubleness of his careers there was the further doubleness that he wrote both prose and verse, and on these divisions he often meditated, not thinking of himself as a particularly gifted novelist, yet prone to say he was first a solicitor, second a novelist, and only third a poet. Powell calls his concern with 'the double, divided self' obsessional, and traces its recurrence in the novels – *The Second Curtain*, published in 1953, has a hero who resembles what Fuller might have been had he not, on demobilization, gone back to the Woolwich. This alter ego wears a beard to disguise himself, but underneath has the same shyness and lack of self-confidence which, remarkably, characterized the successful author – a man at moments capable of exercising combative authority, and a man at once, as Powell puts it, fastidious and reckless. His recklessness was perhaps shown in his writing the novel *Image of a Society* (1956) about a building society very like the one he worked for. In the end this audacity did not damage his excellent prospects. He must have known he was valued so highly there that he could take the risk. His affection, admiration indeed, for his non-literary colleagues is explained in the final autobiographical volume, *Spanner and Pen* (1991).

One sees how little he had to regret in choosing that career, and how confident he was of his worth. He did not miss the parallel between his life and that of the American poet and insurance lawyer Wallace Stevens. But after all it is not very close; to Stevens the quotidian was a malady, not a stimulus, and his jargon as a poet did not have the same struggle with the constrictions of ordinary language. And Stevens, though equally an inhabitant of the suburbs, was a Harvard man, a *bon vivant* (though Powell really shouldn't compare his poetry to plum pudding) and an altogether grander as well as a more private figure, who wouldn't have dreamed of celebrating the virtues of his non-poetic fellow vice-presidents. The difference between the two is caused in part by temperament, in part by the different image of the poet (and of the society and his place in it) still current in America – more bardic, more privileged, and far less domestic than Fuller's, or ours.

*

Powell benefits not only from the existence of the autobiographies (in which he not surprisingly detects certain reticences) but from access to the poet's long correspondence with his friend Julian Symons. That friendship, going back to pre-war years, makes one reflect on Fuller's luck. He went to no university, was the product of a middle-class provincial childhood and education, and began adult life as an articled clerk in Blackpool, an apparently unconventional preparation for a lifetime of fruitful reading, a confident debut in poetry, and the early acquisition of such interesting and well-known friends as Symons and George Woodcock. But we ought to know that for some poets it is good to be self-taught, to make one's own way; and it was good for Fuller.

It is easy enough to understand that his translation, almost by chance, to a mildly bohemian London milieu did little to suppress what Powell calls 'that familiar, treacherous nostalgia of the self-made intellectual for more demotic forms of art' – meaning Fuller's fondness for the popular tunes and jokes of his youth, perfectly consistent, in later years, with his refined understanding of classical music. He also enjoyed an occasional game of snooker, and the ambience of Charley's caff in Marchmont Street. Powell thinks the choice of Charley's rather than the Café Bleu in Old Compton Street, haunt of the poet Paul Potts, 'defines Fuller's character', since Charley's couldn't possibly be called a 'self-insulating artistic enclave'. It is true that on his visits to the Café Bleu the law student Fuller wondered, as the hours slipped by, when, if ever, its habitués wrote or painted; they were, he decided, 'failures', obviously from him a strong condemnation. Yet playing pinball and listening to jazz at Charley's, though not exactly bohemian, will not easily be seen as a way of affirming promise or achievement. Perhaps Powell is right in saying Fuller preferred it, rather high-mindedly, because it belonged to 'a recognizably everyday world', and it was in that world that he always looked for poems. At any rate it was possible for him to aspire to poetry yet enjoy pinball.

Whether Charley's customers strengthened his early left-wing conviction of 'toiling humanity's essential goodness, its innate wish for advancement', is doubtful. But he might well have felt more at home with them than with high-class intellectuals. As he remarked forthrightly in *Home and Dry* (1984), he was suspicious of upper-class bohemians: 'there is (or at any rate used to be) an area of communication occupied by the lower middle classes characterized by irony, decency and unpretentiousness, and that was what I was used to by birth and upbringing'. Charley's was hardly the place to look for those qualities, but, like the rest of toiling humanity, the young law student had a right to some leisure; and the Blackpool clerk who had passed many hours playing 'office cricket', whatever that is, might well feel that pinball and snooker were as much his privilege as self-improvement. It is another doubling, the dedicated and industrious writer and the cautious skiver – a dualism perhaps more common than Powell allows.

In the years when he was still a big shot at the Woolwich, but also Professor of Poetry at Oxford, a governor of the BBC and a member of the Arts Council, the poet was still, in Powell's formula, 'culturally embattled'. But he still spoke out; his shyness, marked by a reluctance to enter into intimacies, wasn't of the kind to prevent his expressing disapproval or disgust at much that presented itself to his fastidious gaze in the aftermath of 1968. He writes of his 'Colonel (Retired) persona', and his

> Reactionary views, advanced mostly
> To raise a laugh – taken as gospel! –

but he meant what he said, and many disliked the manner he assumed almost in spite of himself. It was what he had grown into, having declined the life of the bearded bohemian.

He was proud of having achieved so much in both the jobs he'd done, and once counselled his Oxford audience not to suppose it impossible to be creative while leading a 'humdrum' life. As he told his largely undergraduate listeners, 'the fact that someone is on hand who has done this may be a kind of reassurance that there is some kind of life to be made without dotty bohemianism or perennial studentship'. By 'life' he meant 'creative life'.

There is justified pride and authority in the claim, but during these later years he partly lost his following. By the end of his life he was lamenting that it was more and more difficult to get his books printed, and he even quarrelled with publishers over this indignity. He was out of fashion because he seemed reactionary and had grown old, but it will not do to blame poets, whatever their opinions, for writing on through their last years; those who do have been rare enough, and sometimes, like Yeats and Pound, they have been far more reactionary than Fuller. Moreover, as we are so often told, the old now form a large and growing constituency and, however edentulous (one of his posh words) they may be, and out of breath while pulling on their socks, they may have some sympathy with the notations of senescence in which he came to specialize – at any rate so long as they retain, as he did, some feeling for that 'dream-soaked gibberish' which a poet may go on struggling to match with the language of the quotidian.

Ern Malley

Ern Malley, a Melbourne garage hand who, like Keats, wrote poems and died at twenty-six, was the invention of James McAuley and Harold Stewart, who also created the poet's dim sister Ethel. She it was who found the poems after her brother's death and, knowing nothing about poetry, in 1944 sent the grubby, coffee-stained pages to the Adelaide poetry magazine *Angry Penguins* and asked for an opinion. So began what turned out to be not an ephemeral joke, a short-running tease, but the most famous literary hoax since Swift tormented the astrologer John Partridge.

McAuley and Stewart were poets of roughly the same age as Ern. When the story broke, they claimed to have written the entire œuvre of Malley in one afternoon and evening. It is possible to doubt the absolute truth of this claim, since at least one of the poems was a serious but discarded early effort by McAuley, and there are unconfirmed reports that other material from his old notebook was transferred to Malley. It is likely that Stewart made a similar contribution. Michael Heyward, author of an intelligent, thorough, and only occasionally over-elaborate study,* knows all this – indeed knows pretty well everything about the case – but still accepts the hoaxers' claim, and Stewart, the surviving half of Malley, continues to affirm it in his voluntary Japanese exile.

The object of the prank was to discredit *Angry Penguins* and its

---

* Michael Heyward, *The Ern Malley Affair* (St Lucia: University of Queensland Press, 1993).

editor, Max Harris, an economics student at Adelaide University. Harris was an enterprising, rather hectic literary man with a taste for Rimbaud, Blake, Surrealism and the current English Neo-Apocalyptic school, whose magazine, *Poetry London*, had covers by Henry Moore. *Angry Penguins* had covers by Sydney Nolan, later to become the most celebrated of Australian artists, and a lifelong admirer of Ern Malley.

Harris's response to the poems was immediate; he had no doubt that Australia had found its poet, and that he, given a glorious opportunity to make the fact public, was the right impresario. The poetry was strange but certainly modern. The dead poet had left a powerful 'Preface and Statement': 'These poems are complete in themselves. They have a domestic economy of their own and if they face outwards to the reader that is because they have first faced inwards to themselves. Every poem should be an autarchy . . . Simplicity in our time is arrived at by an ambages . . .' Delighted, Harris fell upon the verses:

> There are ribald interventions
> Like spurious seals upon
> A Chinese landscape-roll
> Or tangents to the rainbow.
> We have known these declensions,
> Have winked when Hyperion
> Was transmuted to a troll,
> We dubbed it a sideshow.

There were passages in which he could trace the influence of Mallarmé:

> The solemn symphony of angels lighting
> My steps with music, o constellations!
> Palms!
> O far shore, target and shield that I now
> Desire beyond these terrestrial commitments.

There was the enigmatically Shakespearian 'Boult to Marina':

Only a part of me shall triumph in this
(I am not Pericles)
Though I have your silken eyes to kiss,
And maiden-knees
Part of me remains, wench, Boult-upright
The rest of me drops off into the night.

What would you have me do? Go to the wars? . . .

And carefully placed on the top of the pile was the best poem in the collection.

Nobody had the slightest idea that the act of sending a bundle of fake poems to an obscure poetry editor would excite the wartime press not only of Australia but of the anglophone world at large; and, to give the hoaxers their due, they couldn't have foreseen that Harris would suffer so much from ridicule, most of it of course totally ignorant, for the hoaxers acquired allies they could not have wanted in the popular press and the poetry-unloving Australian public. Worse still, Harris had to stand trial for publishing obscene poems, not least 'Boult to Marina'. Heyward gives a good account of the trial, surely one of the most preposterous in the preposterous history of such prosecutions. The evidence of Detective Vogelsang, the principal prosecution witness, was to be discussed with hilarity for years to come. It was he who, among other perceptions, found the word 'incest' to be indecent, though he confessed he did not know what it meant. Sniggering in court, no doubt; but the trial was still a cruel ordeal for young Harris. Apparently he narrowly escaped a charge of blasphemy, which would have been even more serious.

Harris did well enough at the trial, and Heyward gives him due credit for his general demeanour throughout the protracted and sometimes rather frightening events of those months. He was an excitable fellow and often tiresomely flamboyant; his novel *The Vegetative Eye* was a grotesquely affected and truly awful book. It is easy to see why the learned and satirical McAuley, always, in matters related to poetry, censorious and austere, should want to teach Harris a lesson. But it is to his credit that Harris declined to be put down; hoax or not, these were, he maintained, important poems, and if they were produced unintentionally by rival poets, whose beliefs and works he despised as much as they did his, that fact had no bearing on their quality. Or it merely showed that they wrote better when not constrained by their false conscious assumptions. Harris never lost his faith in his first excited valuation of the Ern Malley poems, which was supported by the powerful voice of Herbert Read in England, and by John Ashbery and Kenneth Koch in the USA. Of course most people, whether they had read the poems or not, were gleefully sure that Harris had been had. It may be that nowadays fewer readers would feel so confident that he was absurdly wrong.

It so happened that I was in Australia during much of 1945, for no better reason than that the aircraft carrier I served in was dispatched from the Atlantic theatre, which was closing down, to the Pacific, which wasn't. Henceforth we would be based on Sydney. Almost on arrival, and entirely by accident, I met A. D. Hope, then around thirty-five or -six, with a big underground reputation as a poet, his work mostly erotic but severely traditional in form. At that time his reputation depended more on his performances as a reviewer of exceptional ferocity. But his verses circulated in a pamphlet, printed on brown wrapping paper and shared with two other, less impressive, writers. To a very young man with his own poetic aspirations Hope was a most impressive figure, wild in behaviour but quiet of speech, with that soothing accent Australians develop after a couple of years at Oxford.

Since I occasionally stayed at the Hopes' place in Manley, near Sydney, I soon came to know James McAuley. He was about ten years junior to Hope and although of strongly independent intellect he tacitly regarded the older man as his mentor. McAuley was at this time, rather reluctantly, in the Army. He had been in New Guinea, but much of his service had been in sedentary jobs, and he had been able to carry on with his poetry and his other comparably severe intellectual occupations. Conversation between the two poets, despite the flow of liquor, was impressively learned and lengthy, with Mrs Hope and me for the most part discreetly silent.

Hope had been a pupil of Christopher Brennan, a dissolute poet of immense and arcane learning and, rather improbably, once a frequenter of Mallarmé's Tuesday salon: a *mardiste*, no less. He taught French at Sydney University, and was said to have lectured propped up by two porters. Brennan's poetry was at that time practically unobtainable, and this was regarded, at any rate by poets, as a national scandal, for he was declared to be the true father of Australian poetry. Much later his collected poetry was published, but it failed to set Sydney Harbour on fire, perhaps because the mood had changed and Australians no longer cared to think of themselves as second-rate Europeans, needing to re-establish in exile the culture they had lost; or perhaps because Brennan's reputation had owed something to the principle *omne ignotum pro magnifico*, and faded a little when the work became generally available. Fifty years ago there was no doubt in Hope's mind, or McAuley's, as to the identity of their cultural heritage; they took pride in their European learning, and at the same time deplored both the ignorant antics of exhibitionist fellow poets and the philistinism of Australian life generally. Curiously enough, Max Harris and his friends and contributors had some similar aspirations, despite their different methods and attitudes. They latched on to British and European intellectual fashions, but did so in a sophomoric way that disgusted Hope, who wrote a savage review of *The Vegetative Eye*. He was naturally sympathetic to the Ern Malley 'jape', and I have always suspected that he played a bigger part in it than he acknowledged, or than Heyward claims.

I never met Stewart, but recognize the McAuley I knew in the ample biographical account that Heyward provides. He was an intellectual hard man, with a deploring satirist's face, a brow of contempt: there was in his manner a sort of perpetual reproof, kept ready, as it were, to deal with those manifestations of intellectual softness or vacuity that are always, given the decadent state of our culture, on the point of occurring. He was extremely well read and was also a musician – a good jazz pianist – and for these reasons agreeable company; but he seemed to have a permanently exacerbated sense of being surrounded by fools and ignoramuses. He was later to convert to Roman Catholicism, move rapidly to the right, and edit the CIA-sponsored journal *Quadrant.* *

He and Stewart already knew each other, but were brought together in the Army by an extraordinary man called Alf Conlon, who ran a sort of autonomous army unit and made it his business to keep talented young men out of danger. It was on an idle afternoon in Conlon's outfit that Stewart and McAuley compiled the Ern Malley poems. Early accounts claimed that they had thrown in anything to hand, for instance sentences from an official report on the lifestyle of New Guinea mosquitoes. This they had indeed drawn upon; but the implication that all of the Malley poems were made up of such random scraps is false. There are parodies, more or less remote, of Mallarmé, Pound and Eliot – they might even be called, more grandly, 'allusions' to those poets – and there are even McAuley parodies of Stewart and vice versa. They may have worked fast, but they were so talented and so habituated to poetry that they failed to produce the total garbage they had intended.

This made the hoax a bit unfair. Harris had his faults, but he wasn't totally wrong to find merit in Malley. He did go over the top, proclaiming his discovery of a great poet, conducting an earnest correspondence with Ethel about her genius brother, producing a special edition of *Angry Penguins*, and, later, a slim volume of the collected Ern Malley called *The Darkening Ecliptic*. He fell, but not so hard that he deserved the fate he got. It was particularly gross that the final revelation of the hoax was made in a supplement of the *Sydney Sunday Sun*. This was simply throwing him to the philistines, natural enemies of the small artistic community – the 'wowsers', as Australians used to call them. They needed no inducement to jeer at poetry and were not up to discriminating between Harris's take

* For information about McAuley's later life, and his political connections, see Cassandra Pybus, *The Devil and James McAuley* (St Lucia: University of Queensland Press, 1999).

on European modernism and the more researched and temperate lucubrations of Hope and his friends – who, incidentally, cannot have thought they themselves would have fared any better at such hands.

The hoaxers produced effects they had not meant to cause, but they must have known that they had cheated by attributing good poems or lines to Malley. To fool Harris honestly they should have taken care not to include anything of merit, but they may have suspected that they wouldn't get away with that. The Ern Malley hoax was not quite the knockout it seemed at the time, and there was a degree of arrogance in its perpetrators, and even a certain blindness, for they might have been expected to see that they had worse cultural enemies than the poets they disagreed with. Yet it was good, in the midst of the Pacific war, to find such people – so talented, so serious about poetry, that they could not be anything but savagely derisive of men with pretensions to culture who were in fact – as they believed – its enemies. Of course I was very young, but I was right to be impressed.

When I flew back to England in December 1945 I left behind with my luggage a complete set of Ern Malley documents: the famous issue of *Angry Penguins*, a copy of *The Darkening Ecliptic*, reports of the Harris trial at Adelaide, even the scarce and crumbling brown-paper pamphlet of Hope. All were lost with the rest of my gear, so I never wrote, as I'd intended, about the case. Heywood, who wasn't even born at the time of the hoax, knows a great deal more about it – about the authors and their methods of composition, about Conlon, and about Max Harris and his circle and his backers. He has done a good and even an important job, but all the same I think he misses some things. All will admit that the opening poem 'Dürer: Innsbruck, 1945' is at least not bad and might be thought better than that:

> But no one warned that the mind repeats
> In its ignorance the vision of others. I am still
> The black swan of trespass upon alien waters.

An editor might reject that poem, the first in the collection, but could not be expected to see it as a hoax, an attempt to show that he or she lacked all discrimination. Heyward is good at spotting sources but occasionally makes the mistake of believing that having done so he has demolished the dependent poem. So an ingenious Audenesque pastiche, 'Rise from the wrist, o kestrel', and the Poundian quatrains of 'Poetry: the loaves and fishes' are dismissed simply as jokes about rhyming. Oddly enough, some of Hope's finest poetry, greatly admired by McAuley, is pastiche, for instance the beautiful Venetia Digby verse-letter, modelled on an early-seventeenth-century epode form. McAuley was a cradle classicist, and must have known such things could be done. 'Boult to Marina' is also, I think, a real poem; it got Harris into trouble because it was foolishly accused of obscenity, not because he was wrong to like it.

Of course there's a lot of rubbish in *The Darkening Ecliptic*, but people would not now attend to it if it had been all such. It has gone into several editions, it has been the subject of lengthy investigations on Australian radio; it appears in anthologies of Australian verse, and it is here reprinted in full by Heyward. It is continually discussed by a new generation of Australian poets.

Meanwhile the fame of Hope, now a very old man,* seems a little dimmed, McAuley is dead, and Stewart, who good-humouredly but detachedly obliged Heywood with his memories and present views of the affair, has moved into another world. I last saw Alec Hope in 1988; he sat, benign but still sharp in spite of his deafness, in the big A. D. Hope Building at the National University in Canberra. Among other things I asked him what had become of Cordukes. Cordukes was an amiable timber merchant with an interest in poetry. I met him on my first night in Sydney, when he nearly ran me down. He stopped to expostulate and we fell into conversation, as a result of which I got to know his interests and could share the hospitality he extended to poets. I had heard that right after the war he risked his all on a cargo of Russian timber, which the Sydney dockers refused

---

* He died in July 2000, in his nineties.

to unload; the ship went home to Russia and Cordukes immediately disappeared from the scene. So I asked my question; Hope, who probably hadn't heard the name for forty-odd years, softly replied that he had no idea. Yet generous amateurs and benefactors of poetry are not so common that poets should forget them. I, of course, remembered Cordukes because it was he who introduced me to Hope, and so to the hoaxer McAuley.

McAuley I saw on a hectic day in 1967 – another hoax had been exposed: the covert funding by the CIA of certain magazines. We met in the office of *Encounter*, a journal from the same stable as *Quadrant*, the one he edited. He was moderately cheerful; twenty-odd years had, it seemed, reduced his abrasiveness, perhaps his poetry also. I don't think we talked about old Sydney and the hoax – he must have had enough of it by then. He died in 1976, in his late fifties. There is a sense in which young Ern Malley, saved from oblivion by his barely literate and wholly fictitious sister Ethel, with some help from Harris and the hoaxers and even the *Sydney Sunday Sun*, has unexpectedly stayed young and lively while his betters have declined into old age and the only end of age.

On a New Way of Doing History

An increasingly influential group of American academic literary critics has decided that history – cultural history – so long neglected, it is said, by earlier influential groups – is now its most urgent business. The English Renaissance has been chosen as the period promising the best return on an investment in new historical techniques; so the reign of Elizabeth I is now all the rage in late-twentieth-century California, and especially at Berkeley, where the movement called the New Historicism originated.

Richard Helgerson,* a professor at Santa Barbara, makes a point of occasionally distancing himself from other New Historians, but his methods and his terminology undoubtedly presuppose some acquaintance with theirs, and readers lacking that qualification may need a preliminary briefing. The best way to get it would be to read the works of the *chef d'école*, Stephen Greenblatt, though it must be said that, in the dozen years since his book *Renaissance Self-Fashioning* launched (without actually naming) it, the movement has acquired considerable diversity in the hands of enthusiastic disciples, not all of whom can think, or write, as well as he. Moreover its programme has continued to evolve in response to comment, some of it hostile, and theories justifying its procedures have grown more refined and elaborate. Still, the movement can be characterized, serviceably if crudely, in some such way as this.

* *Forms of Nationhood: The Elizabethan Writing of England* (Chicago: University of Chicago Press, 1992).

It calls for a renunciation of the supposed anti-historical bias of the formalisms that for so long dominated American criticism. More positively, it seeks to establish new ways of writing history. Old-fashioned historians failed, it is alleged, to take account of the complexities of the social, political and economic forces at work in any particular period. They were blind to the ceaseless interrelations or 'negotiations' between all manner of contemporary social and cultural practices, and therefore could not know much about the ways in which individuals were subjected to those forces. Moreover the old historians remained unconscious of the limitations imposed on their own vision; for they too were constituted and constrained by the prevailing network of social and political practices. Since the individual is little more than a place where these discourses intersect, they condition whatever he or she thinks about anything, including the past.

By detecting the hitherto unsuspected interplay between a period's discourses one can hope to avoid old errors. For example, historians used to see past literature as somehow, like themselves, exempt from the flux of time. When the documents they arbitrarily classified as literature referred to historical events, it was naively thought that those events were simply reflected in the literature as in a steady, distortion-free mirror. The new understanding is that literature is just as involved in the interplay of discourses as everything else, including books from which we choose to withhold that honorific description. All texts interact with one another; all are discourses, social practices related to dispositions of power. Consequently criticism can no longer reserve for 'literature' the special treatment accorded to autonomous aesthetic objects, while regarding the rest as having only some inferior or contributory kind of interest. By disallowing aesthetic privilege, critics now find new things to say about Elizabethan writing.

Their methods and assumptions derive in part from the anthropology of Clifford Geertz, who uses the technique called 'thick description' and relates a particular cultural phenomenon, such as Balinese cockfighting, to the entire cultural complex of the society; and from early and late Michel Foucault – from the earlier books in which he insisted on the discontinuity of epochs, and the later ones which emphasize the relations of discourse to power. These authorities, and others also regularly cited, are recent, and so, it seems to be assumed, is the discovery that writing history is a very problematical business. Yet it is not true that philosophers of history have only recently become aware of the problems facing all who would speak, from the present, about the past. They have long been asking questions about where and when history happens – in the historian's head? Out there? Now or then? Both? They have talked subtly and at length about the peculiar problems of historical narrative and interpretation, and of course about the 'negotiations' between base and superstructure. So what is so new about the new movement? It really comes down to the claim that, whereas old historians assumed that there was a body of historical fact to which literary works might refer, but to which these works didn't themselves belong, it is now understood that the chief interest of those works, stripped of the special status conferred on them by a detected ideology, lies in their participation in the multiple discourses of the culture.

This view seems to be held, with here and there some backslidings and qualifications, by the whole school. It certainly requires a new direction of interest, for the dominant discourse tends to be political. What the new historians do to the familiar texts is to tease out of them unsuspected hierarchical, sexist, imperialist senses or implications. One practitioner expressly states that his purpose is 'to overcome some of the depoliticizing tendencies of [the] discipline' and to show the plays of Shakespeare 'as a series of semiotic events, the staging of cultural materials, the mobilization of political representations'.*

Jacob Burckhardt long ago gave the world the idea that the Renaissance saw the birth of individualism. As Jean E. Howard has

---

* Leonard Tennenhouse, *Power on Display: The Politics of Shakespeare's Genres* (London and New York: Methuen, 1986).

remarked, in an interesting discussion of this new kind of history,* Greenblatt prefers to think about the gap between the Renaissance ideology of freedom and the actual status of people at the time, considered as constructions of ideology and subjects of power. And if we think thus we cannot help reflecting on our own situation, which, despite period differences, is quite similar. Foucault insisted on the discontinuity and incomparability of epochs, but these followers of his cannot help seeing a parallel between the Renaissance – standing between the Middle Ages and the modern world – and our own transitional period between an old and a new order. So the interplay of Renaissance discourses, though culture-specific, has something important to tell us. All texts, for us as well as the Elizabethans, have their true sense only as con-texts. According to the New Historicist Louis Montrose, the pedagogical benefits of such studies are that teachers can now show their students how they too are at once sustained and constrained by the 'regime of power and knowledge' that happens to obtain in their time.†

Since all discourses interact equally you can talk, as for example Greenblatt does, about the relation between the Elizabethan practice of exorcism and Shakespeare's *King Lear* without assuming that the play is somehow more valuable than Samuel Harsnett's *Declaration of Egregious Popish Impostures*. This is a work well known to scholars, though not read by all who cite it, as a minor source of Shakespeare's play (it provided the names of Mad Tom's devils). Now it is seen less as a source than as a partner or opponent. In principle at least, the old privileges of the tragedy, conferred on it, we are told, by obsolete bourgeois ideologists, are abrogated. Greenblatt is famous for the daring of his discursive collocations, often beginning with an anecdote that seems very far away from the 'literary' text he intends eventually to discuss, then bringing the two together with a pleasing flourish; the effect is rather like that of a

* Jean E. Howard, 'The New Historicism in Renaissance Studies', *English Literary Renaissance*, 16 (1986), 13–14.
† Louis Montrose, 'Renaissance Literary Studies and the Subject of History', *English Literary Renaissance*, 16 (1986), 5–12.

startling metaphor or conceit, which can provide illumination, in this case of the discursive interrelations that constituted Renaissance culture.

It must, however, be said that some New Historicist socio-practical manoeuvres are less beguiling than Greenblatt's. We are told, for instance, that when Petruchio, in *The Taming of the Shrew*, starves Kate and keeps her awake he is treating her 'as if she existed in denial of the material practices of the body'. A reading of T. H. White's *The Goshawk* suggests that he is taming her exactly as hawks were tamed. When, at the end of the long battle of will and endurance involved in the training process, she comes to his call and attacks not him but his prey, she is behaving like a successfully trained falcon. This doesn't make his behaviour any more admirable, but it does bring in a 'discourse' of sport which explains more than a flurry of jargon that neglects the obvious in a quest for novelty. We are told by the same author that Gloucester in *King Lear* is blinded as a punishment for the offence of preferring his illegitimate to his legitimate son, so foisting an outsider into the aristocracy. That the intrusive bastard, Edmund, is a friend and ally of the people who are putting out his father's eyes (they even address him by his father's title) here becomes irrelevant: what is important is that their crime should be understood as the representation of a politics the author happens to want to see represented – it 'purified the aristocratic body'.* This is new, certainly; whether it is sensible is a question. The web of New History is, as Shakespeare remarked of life, a mingled yarn.

Helgerson's plan is to describe the interaction of 'different discursive communities' on a larger scale than usual. He wants to show that the discourses of his choice together constitute 'a concerted generational project', or what he rather grandly calls 'the writing of England'. The project goes beyond mere literary history, for it involves the complex relation between this nationalist enterprise and the sources of political power. These are identified as the monarchy, whose absolutist

---

* Tennenhouse, *Power on Display*, p. 138.

claims these new writings effectively contest, and the rival forces of the aristocracy and the rising mercantile classes. To this end Helgerson's six long chapters study poetry, the law, chorography (mapmaking and related activities), voyaging, the theatre, and religion, always with the representation and distribution of political power in mind.

This is clearly a bold enterprise, and the results are often interesting, though not always convincing. It may seem a little harsh, when so much is included, to criticize the book for what it leaves out; but its peculiar omissions, along with a habitual far-fetchedness in the treatment of what it does include, are its principal faults.

First a word on the far-fetching. One of the dangers of this kind of history is a tendency to emphasize newness by claiming high importance for matters alleged to have been neglected hitherto. For example, Helgerson makes large claims for his novel view of the youthful Spenser. There was a time when some young poets were wondering whether the adoption of quantitative verse might be what English poetry needed to bring it up to scratch. Spenser gave the matter some thought, and while doing so exclaimed in a letter to his friend Gabriel Harvey, 'Why, a God's name, may not we, as else the Greeks, have the kingdom of our own language?' Helgerson insists at length on a new interpretation that gives this remark very grave import. After much far-fetched glossing of the words 'we', 'kingdom' and 'language', he concludes that we have here a quasi-royal Spenser ('we') talking about his aim to 'govern the very linguistic system, and perhaps more generally, the whole cultural system' of England.

It is unlikely that Spenser had any such plan in mind. The argument was about the prosodic difficulty of reconciling Classical quantities with ordinary English pronunciation. What Spenser is saying is that the Greeks sometimes imposed quantity, as it were by force, on language that resisted it. Why should not quantity be imposed on English in the same way, as it were by force? 'Rough words must be subdued by use.' The idea, perhaps not wholly serious, is that after all the language is ours and we can push it around a bit if we choose, just as the Greeks did theirs.

Here, and in his treatment of Harvey's bantering replies, Helgerson seems to me to mistake the tone entirely; his tremendous implications are interpretative fantasies. We are asked to believe that an argument occurring within a small group of poets about the relative merits of 'Classical' and 'Medieval' verse (the work of 'bold rhymers') was of vast cultural and political significance. In opposing Spenser's suggestion, Harvey is said to be resisting his 'version of the absolutist cultural politics of antiquity . . . Here Spenser and Harvey together discover, almost inadvertently it would seem, an oppositional politics of national literary self-representation.'

Spenser soon gave up quantity and got on with his 'Gothic' rhyming, which hardly suits the argument that he had a humanist preference for the Classical over the Medieval; but you can always say, with Helgerson, that presence depends on absence, so that what is not so is as important in its way as what is. This device facilitates a good deal of conjuring with 'systems of difference', thus: Classical epic and Medieval chivalric romance coexist in *The Faerie Queene*. The Virgilian aspirations and the ceremonial cult of the queen stood on one side of the difference, and 'Gothic' romance, representing the aristocratic opposition which favoured 'a partially refeudalized English polity', stood on the other. Spenser sympathized with the refeudalizers, so he never brings the Faerie Queene into the poem: it is therefore legitimate to speculate that some of his less admirable females as well as his good or heroic ones may be covert representations of Queen Elizabeth. The important figure of Duessa, Una's opponent, might be hard to work into this theory, but she seems, discreetly, not to be mentioned. Perhaps we are to assume that her absence from this surely absurd conjecture is as important as her presence would have been. We can bear to be reminded that the great poem has multiple political bearings, but these selective over-interpretations are hardly the way to do it.

The chapter on legal discourse is, however, fascinating. Roman law had been revived in Europe, and it seemed to some humanists in the time of Henry VIII that England, which had been part of the Empire, should receive it also. Helgerson is interested in the later contest between common law and royal prerogative – judge-made law versus king-made law. Here he identifies, more plausibly, another clash between Classical and Gothic or Medieval, the former favouring the absolutism to which James I aspired, the latter attentive to the rights of the subject, and insistent that the monarch remain under the law.

The great Edward Coke, in defending the common law against the king's prerogative, can quite intelligibly be said to have written the law of England. True, he depended partly on the bogus argument that English law, descending from the legendary Trojan emigrant Brutus, was actually more ancient than the Roman; but in his *Institutions*, as unwieldy as they were authoritative, he codified English law – and paradoxically, by writing down 'unwritten law', provided a satisfactory native rival to the *Institutes* of Justinian. 'Each', says Helgerson in a characteristic sentence, 'is ideologically motivated, and each depends on the other (even if only as a signifying absence).' But he does illuminate the issue – the conflict between the absolutist tendencies of James I and Coke's common law was of real constitutional importance. Of course nothing is quite simple in matters of this kind: Coke thought well of the Court of Star Chamber, a prerogative court, though only so long as the monarch never showed up; the royal presence in it was merely symbolic, and the law was left, as Coke thought it should be, to learned judges. Later, when the monarchy was overthrown, the Commonwealth was quick to abolish Star Chamber, but Coke preferred, as Helgerson puts it, not to weaken the 'oppositional prerogative'. This is right, I think, and it might have been worth considering the degree to which 'oppositional' options sometimes continue, for whatever reasons, to be respected – the Classical bias in English culture did not, after all, cease with the victory over absolutism. What is not right is the unbalanced claim that Coke's important defence of native law is to be thought of as having the same kind of effect as the defence of English verse against the classicizers, since both are ways of 'writing England'. One is, one isn't; these discourses won't negotiate.

The chapter on maps is also very good. Helgerson shows that royal emblems and portraits gradually disappeared from maps, which thereafter bore the names of their true makers. Place names now crowded in, for the nation, no longer concentrated in the monarch, insisted on its diversity. It was 'writing itself' against monarchical presumption. Individual historians and geographers asserted their rights, and those of the land at large. And thus 'royal power [was] disabled'. But it fought back: James hated maps, fearing that they would make the land seem more important than the crown. Chorography became a political, even a 'Whiggish', act. All this is new, at any rate to me, and seems largely acceptable.

The chapter on voyages compares the mercantilism of the rather belated English ventures with the more aristocratic ethos of the Portuguese, at any rate as professed in the epic of Camões; the English were clearly more interested in profit than in honour or the augmentation of royal power. 'Vent and commodity', in Hakluyt's words, were the main point of voyaging. 'Commerce is the life of England and the world'; that granted, one might as well add token words about the Queen's 'honour, reverence and power', and the virtuous spread of Christianity.

Helgerson duly explains that the financing of the great expeditions altered social balances, mingling aristocrat and merchant. Yet here again old historians might complain of puzzling omissions. Very little is said about the enormous and rapid transformation in the life and culture of London consequent on these and other mercantile ventures; perhaps it is old history, or too well known to deserve New Historical attention. At the beginning of Elizabeth's reign England was a poor country, well behind its European rivals in technology and production. By the end of the reign London was rich and powerful. Profits, from voyages and from domestic enterprise, could be fantastic. Old historian J. M. Keynes pointed out in his *Treatise on Money* that with the profit on Drake's venture in the *Golden Hind* Elizabeth 'paid off the whole of her foreign debt', which was considerable, and had a nice sum left over to invest in the East India Company, so preparing the way to the larger empire of the future. For other speculators, though not for the poor, who were badly hit by rising prices, the London market, usurping the position of Antwerp, created vast wealth: 'never in the annals of the modern world', said Keynes, who did not live to see the international markets of today, 'has there existed so prolonged and so rich an opportunity for the business man and the speculator'. These new riches founded what might be called the discourse of proto-bourgeois luxury. Ostentation in dress, hair-styles and weapons spread throughout society, and so did the expen-sive tobacco habit. The plays that exposed or satirized City greed and display – Jonson's, and later Massinger's and Middleton's – get no mention here. Indeed it is extraordinary how lifeless this New History can seem – a bloodless ballet of social practices, danced high above the scams and the traffic jams, the noises of dog eating dog, in the City where they are said to interact.

There follows a chapter on Shakespeare in the currently fashion-able disparaging manner. Socially insecure, the playwright sought to be taken up by the aristocracy. He progressively excluded the com-mons from his stage, and when he showed the populace at all it was engaged in 'demonized revolt'. The success of his social climbing was such that he eventually secured the position he now holds in bourgeois aesthetic valuation. Yet there were other theatres than his, now neglected, which had a different attitude to the commonalty – which dealt in carnival, and relished popular sentiment. These the bourgeois Establishment has preferred to ignore.

Much is made of the replacement in Shakespeare's company, around the turn of the century, of the clown Will Kemp by the fool Robert Armin. Was the departure of the more popular, 'broader', comic related to the dramatic dismissal of Falstaff, played by Kemp? Well, no, 'but the fictional event does have a proleptic relation to the factual one' – another of those hocus-pocus passes that enable the writer to say what he wants to say even though he knows better. 'Clown' and 'fool' aren't all that sharply distinguished in Shake-speare's terminology – Lavatch in *All's Well* is called 'Clown' throughout, yet he is obviously the Countess's fool. Of course there was some difference, and Armin had a distinctive style, of which Shakespeare, who wrote for his actors, took account when writing

Feste and the Fool in *Lear*. But to make Armin out to be another sign of Shakespeare's 'infatuation with kingly power' is excessive. So is the notion that by losing 'the common touch' Shakespeare eventually excluded the commonalty from the canon of literature. 'Shakespeare stood, as he stands today, for Royal Britain, for a particularly anachronistic state formation, based at least symbolically on the monarch and an aristocratic governing class.' There is little evidence that modern royalty would agree that he stands thus, and it is now a long time since Britain had an aristocratic prime minister. It is hard to imagine that Heath, Wilson, Callaghan, Thatcher, Major and Blair, to say nothing of the hereditary peerage, think of Shakespeare as contributing to their discourses of power. Their opinion, at least in private, is more likely to have been that of George III: 'Was there ever such stuff as a great part of Shakespeare?'

Again, too much is left out. *Coriolanus* is unkind to the mob but unkind also to the aristocracy, and Shakespeare, as Wyndham Lewis remarked, knew a lot about really nasty supersnob aristocrats and remembered them in his plays. It is a real difficulty to distinguish what Dr Johnson called the praise 'paid by perception and judgement' from that which is 'given by custom and veneration', but it is not a difficulty admitted by Helgerson, who only rarely hints that the plays are of any value except for what they seem to reveal, willy-nilly, about the contemporary conflict between absolutism and popular nationalism, and about the bardolatrous machinations of later ideologists.

The chapter about religion makes its point by comparing the apocalyptic populism of Foxe's book of Protestant martyrs at the beginning of James's reign with the suaver conservative apologetics of Hooker at the end. They are said to offer 'differing discourses of nationhood'. Indeed they do. It is possible that both Foxe and Hooker, each in his own way but also by expressing oppositional attitudes, played a part in opening up 'a discursive space' for future generations. For, as Helgerson remarks, there were and are 'competing and even contradictory ways of being English'; that is, 'most literate and mobile Englishmen belonged to several discursive communities, were traversed by a plurality of nationalist discourses'. And so they are still, though they might not put it just like that.

It seems sad that a scholar who obviously knows how to find things out, and can obviously write, should feel compelled to deal in imaginary *trouvailles*, and to use this modish jargon. For it is surely not impossible that lively cultural history could be written, and indeed better written, if the desire to astonish by novelty were moderated, and the new cant were given up altogether.

Shakespeare at Work

John Jones, sometime Professor of Poetry at Oxford, has written a number of good, idiosyncratic books on topics as diverse as Greek tragedy and Wordsworth, together with an excellent novel, *The Same God*, published in 1972 and apparently without a successor. He has now produced a good, idiosyncratic book on Shakespeare.* In the nature of the project he can't avoid technical questions, and readers new to the complex problems of Shakespearian texts may find some parts hard going, but Jones avoids all temptation to be impressively professional and bejargoned; and his book is indeed so courteously written, so curiously intimate in manner and so engagingly clear and resourceful in argument, that anybody with a genuine interest in Shakespeare, and particularly in *Hamlet*, *King Lear* and *Othello*, should read it for pleasure and then reread it to pick quarrels about details.

Jones's material is drawn principally from readings in earlier Shakespearian texts that differ from those of the collected edition, the Folio of 1623. His method is demonstrated on the first page by this example:

SHALLOW. O, Sir John, do you remember since we lay all night in the Windmill in Saint George's Field?
SIR JOHN. No more of that, *good* Master Shallow, *no more of that*.
SHALLOW. Ha, 'twas a merry night! And is Jane Nightwork alive?
SIR JOHN. She lives, Master Shallow.

* *Shakespeare at Work* (Oxford: Clarendon Press, 1995).

The italicized words, found in the Folio, are not in the Quarto of 2 *Henry IV*, published in 1600 – a text almost certainly derived from Shakespeare's autograph. The fuller text can therefore be taken either as evidence of revision or as suggesting that the printers of the Quarto for some reason omitted the italicized words. In this instance the first is the more credible explanation; somebody, probably Shakespeare, had touched up the old text. Here he is, then, snapped at work.

Not all the alterations in the Folio are so manifestly Shakespeare's own second thoughts, and of those that seem likely to be so not all can be represented as improvements. Some are journeyman expedients to meet needs that became evident in rehearsal – giving a character a bit more time to get to his mark, etc. But many are a good deal more than that, and some sound (to experienced and sensitive ears) so much like Shakespeare that it would be perverse to attribute them to anybody else. So this Shallow–Falstaff dialogue is offered as a tiny but persuasive instance of Shakespeare revising his own play, not to meet some momentary theatrical need but simply to improve it. Plausible as this may sound, it runs counter to the scholarly opinion, until recently stubbornly held, that it wasn't Shakespeare's practice to rehandle his material.

Lately this view has been repeatedly challenged, as it now is by Jones; and common sense is surely on his side. Shakespeare was acting in and doubtless directing the plays, and might, almost in the ordinary course of business, see ways of improving them which are reflected in later texts. Of course the proofs are difficult, and are often reduced to flat declarations that such and such a new reading is unmistakably 'Shakespearian'; this is what Jones says about the little change in Falstaff's reply to Shallow. But more could be added in his support. Falstaff in the later version is more uneasy, less willing to be reminded of that episode in the windmill with Jane Nightwork; he has had many more subsequent escapades than Shallow, whose senile memories of juvenile debauch make Sir John a little uncomfortable. Shadows are beginning to thicken around him. Or whatever; anybody could produce other reasons for admiring these additions.

On the other hand it might still be maintained by stubborn anti-revisers that they are merely instances of theatrical sophistication, the work of intrusive, self-indulgent actors. And there are certainly cases where that kind of explanation is more plausible than it is here.

Conflicts of opinion naturally get sharper when the decisions that have to be made involve the substance of *Othello*, *Lear* or *Hamlet*. They call for delicate apprehensions and tactful demonstration, and occasionally some polemical vigour. For what it is worth, my opinion is that Jones is rarely wrong in his sense of what is Shakespearian; he recognizes a quality he calls 'poise', and repeatedly displays a sense of what I can only call the presiding personality: nobody else would have done precisely *that*. For all his scrupulous documentation it is on this kind of perception that he has to rely, and it is on the authority of such perceptions that the reader in turn comes to depend.

He starts his detailed inquiry with the sole extended passage of writing that is almost certainly in Shakespeare's own hand, namely three pages, 147 lines, in the manuscript play *Sir Thomas More*. This play, never printed or performed, was mainly the work of two or three minor dramatists of the period – it was not at all unusual to patch plays together in this way. Their first attempt ran into censorship difficulties, and at some point the manuscript was revised (though, curiously, not in ways calculated to appease the censor) and Shakespeare seems to have been one of the revisers.

Nobody can say why he took on this job at a time when he must already have had a heavy workload, but there is unusual unanimity among the experts that the lines are in his hand as it is known from other sources, and that some idiosyncratic spellings, strange even in that age of 'spell-as-you-please', as Jones puts it, support the attribution. Moreover the crowd scene, with More restoring a potentially dangerous mob to order, is very much in Shakespeare's line. So the manuscript offers a picture of Shakespeare 'composing fluently, making the slips that go with speed'. His text suffered some alteration by another hand that was perhaps preparing the play for the stage, and occasionally got muddled by the untidiness, and the already existing changes and insertions made by Shakespeare. Here is a unique piece of evidence – a longish passage of Shakespeare seen in its transition from first thoughts to theatrical text.

Everywhere else it is more a matter of tactful conjecture. Sometimes one can be fairly sure what has happened; for example, in the Quarto of *Richard II* we read the line 'Cry woe, destruction, ruin and decay', which, though perfectly serviceable, is replaced in the Folio by 'Cry woe, destruction, ruin, loss, decay', and Jones feels sure that the change, by which 'the line's rhythm grows more subtle and more grand', is by Shakespeare. On the other hand he explains the Folio deletion of a passage in III.ii of the same play by describing the four cut lines as 'dramatically inert', which they aren't, since (in my opinion) the next speech plainly follows directly from them and not from the line that precedes the cut:

BISHOP. Fear not my lord. The power that made you king
　Hath power to keep you king in spite of all.
　The means that heavens yield must be embraced
　And not neglected; else heaven would,
　And we will not; heaven's offer we refuse,
　The proferr'd means of succour and redress.
AUMERLE. He means, my lord, that we are too remiss,
　Whilst Bolingbroke, through our security,
　Grows strong and great in substance and in friends.

Whether or no the italicized lines, found only in the Quarto, are so much flatter than the verse on either side of them, the Bishop is saying that although heaven has the power to keep him king it's up to Richard to do something to help. This, and not the suggestion that heaven will do it all on its own, is the point Aumerle is summarizing. So whoever made it, and for whatever reason, the cut is actually inept. It could be by a ruthless prompter rather than a dramatist weeding out dull lines.

On the whole Jones avoids idolatry, sensibly remarking that not all authorial revision need be for the better, and also allowing for the fact that the pen that alters one thing is likely, redundantly, to alter others in its vicinity; but here and in some other places he does seem to give the Bard the benefit of any doubt. (Excepted from this rule of charity is *Troilus and Cressida*, a play with which Jones is uncharacteristically and unfairly impatient, dismissing it as 'a lofty romp'.)

The bulk of the book is devoted to *Hamlet*, a play that is a paradise to bibliographers but a nightmare to many editors. There are three versions, a quarto of 1603, a second quarto of 1604/5, and the Folio of 1623. The first, based on memorial reporting, is without authority, though in several ways useful. From the 1930s until recently it was commonly assumed that Q2 ought to be the copy-text, as closest to Shakespeare's autograph. The view now taken is that Q2 represents a draft, quite close to final but later revised for performance, so that the differences between Q2 and F, which are considerable, ought usually to be resolved in favour of F. The texts of the play most of us grew up with tend to insert bits of F into Q2, so providing a composite version which was never performed. Jones is, of course, a Folio man. Strictly speaking, the great soliloquy 'How all occasions do inform against me', which is not in F, should be omitted from modern editions (as indeed it is from the recent Oxford versions, for which Jones has a not uncritical fondness). Incidentally, it is also absent from Q1, which offers, though unreliably, an idea of what was performed in the first years of the play's existence.

Jones argues that it was cut because there had already been quite enough of Hamlet lamenting his procrastination, especially in the earlier soliloquy 'O what a rogue and peasant slave am I!'. 'Having written these two soliloquies, Shakespeare saw that he had made a mistake', so he threw out the final soliloquy (which is in any case oddly placed; Hamlet says he has 'strength and will and means' to kill the King when he is on his way to England, under guard and for the first time quite unable to get at Claudius). To make up for the loss, and give the play a better balance, he inserted in the already enormous and wonderful II.ii a long and remarkable passage of dialogue about Denmark being a prison.

Jones's reasons are interesting in their way, but reasons in these cases are as plentiful as blackberries, and I think his work best not on large conjectures about the dramatist's concern for balance and so forth, but on small details, like the difference between 'What's Hecuba to him or he to her?' and 'What's Hecuba to him or he to Hecuba?', preferring the second (F), which he regards as a revision, though editors often think it a corruption. Another instance is his admiring acceptance of the F revision in the following passage, at the end of the play within the play:

OPHELIA. The King rises.
HAMLET. *What, frighted with false fire?*
GERTRUDE. How fares my lord?
POLONIUS. Give o'er the play.

Hamlet's line here is not in Q2. Jones believes this change was made between the writing of the scene and its performance (the 'pirates' of Q1 remembered it, so it must have been there by 1603). Of course it could simply have been left out of Q2 by a compositor; Jones cannot insure against that possibility, so that his praise for this 'afterthought' could conceivably be misplaced. But, as he remarks, he is always dealing with probabilities rather than certainties. He approaches certainty, however, in some subtle readings, as in his comment on the passage where F inserts the words 'lawful espials' into a speech of Polonius, thereby disturbing a perfectly good iambic pentameter and making necessary a short line which isn't filled out. Here it is necessary to explain why the addition was worth the disturbance, and Jones explains it.

What gives one confidence is the author's well-expressed sense of the general mood of the play as 'flecked with high spirits and a vastly intelligent, piercing levity . . . the play is in a state of revolt against the more obvious of its own decorums'. It is this mood that is served by 'lawful espials', and it is his understanding of it that makes everything Jones says about the play so absorbing, whether or not he is right to treat Q2 as a provisional version, subject to the corrections recorded in whatever was the principal copy for F, presumed to be of theatrical provenance.

The case of *Lear*, at present the subject of much throwing about of bibliographical brains, is different. Current expert opinion prefers to think the Quarto of 1608 to be not a working draft but a distinct version of the play, and the Folio a complete reworking; which is why the Oxford Shakespeare sets out both texts in full. Jones compares them to the distinct versions of Wordsworth's *Prelude*, of 1805 and 1850. He does consider the possibility of a lost original behind both versions but dismisses it. I have doubts about the rightness of this, and am not convinced that the revision thesis necessarily rules out the lost archetype; but there is not space, and perhaps not enough readerly patience, to argue the point here.

Possibly these doubts explain why I feel more sceptical about Jones's *Lear* than about his *Hamlet*. Consider these famous lines (V.ii):

> Men must endure
> Their going hence even as their coming hither.
> Ripeness is all.

Edgar has parked his blind father under a tree and gone off to battle, promising that if he returns he will bring comfort. But the battle is lost; he returns without being able to offer any comfort at all, except for the *sententia* recorded above. The Folio completes the concluding line by making Gloucester answer 'And that's true too', which Jones, unable this time to think of a reason why Shakespeare might have added these words himself, calls 'a pointless enfeeblement', perhaps the work of a compositor needing to 'stretch' his copy.* But this bibliographical conjecture seems to be necessary only because Jones happens not to approve of the additional words. Can this be out of misplaced reverence for the wisdom of Edgar's remark 'Ripeness is all', and indeed for the wisdom of the Bard? Consider what Edgar

---

* This occurred quite often in the printing of the Folio. The copy was cast off to make for economy in composition (more than one compositor worked on the job), and if the casting-off was inaccurate a compositor would have to 'stretch copy' to fill his page, or compress it if he had more than there was normal space for. He would do this by printing verse as prose to save space, or prose as verse to lose it. There were other such expedients, but I doubt if the compositors often wrote new copy. However, Jones seems to believe that one may have done so here.

then says: 'Come on!' He's in a hurry, uttering not great truths but a perfunctorily consoling commonplace; Gloucester, wearily and reluctantly following his son, recognizes it as such, no doubt feeling quite ripe enough already. To read this extraordinary little scene otherwise is, I think, to risk devaluing the play. This seems true also of a rather far-fetched idea that in cutting the scene (IV.iii) in which Cordelia is described in rapt tones, rather like a heroine of romance – or, as some have said, like the Virgin Mary – Shakespeare was acknowledging that his Romance was to come later in his career, not just yet; as if he was already, like Dowden, dividing his life into phases, and didn't want to get 'On the Heights' too soon. But such lapses (as I think them) are invariably engaging.

The two versions of *Othello* present different problems; the play was published in a quarto in 1622, very shortly before it appeared in the Folio. Jones thinks the version performed for James I at the Banqueting House in 1604 was substantially the Quarto text. In 1606 Parliament passed an act restraining profanity and blasphemy in the theatre, so that thereafter existing plays had to be revised to eliminate oaths and other language that might be called blasphemous or profane. The Quarto of *Othello* has fifty-two oaths, such as 'Sblood' or 'Zouns', while the Folio has none. The argument is that in going through the play to clean it up in this respect the reviser made a good many other changes as well. This person was Shakespeare, and Jones thinks that some time after May 1606, when the act of Parliament became law, he wrote out the whole play afresh. On this view the *Othello* Quarto, unlike *Hamlet (Q2)*, represents a satisfactory version that had already been acted; and the Folio offers a complete reworking of it. There are many small changes, on which Jones is very acute, and one large one, the addition of the Willow Song (the alternative explanation, that it had existed but was for some reason left out of the Quarto version, is, I agree, less probable). Following a hint of Neville Coghill's, Jones takes this striking addition as part of a rethinking of the role of Emilia, who is also given, at the end of Act IV, a splendid new eighteen-line speech ('But I do think it is their husbands' faults/When wives do fall . . .') which is even more plausibly part of such a plan. Here, as elsewhere on *Othello*, the argument seems very convincing, and it seems a shame that Boito and Verdi, to whom the added Willow Song passage was such a godsend, should have cut the role of Emilia so heavily.

Anyway, Jones is right that the 160 lines of F that are missing in Q make a deal of difference. And about such differences this book, which is a work of literary criticism in its detective mode, has more of interest to say than any other I know. Few readers, glancing past the sigla in the footnotes of their copies, can ever have expected that much delight and wisdom might be got from them, and many rewards in the forms both of agreement and of dissent. And how rare a pleasure it is actually to admire a book on Shakespeare!

Romantic Revisions

The time is almost past when writers copiously provided the curious, at least as interested in process as in product, with drafts showing corrections by one or more hands and interestingly rejected alternative readings. Poems are still drafted, of course, and corrections are made, but they won't show up in computer files, where all traces of a poem's trajectory from conception to birth can be, and usually are, erased. Research into the ways in which authors revise their work, or allow others to do so, will usually have to be content with material written during the epochs of pen and typewriter. All is not quite lost, for there will remain variations in different printed texts, early versions in periodicals; but there will be less to work on, and this book* is evidence that we'll be a little the poorer for it.

W. H. Auden became convinced that in some of his pre-war poetry he had been telling lies or advocating causes in which he no longer believed. Indeed he had come to think that it had been wicked to write in support of such causes. Poetry itself was suspect: 'Nothing is lovely,/Not even in poetry, which is not the case,' he decided, and it is difficult for poetry to be nothing but the case. Auden altered some poems in an attempt to bring them closer to being so; others he eliminated from his canon as beyond repair. Some of his alterations were so perverse that it sometimes seemed he was now simply missing the point of the original, as when he took the celebrated line 'We

---

* Zachary Leader, *Revision and Romantic Authorship* (Oxford: Clarendon Press, 1996).

113

must love one another or die' to be a mistake, and preferred 'We must love one another *and* die.' Later he struck down the whole poem, as he did others, among them, it is still possible to argue, the finest of their period.

Auden's scrupulous editor and executor, Edward Mendelson, has invariably respected and supported the poet's decisions, but manages to have it both ways by including in a separate volume, *The English Auden*, the original versions of poems that were later either revised or rejected. This expensive option is not available to all editors. Yeats, though not in the same way anxious about having said what might be thought not the case, was another reviser, sometimes drastically altering early poems. His editors, Allt and Alspach, dealt with the problem by producing a large so-called 'variorum' edition, recording all printed versions but giving precedence to the last ('The brawling of the sparrows in the eaves,/ The brilliant moon and all the milky sky,/ And all that famous harmony of leaves,/ Had blotted out man's image and his cry') and relegating the original to the footnotes ('The quarrel of the sparrows in the eaves,/ The full round moon and the star-laden sky,/And the loud song of ever-singing leaves/ Had hid away earth's old and weary cry'). In hectic later years Yeats disowned the weariness of his twenties but still thought of this poem, revised and updated, as a necessary constituent of his œuvre. He admitted that it belonged to a group of poems so much altered as to become 'altogether new poems. Whatever changes I have made are but an attempt to express better what I thought and felt when I was a very young man.' Some thought this mere falsification, but he answered them thus:

> The friends that have it I do wrong
> Whenever I remake song,
> Should know what issue is at stake:
> It is myself that I remake.

These lines were written in 1908, but the idea that in his revisions he was remaking himself as well as the poems persisted; thirty years later, near death, he prays 'Grant me an old man's frenzy, / Myself I must remake . . .'

It is this doubleness – the desire to keep what belonged to an earlier phase of existence yet change it to make it comply with a different self-image – that makes it difficult to decide what to do with Wordsworth, another keen reviser, and a harder case than Yeats. *The Prelude*, for instance, remained in manuscript, indeed in a good many variant manuscripts, until after his death. This multiplicity creates all sorts of problems, and they are among the issues meditated in Zachary Leader's carefully written book.

He has two objectives. At a rather abstract level he wants to know what notions of identity underlie the assumption that a poet in his twenties could be identical with the poet who, in his seventies, was still tinkering with his early writings as if they were essential to the expression of the singleness of a life or a life-work, rather than leaving them alone as virtually the work of a different person, or at any rate of a person in no need of being assimilated to a later version of itself. Secondly he proposes to examine what actually happened in the process of certain revisions in the poetry of Wordsworth and Byron, the Shelleys, Clare and Keats. In carrying out this second part of his work he has to take into account a fact of special interest to some modern bibliographers: other hands than the writer's have often played a considerable part in the revisions.

Leader starts from the position that a preference for earlier, if possible the earliest, versions is evidence of what he thinks of as a (false) Romantic notion: that closeness to the original moment of inspiration is the best determinant of the right text. This opinion unconsciously echoes Shelley's famous notion that 'the mind in creation is as a fading coal . . . When composition begins, inspiration is already on the decline' – whence it follows that all the 'labour and study' later bestowed on a poem merely take one further away from that precious but already fading original inspiration.

In contesting this view of the matter, Leader aligns himself with the modern critical school associated with the name of Jerome

McGann and with his attack on what he calls 'the Romantic ideology', a disease of the original Romantics from which all criticism of them continues to suffer, or anyway did so continue until McGann and his friends administered a purgative cure. Much of what this school says I myself think erroneous, but Leader is not interested, here at any rate, in its New Historical bullying; his point is simply that there is something false in the cult of the original unrevised version.

He takes issue with Stephen Gill, whose Oxford Authors edition of Wordsworth prints the poems 'in texts in which their original identity is restored'. Thus all the 'secondary' work that resulted in the final authorized text, the six-volume *Poems* of 1849–50, published at the very end of the poet's life, is ignored. Yet Wordsworth always assumed that the child is father to the man, the neophyte poet to the aged laureate. Gill's defence is that to give the preference to later, much changed, versions creates a false idea of what the poetry looked or felt like to Wordsworth's immediate contemporaries when it first appeared, and obscures our view of his development. Leader has no difficulty pointing out confusions in Gill's practice, but his main objection is that there is no good reason to believe the revised versions to be less worthy than the original effusions. He allows that Wordsworth himself caused some of the confusion, because although he manifestly believed in revising he did talk about the value of the spontaneous overflow of powerful feelings. But he evidently took the un-Shelleyan view that there was a secondary phase of creation as important as the first, which Leader also believes.

The truth is presumably that there are two extreme positions, one emphasizing the labour of the file, the other the valuable initial glow of creation. Between the two most writers oscillate; some may incline more towards the Shelleyan idea, others more to Horace's. But most know that both the delight of the *donnée* and the less joyous pleasures of revision actually work together. Valéry thought poorly of the initial flourish, what you were given, for which you deserve no more credit than the Pythian oracle did for relaying the divine message; the real work of the poet comes later. And few poems reach print unrevised, though some are more spontaneous than others. It is curious that Wallace Stevens, who rarely suggests the poetry of flashing eye and floating hair, was in fact a very spontaneous writer and did very little revision, as if, for him, the primary and secondary processes were virtually one and the same. Wordsworth, on the other hand, revised obsessively, and his revisions reflected his changes of opinion, especially his political opinion, over a very long period. Leaving out technical matters of bibliography, some will prefer the early, some (probably rather fewer, in Wordsworth's case) the late. And there are all those other intermediate versions, which may one day be represented by hypertext, the reader at his console picking and choosing among all the variants. But Leader argues, reasonably, that these plural texts are not likely to be of much use to people who simply want to read Wordsworth and leave it to the experts to give them a text.

Leader maintains that Wordsworth in his revisions has 'an underlying coherence of purpose', and indeed this is what the poet himself affirmed. He accepted that youthful enthusiasm naturally gives way to mature reflection, and saw no reason to be ashamed that he had turned against 'France, and her Rulers, when they abandoned the struggle for Liberty, gave themselves up to tyranny, and endeavoured to enslave the world'. This change of attitude is reflected in the revision of *The Prelude*. Whether you prefer the early versions or the later depends partly on whether you want to see the poet's years 'bound each to each', as he did, or prefer the younger Wordsworth before 'mature reflection' disappointingly altered his character and dimmed his youthful fire. Leader has very carefully considered the whole question; he won't always win agreement, but what he says demands a comparably scrupulous attention.

Byron provides a contrast. He did very little revision, being lazy, preternaturally fluent, and aristocratically hostile to the bourgeois glamorizing of integral selfhood, the Romantic cult of organic wholeness, and pretentious claims for the sedentary trade of writing ('who would write who had anything better to do?'). This was the 'affected coolness' of which Keats complained. Byron took care to read proofs, but did little by way of correction before that stage. He allowed Mary Shelley to make prudential changes in his manuscripts, and left the rest in the hands of the publisher John Murray and his advisers: 'Ask Mr Gifford and Mr Hobhouse, and, as they think, so let it be.' To some extent this kind of interference, sanctioned as it was, justifies talk about replacing the author with Foucault's 'author-function', a term designed to account for the part played by friends, advisers, proof-correctors, publishers and so on – every hand that touches the work in the course of its production. But I don't see this catching on with the laity, or any who persist naively in imagining that in all great works of art they can perceive what Wallace Stevens called a presiding personality.

Coleridge heavily revised *The Ancient Mariner*; should we be offered everything, hypertextually, or be content to let editors choose a version? Do you find the later version 'richer, more complex', like Jack Stillinger and Zachary Leader; or decide, with William Empson, that it has been mangled 'for reasons of conscience'? It is not easy to make out what Coleridge thought about the unity of the self, but surely having a sense of it is consistent with occasional changes of mind. His practice suggests that he at least thought of the body of his poetry as capable of achieving integration. In practice some of the changes he made seem to be the result of political prudence, some smack of prudery; it would be hard to say which version would contribute more to the achievement of those Romantic ambitions, the integral life, the organic whole. The story of the person from Porlock who caused Coleridge to break off 'Kubla Khan', and so forfeit his primary inspiration, obviously illustrates another Romantic illusion: the fading-coal theory. Coleridge's texts, unlike Byron's, are highly unstable; editors have not yet solved all the problems and, short of hypertext, perhaps never can.

The textual history of Mary Shelley's *Frankenstein* is typically complex but in detail unusual. P. B. Shelley made many changes in the original manuscript and the proofs – changes that seem by no means always to be improvements. It would not have been easy for the youthful author to resist these corrections even if she'd wanted to; Shelley was older, more eminent, and also a man, whereas she was merely an inexperienced young female, self-described as 'a silly goose'. But Leader convincingly criticizes the strong-feminist version of this relationship, arguing that the novel actually contests the Romantic 'Promethean' view of the author, an attitude Mary understood very well because she lived with Shelley. After his death she in her turn had some power over her husband's poems. In such cases writing does in a sense become a 'genuinely social activity'.

John Clare's dealings with his publisher John Taylor provide a variation on this theme. Clare's peculiar circumstances resulted in revisions that were necessarily 'social', but modern editors have a persistent tendency to revert to the earliest unsocial text, which they regard as more 'authentic'. Leader wants to know 'what is the nature of the evidence that Clare would have preferred manuscript versions of his early poems – unpunctuated, misspelled, ungrammatical, metrically defective, irregularly rhymed, poorly structured, repetitive' – to the versions printed by Taylor. Until he went mad Clare expected and wanted his poems to be revised, and Taylor, though sometimes cast as the interfering bourgeois publisher, was actually never too keen on the job. On Leader's view, critics who ignore these facts are still under the Romantic illusion that the poet is a solitary genius, still unreasonably favouring primary over secondary process, still unwilling to take into account the 'social' aspects of that process.

Taylor, here defended against these primitivist 'victims of the Romantic ideology', was the publisher who took on Keats when his first publisher dropped him, and Keats also underwent revision at Taylor's hands and those of his advisers, Reynolds and Woodhouse. Keats was not himself a great reviser, but on the whole approved the alterations they made, often with a view to getting him a less critical hearing and to nullifying his dangerous association with Leigh Hunt. Keats even apologized for giving Taylor so much bother: 'I did very wrong to leave you all the trouble of Endymion.' Of course that poem still got a critical drubbing, and the revision of Keats's next book in 1820 was in large part devoted to the elimination of

Endymion-like gushings and lusciousnesses. Once again other hands than the poet's intervened between manuscript and print. Keats had to be helped to be 'manly'. He responded to this advice, and to the changes proposed, with some enthusiasm, while professing to despise the audience these changes were meant to placate. Thus, to use a word that interested him, he acquired, under social pressure, a revised *identity* as well as a revised text and a new respect for the 'secondary' creativity of revision.

Leader develops these points in great detail, with many long footnotes – happily, for once, at the foot of the page. His arguments have implications that go beyond the Romantic authors he concerns himself with. Conventions of self-understanding change; and if we are to believe Charles Taylor's argument in *Sources of the Self* the change speeded up remarkably during the Romantic period. Of course it is rare (though not unknown) for a poet to abandon his or her youthful work entirely; it may be thought of as juvenilia, failing to meet the standards of the mature writer; still, though only faintly, relevant, still not quite dispensable, it may find a place in an appendix. And we are all so infected by the Romantic ideology that we have what seems a fairly clear, though some would say a hallucinated, view of the wholeness as well as the inspiration of Yeats, of Wordsworth, of Keats, author-functions though they may be; just as we have a view of our own selves as forming a continuum, from youthful immaturity to ancient resignation. Others took a hand in that process, but we think we know we somehow made and remade ourselves. Is this a Romantic fallacy? If so it was shared by many writers before Romanticism came in (Pope, for instance, carefully recovering and rewriting his correspondence) and by many lesser souls, all of whom unsophisticatedly see themselves as single persons. Some of them even live with the rather awful idea that at some future moment they will be asked to account for what they made of the selves they started with. Shakespeare wrote, of a unique occasion, that Property (the personified idea of what is proper to a person, what makes that person distinct and individual) was appalled to discover that the self was not the same. We also feel that such a metaphysical discovery would be pretty appalling, that generally the self is the same, yet malleable, revisable, remakable – and usually, perhaps always, we arrive at that comfortable conviction with social assistance.

English Gnostics

A. D. Nuttall is probably the most philosophically-minded of modern literary critics, and he has the additional merit of assuming that at some level philosophical (or theological) problems are of importance to everybody – an assumption that operates even when he is applying his mind, and his exceptional erudition, to such matters as the presence of Gnostic speculation in Marlowe, Milton and Blake.* The justification for this belief is that almost everybody, often at an early age, has wondered how a God officially certified as good in all possible ways can coexist with a creation that is manifestly not so.

This puzzle is generally known as the Problem of Evil, and Nuttall says it worried him as a child, having no doubt been instructed, or allowed to believe, that in spite of evidence to the contrary God is good as well as omnipotent, and that ours is the best of all possible worlds. Most people soon put this problem aside and get on with their lives. Some, less quiescent, consider the matter in the light of such works as Leibniz's *Theodicy*, and Voltaire's satirical response to it in *Candide*. But there is another venerable way of looking at it, invented by heterodox thinkers in the early days of the Christian era. Gnosticism avoids our problem by holding that the world is not the work of a good god at all, but rather of an evil power, the Demiurge, who has been falsely represented as a good god and could be identified

---

* *The Alternative Trinity: Gnostic Heresy in Marlowe, Milton and Blake* (Oxford: Clarendon Press, 1998).

with the God of the Old Testament. The consequent doctrinal ramifications are endless, and whenever the question came up it was likely that certain aspects of early Gnostic thought would be aired again.

The early Gnostics had considerable success, and if the views of Marcion, in the second century, had prevailed (as they might well have done) the Old Testament, a celebration of the bad god, would have been banished from Christian Bibles. For he was a god of Law, an intolerant and capricious dictator who was wholly responsible for the evil of the Creation. Only a part of the New Testament, certified as purely concerned with Love, was to be used – some Pauline epistles and a reduced version of Luke's gospel. One effect of Marcion's efforts was to prompt the orthodox establishment to set about defining a rather more copious biblical canon. In the end Marcion, and many much wilder Gnostics, lost the struggle with orthodoxy so completely that few traces of their writings survived; their ideas were known only by their citation in the works of the orthodox Church Fathers who triumphantly refuted them. But more direct light on Gnostic speculation was provided by the discovery, in 1945, of a cache of Gnostic writings at Nag Hammadi in Egypt, and since then Gnosticism has been intensively and sympathetically studied.

The eclipse of this rival form of Christianity by a politically well-organized Church has been much regretted. Elaine Pagels, in her book *The Gnostic Gospels* (1979), calls it 'an impoverishment of Christian tradition'. Nuttall says its defeat 'is of some interest because in one respect orthodox Christianity seems philosophically more vulnerable than Gnosticism'. He means that none of the Christian answers to the Problem of Evil really works. They include the notion that God leaves evil in the Creation simply because, for reasons secret and inscrutable, he chooses, in spite of being good and powerful, not to remove it; or that evil is there to promote wisdom by enabling us to distinguish good from bad; or that it is a necessary consequence of our being granted free will. None of these, except possibly the second, is very convincing except to the apologists themselves.

Gnosticism does not need these excuses since it regards the whole Creation as evil, and the work of a corrupt Demiurge.

This, as Nuttall says, 'fits the facts' or 'saves the appearances'. Gnosis is knowledge not of the physical but of the supernatural world. Knowing that knowledge is a good enables the adept to believe that the Serpent who persuades Eve and Adam to eat of the Tree of Knowledge is a beneficent snake. One Gnostic sect even identified the Serpent with Christ, going disguised about his work of undoing the wicked ukase of the Father. This of course sets the Son against the Father, and lays the foundation for the 'Alternative Trinity' of Nuttall's title.

It may be that the Gnostic formulation, stripped of its allegorical apparatus, is rather closer to the feelings of ordinary people than official Trinitarianism. It also accounts for the general approval nowadays given to the dissident theology, the revived Gnosticism, of Blake: 'The vision of Christ that thou dost see/ Is my vision's deepest enemy.'

The purpose of Nuttall's book is to show how Gnostic principles are manifested, or can be shown to be present, in the work of Marlowe, Milton and Blake. The treatment has all his usual good-tempered energy and his gift for lateral thinking, which occasionally leads him into digression. There is one interesting digression on epic similes, some of which benefit by what he calls 'homologation' and some of which do not. The matter is too complicated to be expounded here, but the principle of homologation operates not only in certain similes but in the book itself, bringing together materials that may at first seem to have a rather remote relevance to the argument.

In the end it does all hang together homologously. Nuttall singles out C. S. Lewis as a typical opponent. Lewis was certain that in Elizabethan and early Stuart England some thoughts that later became possible were still unthinkable, and should therefore be ruled out of consideration. *Paradise Lost*, properly read, need present no difficulties to perfectly orthodox Christians. And Blake, who said 'the Creator of this World is a very Cruel Being and being a Worshipper of Christ I cannot help saying the Son O how unlike the Father', simply represented a kind of thinking that was, in Marlowe's time or even Milton's, unthinkable. Nuttall's point, of course, is that however the ideas were transmitted it was at no time impossible to regard the Father as cruel and the Son as his enemy: Love as the enemy of Law.

Marlowe's Faustus sells his soul to the Devil for knowledge and power, and the fact that God condemns this bargain shows that he prefers human beings to be ignorant, as he proved when he placed his ban on the Tree of Knowledge. Marlowe, along with others of his time, found the idea of new knowledge – of a magic that was on the verge of becoming science – very exciting. Confidence in the powers of the human mind and the possibilities offered by its acquisitions was now so strong that some found the Calvinist doctrine of total depravity, at that time endorsed by the Church, very distasteful, preferring to believe that despite the Fall man was still capable of exploring the Creation in detail.

As Nuttall remarks, Faustus' punishment is tragic in a sense impossible to Calvinism; the question whether he will be sent to hell, the question on which the tragedy turns, would be meaningless to a Calvinist, who is sure that such decisions are taken long before the person concerned is born. The only question for Calvinists watching *Dr Faustus* would be whether the play would show whether Faustus had been damned from eternity (always already, as the phrase goes) or not. If not, not; if so, too bad. Along the way Nuttall wonders why Calvinists, their ultimate fate already sealed, didn't become 'passive libertines', as some Gnostics did in earlier times, since nothing could be done anyway to change their ultimate fate and they might as well enjoy themselves as long as they could. However, as Faustus reminds himself at the outset, the wages of sin is death. Will he abjure magic and repent? The question is settled in advance by Calvin: if repentance happened to work it would do so by the gift of prevenient grace, itself foreordained from the outset. But in Marlowe's play that view is countered by another, essentially Gnostic, idea. Despite the power of the Calvinist position Marlowe is, in the end, on the side of knowledge, the cause of Christ against that hidden tyrant. Finally Faustus is forsaken much as Christ was forsaken on the Cross. There are, of course, deviations from the older Gnostics, who despised the nature that Renaissance magician-scientists rejoiced in exploring; the knowledge they sought was not natural. But the recurrent Gnostic rebellion against Jehovah is there all the same.

The chapter on Marlowe is the most difficult in the book. It has to consider all sorts of issues like the Calvinist philosophy of time, and the differences between various alternative trinities, as they declared themselves in the peculiar climate of sixteenth- and seventeenth-century opinion. With Milton the issues seem simpler, perhaps because they have been debated, though not in these terms, so many times before. *Paradise Lost* announces itself as a theodicy – it means 'to justify the ways of God to men'. Nuttall believes in the authenticity, at present disputed, of the treatise *De Doctrina Christiana*, and accepts that it is roughly contemporary with the poem, though he wisely does not expect the theology to be identical in both cases. Milton was not a Calvinist; he believed in free will and so was opposed to Calvinistic ideas of predestination. But this attitude, according to Nuttall, presented some difficulties when enshrined in a narrative about the Fall. One venerable problem is that for Adam and Eve to make their fatal choice they must have been corrupt already. St Augustine thought so, and the difficulty does not go away; Auden expresses it as a paradox:

> Since Adam, being free to choose
> Chose to imagine he was free
> To choose his own necessity . . .

But Nuttall denies that one can explain sin as a simple consequence of free will. His answer, in short, is that Milton found himself unable to resist the idea that in defying the divine ban and choosing knowledge Adam and Eve were right; the advice of Satan was sound, and indeed there may be a touch of the old Gnostic identification of the Serpent with Christ, for in the end the Fall was Fortunate and made possible the Redemption.

Yet Milton could not quite ignore the implication that to reject predestination was to limit the power and majesty of God. There is a tricky moment in the Argument to Book V, where Milton writes, 'God, to render man inexcusable, sends Raphael to admonish him . . .' Of course God foreknew that Adam would eat the apple; but foreknowledge, as God explains in Book III, doesn't put it out of the power of Adam and Eve not to sin, even though in some sense they were bound to:

> If I foreknew,
> Foreknowledge had no influence on their fault,
> Which had no less proved certain unforeknown.

Nuttall's pages on this crux, and on the Fortunate Fall, topics familiar to all who have studied Milton, are full of intellectual energy and novelty. When Pharaoh might have obeyed God and let the Israelites go, God hardened his heart and caused him to refuse, so forcing him to sin and to extend the list of disasters that fell on the Egyptians. Since Milton's God rendered man inexcusable, and therefore to 'deserve new torments', Shelley was justified in calling Satan morally superior. A residual Calvinism causes tension or even confusion in Milton's narrative. There are attempts to suggest prior corruption (Eve's dream in Book IV, for instance) but in the end 'the myth designed to account for the origin of evil has had to presuppose, as occurring at an earlier point in the story, the very element whose first appearance it purports to explain'.

Fortunately the Fall turned out to be Fortunate. Moreover it created the state of affairs celebrated by the poet years before in a famous passage in *Areopagitica*, where he refuses to praise 'a fugitive and cloister'd virtue, unexercis'd and unbreath'd, that never sallies out and seeks her adversary, but slinks out of the race, where the immortal garland is to be run for, not without dust and heat'. The Milton of *Areopagitica* had little doubt that good came of the eating of the apple:

It was out of the rind of one apple tasted, that the knowledge of good and evil, as two twins cleaving together, leaped forth into the world. And perhaps this is that doom which Adam fell into of knowing good and evil; that is to say, of knowing good by evil. And therefore the state of man now is: what wisdom can there be to choose, what continence to forbear, without the knowledge of evil?

Evidently the twenty years or so that intervened between the prose work and the epic had not changed Milton's belief that the knowledge of good is inseparable from the knowledge of evil, so that in a sense the choice of Adam and Eve was between a sort of ignorant inertia and a virtuous encounter with the world, an encounter ultimately to be rewarded with 'a paradise . . . happier far'. It is at this point that we again encounter Gnosticism. Milton's alternative trinity is a complicated affair because he was an Arian, believing the Son to be subordinate to the Father, so that the task of making Christ (who by general consent gets a rather poor showing in the poem) the successful antagonist of the Father is difficult. It is not enough to say that Adam and Eve reasonably wanted to know, and that it was simply wicked of God to make knowledge a forbidden thing. Milton's God, who must be allowed some authority, says that it would have been better for them to know good only, without knowing evil, but he does not explain how this could have been done. And for Nuttall there is the further problem that Milton seems in no doubt that the Serpent Satan, though in some ways very attractive, is very wicked.

I am merely glancing at Nuttall's very bold and complex rumi-nations on *Paradise Lost*. What they tell us, to put it crudely, is that Milton could not avoid an extremely difficult encounter with the problems we have all spotted but prefer not to go into. I have not mentioned them all; for instance, there is the question how the world could be created without diminution of the divine substance and why, despite its necessary inferiority, it could still be called good. Milton mentions Gnosticism in his theological treatise, but as to the possibility that the world was created by an evil god he simply says that it is 'intolerable and incredible that evil should be stronger than good and should prove the supreme power'. He is driven by his own love of knowledge to approve in some sense the choice of Adam and

Eve, but cannot say that it was a blow struck at Jehovah, any more than he can elevate the Son over the Father. What we are seeing is a treatment of the evidence that persuaded Gnostics to take such positions, not a proof that Milton was Gnostic; indeed he was trying to work things out without the drastic abandonment of more orthodox Christianity to which that evidence might have led. His will or need to believe God good was simply too strong.

With Blake we are, despite some of the author's disclaimers, in a different world. His historical connection with certain Gnostic-like seventeenth-century sects, such as the Ranters and the Muggletonians, has been established by modern scholars, notably E. P. Thompson and A. L. Morton, and antinomian traditions of a Gnostic flavour survived into Blake's time and beyond. They treated the Old Testament God as a Demiurge, an evil creator, and claimed personal inspiration and complete liberation from the Law, not least as it bore on sexual conduct. The celebrated Abiezer Coppe, of Merton College, author of *The Fiery Flying Roll*, would have had little difficulty in understanding 'The Everlasting Gospel', and indeed Nuttall detects a similarity of styles in Coppe and Blake. He studies the relation between Blake and Milton, who did argue in the *De Doctrina* that the old Law had been abolished; Blake agreed, but deplored Milton's continuing respect for the Father. Satan is now the unacknowledged hero of the story told in *Paradise Lost*. Milton was of the Devil's party without knowing it, and the difference between them was that Blake did know it, and acknowledged the goodness of Satan. 'In the book of Job Milton's Messiah is called Satan,' says Blake. 'For this history has been adopted by both parties.'

Milton would not have approved of Blake's antinomian extremism – 'Sooner murder an infant in its cradle than nurse unacted desires' – nor, perhaps, of the proliferations of Blakian mythology, which more resembles the fantasies of the early Gnostics than Milton's more restricted Christian mythology. But although their solutions were different it can be said that in some sense of the term Milton and Blake, and even Marlowe, do suggest an 'Alternative Trinity'. Much of the pleasure offered by this agreeably argumentative and learned study derives from the author's own power of scholarly fantasy; but it remains true that he is, in the last analysis, treating a topic in which all can be, or have been, interested, namely the problem of the origin of evil and the problem of a world so little in accord with our wishes for it – so beyond our powers of understanding that we cannot help being interested in what great poets have to say about it. It seems these three all at least considered the Gnostic way out, and the modern revival of interest in Gnosticism may suggest that this is indeed an alternative that could find favour in a new age of secular antinomianism.

Bertrand Russell

This enormous book* covers the first forty-nine years of Bertrand Russell's life, from his own birth in 1872 to the birth of his son Conrad in 1921. It is not clear how many volumes are still to come; this one gives little more than half the life, and there are crowded years ahead, though it is possible they may be less interesting. Professor Monk's much-admired biography of Ludwig Wittgenstein made one feel, for a while at any rate, that the subject's weird ascetic life and his philosophy, which he himself felt sure no one would understand, could be represented as an intelligible whole. Now he turns to Russell, another baffling philosopher, but one who enjoyed or endured a far longer, more varied and more public life, and documented it with almost incomparable abundance. The archive at McMaster University contains about 60,000 letters, a high proportion of which must be love letters; and among Russell's 70 books and 2,000 articles (the bibliography of Kenneth Blackwell and Harry Ruja lists over 3,000 items) many are autobiographical in character.

Russell was, on occasion, capable of unusual generosity and courage, but it must be said that one closes this volume convinced that some of the harsher opinions of his friends were justified. There was a celebrated moment when he asked G. E. Moore point-blank if he liked him, and Moore, after protracted deliberation, replied 'No.' Clifford Allen, with whom for a time he shared a Battersea flat, found him to be 'very childlike in his engrossment with his own emotions,

* Ray Monk, *Bertrand Russell: The Spirit of Solitude* (London: Cape, 1996).

virtues, vices, and the effect he has on other people'. The actress
Colette O'Neil, wife of the actor Miles Malleson, wrote a novel *à
clef* in which a character based on T. S. Eliot called Russell 'a man
exhausting other men by his intellect; exhausting women by his
intensity; wearing out his friends, sucking them dry, passing from
person to person, never giving any real happiness – or finding any'.
It is clear from his correspondence with Colette O'Neil (until recently
under embargo) that Russell treated her badly, but that seems to
have been his way with most of his lovers, and there is plenty of
evidence in this book that her judgement, though embittered, was
not unjust.

Monk, who excels, as one might have expected, in the deft exposition of arcane speculations in mathematical logic, is equally
thorough in his treatment of the spiritual and erotic aspects of the
life of his subject. Russell was born into the Liberal aristocracy and
inherited its habits of free thought along with its assumptions of
privilege. The darker side of the inheritance was a lifelong fear of
madness (an uncle became hopelessly insane), a sense that one needed
to struggle to stay happy, and a hidden violence of temper which for
the most part he controlled well enough, though always ready to
believe himself capable of murder. He lost his parents as a young
child, was unhappy with their replacements, and suffered a little
from the administrations of an apparently rather evil tutor; but as a
child he was on the whole docile and clever – in the view of his more
boisterous elder brother, 'an unendurable little prig'. He had a strong
sense of sin, and through most or all of his life felt a need for religion,
though he found its conventional forms quite unacceptable. At sixteen he was already lamenting this lack, and in the course of his life
he often tried to supply it with religions of his own invention, designed
to be proof against his profoundly sceptical temperament.

At eleven he delightedly discovered Euclid, and so inaugurated
what he was to call 'a life of intellect tempered by flippancy', or 'a
life of flippancy tempered by intellect', whichever you choose of the
two versions Monk quotes (and there is a difference). This was an
early epiphany. Russell had a passion for epiphanies – again and

again he suggests that some important decision or discovery struck him like a bolt from the blue. Breaking off his studies to go out to buy a tin of tobacco, he 'suddenly seemed to see truth' in the ontological argument for the existence of God. 'I threw the tin in the air and exclaimed out loud "Great God in boots, the ontological argument is sound". . . So I became a Hegelian.' Finding Mrs Whitehead, with whom he was secretly in love, in extreme pain from angina, he experienced what Monk, though well aware that Russell was 'perhaps over-fond' of retrospectively organizing his past in this way, nevertheless endorses as a genuine conversion experience – one which left him convinced that 'the loneliness of the human soul is unendurable' and impenetrable save by 'the highest intensity of love that religious teachers have preached . . . A sort of mystic illumination possessed me . . .' Yet another epiphany occurred when Russell and Joseph Conrad looked 'deep down into each other's eyes'. At other times whole books presented their arguments to him in the twinkling of an eye (and it must be admitted that when he got an idea he often developed it with prodigious speed). To view one's life as punctuated in this way by uncovenanted transcendental interventions surely indicates a high degree of egotism, but then St Augustine was, on that criterion, a supreme egotist, though that isn't the first thing one wants to say about him.

Plainly there is an analogy between these epiphanic experiences and the experience of falling in love; indeed Russell was clearly conscious of it. Writing to a woman, especially to Ottoline Morrell, he would say that his last night with her had produced in him a change so great and sudden that he had never known the like before. But his attitude to women was complicated; he needed them to console his solitude and to give relief from the intensity of his professional work, but most of all to go to bed with: 'I know that my nature makes it *impossible* for me, however hard I try, to go on long giving *active* love to a person I don't see and have easy sex relations with.' His engagement to Alys Pearsall Smith created expectations of extraordinary passion, but the wedding night was not a success (both were virgins) and his fervid predictions were all falsified; the marriage soon failed, though it was legally ended only after many painful and rancorous years.

Although he had a strong preference for well-educated women (most of whom, like Alys, wanted their own careers) he generally assumed that they were of most use as assistants – researchers, secretaries, admirers of his talk – and not as intellectual equals. 'It is difficult to me to understand a mind so genuinely unaffected by argument as yours,' he tells Ottoline Morrell, who in turn remarks that he expects her 'to be entirely at his disposal, morning, noon and night, and becomes very angry if I am not. He told me that I could never accomplish anything important in life by *my* reading, while I could help him by being with him.'

Of course he did not expect many men to match his intelligence, either. His time at Cambridge put him on terms with the great men of the period, McTaggart, Moore and his collaborator Whitehead, and he early enjoyed the correspondence of such great Europeans as Cantor and Peano; and such, along with a very few more, were the people he wanted to impress with his philosophy. Not even all of these stayed the course. For the rest of the world he wrote popular philosophy, within the capacity even of women, who could not be expected to lie awake pondering the logical status of such propositions as 'The present king of France is bald.' Despite his dependence on women, he accused the whole sex of 'triviality of soul'.

In his letters he spoke copiously and freely to a great many correspondents. It is hard to read the dozens of amorous effusions here quoted without some distaste. The language of love is tediously extravagant, and often deserves the criticism Monk applies to Russell's attempts at imaginative writing: 'weak and affected'. Moreover, though he professed to hate cruelty and dishonesty, he was often disingenuous and cruel in his amorous dealings. His affair with Vivien Eliot Monk calls 'odd and strangely interminable', having discovered that it was by no means a matter of one night, as Peter Ackroyd conjectured in his life of Eliot. It was also, to say the least, opportunistic; he professed to be having it in order to help the Eliots in a time of trouble, and as it ended he told Colette O'Neil, as it were with a complacent sigh, how much he regretted having to break Mrs Eliot's heart. A young American woman, Helen Dudley, whom he met and seduced at Bryn Mawr, travelled to England at his invitation – not without difficulty, for the 1914 war was about to begin – only to find that he had no use for her, being otherwise engaged. He blamed her for the ensuing embarrassments: 'her selfishness does not make me *dislike* her, tho' it might make me hate her if I were made to suffer by it'. So he told his long-term lover Ottoline Morrell, assuring her that he would never 'go an inch beyond friendship' with this young rival. Nevertheless he did, and Helen told the patient Ottoline all about it. 'I broke her heart,' he sighs; and in a sense he did, for it seems Helen Dudley never recovered from the wretchedness he inflicted on her. He hated women to be unhappy, because it upset *him*: 'I cannot endure her misery.' In the time before Dora Black solved some problems by becoming pregnant he was energetically lying to Colette O'Neil, a strong-minded woman who was nevertheless capable of unhappiness. At lovers' perjuries they say Jove laughs, but most do not go so far towards making perjury a profession. Russell's description of the pragmatist F. C. S. Schiller as 'a bounder and a cad' makes one wonder what *his* biography would be like. Russell was fond of a quotation from Jeremiah 17: 'The heart is deceitful above all things, and desperately wicked: who can know it?'

The long affair with Ottoline Morrell was the most important, and it continued despite endless vicissitudes, all perhaps too fully chronicled here. Conducted with the tacit consent of Philip Morrell, who himself had other interests, it did not preclude rival attachments on both sides, and was the cause and subject of hundreds of letters, some celebrating a recent ecstasy, others announcing an end that was always endlessly deferred, like meaning in Derrida. Rather surprisingly in view of the longevity of the affair, Ottoline found Russell physically unattractive; it must have been the wonderful talk, and the extravagant letters, that kept her interested for so many years. With others, such as Katherine Mansfield, the spell worked only for a few moments, but it worked.

To T. S. Eliot he was Mr Apollinax, devouring the afternoon with his dry, passionate talk; but apparently the afternoon wasn't all he devoured with it. And, considering that his lovers were usually married women in permissive relationships, it isn't delightful to learn that he was ferociously and miserably jealous, trying, for instance, to insist that the Morrells should sleep in separate beds, and, during his time in prison, agonized by the thought that Colette O'Neil might have taken another lover.

Monk devotes much of his ample space to the equable description of these goings-on, and is calmly condemnatory when necessary; but of course they would be of small interest if Russell wasn't, for quite other reasons, a great man. It isn't difficult to imagine that the pleasures of logical and mathematical discovery resembled those of sex. Having received an illumination which enabled him to rewrite *The Principles of Mathematics*, a work of some 200,000 words, in less than three months ('one of the most astonishing bursts of intense creativity in the history of the subject'), he described this period as 'an intellectual honeymoon such as I have never experienced before or since'. Like other honeymoon experiences, this one faded into the light of common day – in this case when it was subjected to the damaging scrutiny of Wittgenstein.

Monk remarks on Russell's admirable ability to surrender a cherished position when convinced of his opponent's correctness. In collaboration with Whitehead he laboured long on *Principia Mathematica* – Monk speaks of 'its inexorable growth towards complete unreadability' – only to see its foundations undermined by Kurt Gödel's proof that what they had attempted couldn't be done: 'there can, in principle, be no logical theory within which all truths about numbers can be derived as theorems, all logical theories of mathematics are destined to be "incomplete"'. This conclusive dismissal of its premiss does not mean that Russell's work was without value, for it enabled other mathematical logicians to develop a theory of computing, the practical applications of which are all around us; but at the level of achievement to which he aspired this was a blow, made no more tolerable by further criticism from Wittgenstein.

Russell's relationship with this difficult man must be thought to do him credit. At their first encounter he thought Wittgenstein an odd sort of German, 'very argumentative and tiresome', even a bit of a fool: 'He thinks nothing empirical is knowable – I asked him to admit that there was not a rhinoceros in the room, but he wouldn't.' It was a waste of time talking to him. But before long he discovered that Wittgenstein, really an odd sort of Austrian, was a man devoid of 'the false politeness that interferes with the truth', a man with whom he felt 'the most perfect intellectual sympathy'. While others continued to find Wittgenstein a contentious bore, Russell was happy to become a sounding board for his ideas, and soon began to think of him as a sort of intellectual son, his chosen philosophical successor. Monk believes that he quite failed to understand that there were decisive differences between their philosophies, that 'Wittgenstein was rejecting at its very root the conception of the subject that provided Russell's motivation: the idea that philosophy receives its value from providing us with a glimpse of an eternal, immutable world beyond impulses, passions and ordinary life'. But he loved Wittgenstein's 'theoretical passion', and did not mind that he was a destroyer.

Wittgenstein had come to Cambridge as a pupil, but before long could find no one there of any use to him, not even Russell. The teacher–pupil relationship was inverted, Wittgenstein becoming the master. The moment in 1913 when Wittgenstein demolished his 'theory of judgement' was a genuine though painful turning point in Russell's life. And his delight on learning that his friend – 'glorious and wonderful, with a passionate purity I have never seen equalled' – had survived the war, and that his *Tractatus* – 'a really great book' – would at last be published, is very touching. Russell wrote popular philosophy (wanting to write 'things of human interest, like bad philosophers, only without being bad'), which is something one can't imagine Wittgenstein doing; but Russell had patience and intelligence and a respect for intellectual purity that made him admire and even love Wittgenstein (though Monk seems to doubt whether he ever fully understood him). There is a sharp contrast, which he himself might well have appreciated, between the candour of this response and the devious, hypocritical mess of his sex life.

Russell obviously had a gift for recognizing genius as well as an engaging readiness to accept criticism from people he respected. His enthusiastic admiration for D. H. Lawrence is another instance of these qualities. The initial enthusiasm waned as they planned to work together, but Russell was remarkably patient when Lawrence used the same privilege of plain speaking as Wittgenstein, though in an even more offensive tone:

You simply don't speak the truth, you simply are not sincere . . . you are simply *full* of repressed desires, which have become savage and anti-social . . . the enemy of all mankind you are, full of the lust of enmity. It is *not* the hatred of falsity which inspires you. It is the hatred of people, of flesh and blood. It is a perverted, mental blood-lust.

This letter is profoundly and deliberately offensive. Of course Russell probably knew that Lawrence, particularly in the war years, was prone to writing intemperate letters, but this must still have been a shock, for, as Monk remarks, 'it was as if Lawrence could see straight into Russell's soul and knew what would hurt it most'. Though much the younger man, Lawrence accused Russell of 'the inexperience of youth', knowing little of personal contact and conflict, 'almost juvenile'. Russell, after reading the letter, briefly contemplated suicide, but he recovered and 'was never so vulnerable again'.

Political work, and especially anti-war agitation, were partly what rescued him from this depression. As a politician he was a Liberal in the family tradition, but to particular problems like the war he applied his own mind and came up with highly unpopular solutions. He was by his formation pro-German and rather anti-Russian and did not endear himself to the bellicose public and press by suggesting that the Germans could be expected to behave reasonably if our side showed a comparable desire for peace. Though associated with pacifist causes, he was not a pacifist *pur sang*, believing that some causes had to be fought for, but the present cause was not of that sort. He did oppose conscription, though with a certain distaste for those conscientious objectors who declined any alternative service, finding them 'Sunday-Schooly' and unaware of 'the volcanic side of human nature', a side he considered that he understood very well by introspection. He deplored the Allied refusal of German peace offers, and genuinely hated the savagery of the mob and the dishonesty of the press.

These attitudes divided him from his professional colleagues and his class, as well as from the population in general, and he was being closely looked at by the government. In the end it was an editorial he wrote for *The Tribunal* that landed him in jail. He had claimed that American troops were being used to intimidate strikers, and this was judged an offence under the Defence of the Realm Act. He escaped the arduousness of imprisonment in the second division, and served his term in the first, more comfortably than the conscientious objectors, and with facilities for reading and writing. He suffered mostly from jealous speculations about the possible activities of his mistresses. And he meditated at length on his own character, as well as working on a book at the rate of 10,000 words a day.

Soon after the war he got his divorce from Alys and married the pregnant Dora, who alone among his lovers was willing to give him the child he so longed for. There this volume ends. Perhaps the most remarkable of his philosophical achievements are already recorded here, but almost half a century of celebrity and industry are still to come. This book, despite the *longueurs* of the love letters, provides an extraordinarily full and fascinating account of the earlier phase. Monk understands and admires his man, yet doesn't conceal the applicability of Jeremiah's observation that the heart is deceitful – perhaps not in all things, but in almost all that have nothing to do with the purest operations of intellect.

A. J. Ayer

A. J. Ayer, says Ben Rogers, had 'a pampered upbringing, even by Edwardian standards'.* He suffered much at prep school, then went to Eton, where he suffered less and soon got over it. The next move, to Christ Church, was painless. Oxford gave him Gilbert Ryle as his tutor and appointed him to a lectureship before he graduated. Having volunteered for National Service he was drawn, by the irresistible voice of privilege, into a Guards regiment. Thereafter his military career passed through several glamorous and comfortable stages: he was, in his own words, 'a soldier in England, a British government official in the United States, an apprentice commando in Canada, a civil servant in the Gold Coast, a staff officer in London, a political observer in North Africa, a tourist in Italy and a liaison officer in the invasion of Southern France'. A little later the ambassador, Duff Cooper, declared that he was 'extremely anxious to have him', so Ayer became 'a diplomat in Paris', where he met everybody – Bataille, Artaud, Leiris, Giacometti, Tzara and so on. He had some affairs and developed an interest in existentialism which produced good articles on Sartre and Camus. Times were hard for most Parisians, but Ayer lived in Guy de Rothschild's house in Paris, supported by a butler, a cook and a good cellar.

When this arduous post-war service was over he returned to Oxford, at a time when Oxford philosophy in his view (Ryle, perhaps, apart, and H. H. Price) needed a good shaking. Real philosophy was

* *A.J. Ayer: A Life* (New York: Grove Press, 1999).

what went on in Cambridge. Ayer read Wittgenstein when hardly anybody else in Oxford had thought of doing so. But at Ryle's suggestion he gave up the idea of sitting at Wittgenstein's feet in Cambridge and instead went to Vienna to work with Moritz Schlick – this at a time when hardly anybody in England had even heard of logical positivism. In his early twenties he published what is probably to this day the most widely read work of English philosophy, *Language, Truth and Logic* (1936), and followed it with *The Foundations of Empirical Knowledge* (1940). Late in life he doubted whether much of *Language, Truth and Logic* was right, and complained that students are required to read it primarily in order to pick holes in it; but it survives and sells by the thousand, partly, no doubt, because it is very well written. 'Sixty years on,' says Rogers, 'the book's vigour, elegance and ease are as remarkable as ever. Never has philosophy been so fast, so neat.'

In view of all these successes it may be surprising to find that Ayer habitually thought of himself as an 'outsider' and 'self-made', exaggerating the poverty of his family, looking at the world, as his wife Dee Wells puts it, with 'big desiring eyes', and, despite a career of equal brilliance as philosopher and hedonist, often a little anxious about where he stood on the borders of outside and inside.

Certainly Oxford, despite that lectureship, was reluctant to admit him to true insider academic status. Oxford philosophy was a competitive business; there were certain prizes that one had to win – the John Locke Prize, the All Souls Fellowship – but Ayer's fate was to be pipped by his contemporaries Isaiah Berlin, Goronwy Rees and the slightly younger J. L. Austin. As an undergraduate he had been taken up by Maurice Bowra and acquired a certain celebrity by having a mistress, but this was no help to his professional career. The wind that favoured Berlin and the others seemed set against him.

Despite their differing views on womanizing, Ayer and Berlin seemed at first to have a lot in common. Both were from Jewish families in the timber trade, both were torrential talkers ('always using two words where one will not do'), and both had ways of speaking that were not only rapid but might have been thought affected. Both young men were socially successful, but Ayer was more flamboyant and far more likely to put people off. They were friends but not close, for the difference between their temperaments was great; for example, Ayer was uninterested in his Jewishness, while Berlin of course wasn't.

Despite the clarity of his mind and his prose, Ayer as lecturer was not easy to follow. He was aware of this and tried hard to halt the rush of his language. This ambition he to some extent achieved; in any case, his fame was such that everybody wanted to hear him, and his way of talking came to be part of the attraction. But Christ Church, and Oxford more generally, was still unkind to him. The formidable J. L. Austin began as a disciple but later was hostile; each thought the other overrated. Rogers gives a good account of the running battle between these two; Berlin said 'they were in a state of almost continuous collision', but remembered their jousts as 'true intellectual happiness'. They fought in the ring provided by *Language, Truth and Logic*, the fame of which may in some respects have become a bit of a nuisance. Anyway, Oxford philosophy, while interested in his polemical style, did not want Ayer himself. His book became a historical document; fresh starts were being made, Austin's especially. One rather spiteful colleague later remarked on the coincidence that *ayer* is Spanish for 'yesterday'.

All this was irritating, but there was a world elsewhere, specifically in London. In 1946, at thirty-six, he went to the philosophy chair at University College London. At the time the department was far from famous, but had the advantage of needing energetic reconstruction, and the further advantage of being in London. Ayer agreed with Hume about many things, including, as Rogers points out, the view that the town, not the country, was 'the true scene for a man of letters'. At University College he transformed the department, first by appointing Stuart Hampshire, who happened to have been the co-respondent in an Ayer divorce case. Three years later he recruited Richard Wollheim from Oxford, but thereafter he appointed his own students. Since he was a fine teacher this proved a better idea than might ordinarily be thought. He had a department of varied talents and no orthodoxy except an un-Oxfordian devotion to Russell. The department, housed in Gordon Square, became famous, not least because of the Professor's furious lifestyle. London offered everything: in Gordon Square a stream of celebrated visiting speakers and perpetual high-level discussion; in nearby Charlotte Street, and in milieux much grander, the pleasures of the town, not least dancing and seduction ('great fun', as he and Philip Toynbee agreed). And of course there was Tottenham Hotspur, and Ayer was a pioneer intellectual football fan. However, in 1959 he applied for and got the Wykeham Chair of Logic and went back to Oxford, a place he professed not to like. He was nearly fifty and world-famous, but his election was quite strongly opposed.

Non-philosophers often have trouble making out why philosophers remain fascinated by questions they themselves gave up as hopeless at the age of six or seven: why what is, is; what one can know of other minds than one's own; what it is for words to mean what they do, and the like. Wordsworth was heavily censured by Coleridge for addressing a six-year-old as 'Thou best philosopher', and he may, in that passage of the Ode, have been guilty of a degree of what Coleridge called 'mental bombast', but there is still some truth in the root idea: children sometimes do ask themselves what can be thought of as unrefined philosophical questions about identity, perception, God, and so forth. When shades of the prison house begin to close upon the growing child these naive speculations are abandoned as hopeless or irrelevant. And probably most future philosophers give them up, too; but later they discover that the same questions have been put, immemorially, by persons of admirable intellect, who have also provided languages in which to talk about them. To use or improve or dispute the utility of such languages becomes a job, not quite like any other, but a job all the same, a profession.

For philosophers like Ayer the profession of philosophy is set apart from the rest of life. He was a passionate thinker and debater, but he was equally passionate about pleasure and non-philosophical company. He knew pretty well everybody of importance, and took an interest in literature; he was a friend of e. e. cummings as well as the English poets of the period. He was flattered by Einstein, and fancied that Wittgenstein fancied him. He was certainly vain, yet in some ways strangely modest. He did good work for good causes, mostly left wing and humanitarian. He challenged an Eton statute that enabled discrimination against the admission of Jewish boys, and won.

These benevolent activities belonged, like the pursuit of pleasure, to the hours of the day when he was not doing his job. But mostly, whether at work or at play, he needed to win – whether with women or at chess, or bridge, or Scrabble, or any kind of conversational contest, including philosophical argument. Here, despite their obvious discontinuity, was a connection between the activity of thought and the life of the senses. His philosophical ancestor Hume, in a famous passage, said, 'I dine, I play a game of backgammon, I converse, and am merry with my friends; and when, after three or four hours' amusement, I would return to these speculations, they appear so cold, and strained, and ridiculous, that I cannot find it in my heart to enter into them any further.' But Ayer clearly did not return to find his speculations cold; he wanted ardently to win the truth, and was as hot in the enjoyable pursuit of it as he was in that of girls.

Philosophical minds that are determined to resist transcendental explanations may find themselves obliged to pursue the study of truth by means of logic and inquiry into the language in which statements are made about the world. Most philosophers have humanistic educations and often envy the achievements of scientists, who can make their statements with confidence in their empirical observations. This envy may make philosophers even more impatient with the history of their own subject. Hence the desire, noted by Stuart Hampshire when Ayer recruited him to logical positivism, to 'start philosophy all over again'.

Nothing must be allowed to pass that crosses the line into metaphysics. 'We shall maintain that no statement which refers to a "reality" transcending the limits of all possible sense-experience can possibly have any literal significance; from which it must follow that the labours of those who have striven to describe such a reality have all been devoted to the production of nonsense.' This was the manifesto. The criterion for judging whether apparent statements of fact were or were not nonsense was the 'criterion of verifiability'. Any sentence that fails by this criterion communicates nothing at all, is strictly nonsense. Some positivists concede that nonsense of this sort can nevertheless be important; but Ayer will not have this. God is strictly nonsense, and philosophy has nothing to do with enquiries like 'How should I live?' That is 'ultimately up to us'. But it is still an inescapable responsibility. Rogers detects an inconsistency here. 'We can have knowledge of empirical truths and of the truisms of maths and logic, but not of values' – yet to require individual responsibility is, in the teeth of that argument, to take the position of a philosophical moralist.

Rogers thinks of *Language, Truth and Logic* as a statement of philosophic rebellion analogous to the new poetry of Auden and his friends; it should be seen as a rejection of authority in both knowledge and morals, an attack on the imperialist pretensions of the great philosophers of the past. The attack on ethics and theology and in general the condemnation of all philosophy that goes beyond the evidence of the senses dealt such a blow to the almost canonical *Principia Ethica* of G. E. Moore that 'it never recovered its prestige'. But in this respect Moore still belonged to a very distinguished company.

The doctrine as a whole is of course far more complex and qualified than this suggests; the present point is that the manner is aggressive and competitive, and involves an assault on God, on morality as usually understood, and on many other unverifiables. Although *The Foundations of Empirical Knowledge*, finished while Ayer was doing basic training at Caterham, was well received and thought by experts to be the better book, no future work of Ayer's achieved the fame of his first. Rogers gives an account of them all, as well as of 'a large collection of beautiful and accomplished girlfriends' and wives which testifies overwhelmingly to Ayer's belief that not everybody is monogamous by nature.

Perhaps curiously, perhaps not, several witnesses remark that Ayer was not very interested in other people. 'He was observant about people and a good judge of intelligence,' says Lady Ayer (Dee Wells). 'He did not try to understand them . . . If someone died he would not miss them . . . If a cleaner or a secretary or someone left, he never mentioned them again. It was out of sight, out of mind . . . he did not know what the rest of us were talking about when we spoke of feelings . . .' No wonder he had such difficulty with the problem of other minds.

This is a very good biography in the tradition of Ray Monk's *Wittgenstein* and his *Russell*. Like Russell, Ayer did an enormous amount of living, and Rogers understands its pleasures, its anxieties, its energies and its final exhaustion. Ayer travelled, lectured, broadcast, conversed, it seemed indefatigably; but he could not for ever escape age and illness. His volumes of autobiography were not much admired. Oxford was ungenerous to the end, obliging him to accept a reduced pension.

The insecurity that showed up occasionally through his life did not diminish with age. Anthony Grayling, his last graduate student, provides a touching record of his anxiety at the time of his retirement: ' "One day someone is going to point the finger at me: You are a fraud. You got into Eton and to Christ Church, you were an officer in the Welsh Guards, you became Wykeham Professor at Oxford and you secured a knighthood. But underneath you are just a dirty little Jew-boy". . . . He worried that other philosophers did not think he was as good as he was famous.' In a valedictory talk his limited claim for the achievements of twentieth-century philosophy was this: 'The answers are not much clearer, but the questions are.'

'Other philosophers' did indeed point the finger at 'The Man who Hated Wisdom' (the headline of Roger Scruton's obituary in the *Sunday Telegraph*). But Ayer's friend and pupil Ted Honderich, now himself the professor at University College, was more charitable and also nearer the mark when he spoke of Ayer as a philosopher 'whose audacity was being true to the truth'.

Moral Literacy

Once there were popular books with titles like *Straight and Crooked Thinking*, books in which professional philosophers, avoiding arcane speculation, tried to make the rest of us more sensible by sharing with us their philosophical wisdom. Nowadays such books seem to be less common, and in any case some quite important philosophers, doubting the claims of philosophy to have special wisdom qualifications, would think it presumptuous to write them. Colin McGinn does concede that specialist skills in philosophy don't in themselves constitute a licence to preach or judge ('Morality isn't the kind of thing in which you can have a special expertise') but he seems confident all the same that a professional habit of straight thinking will enable him to advise lay folk whose moral thinking might be crooked, or, as he would prefer to say, stupid.*

He assumes that every sensible person would rather be thought to be doing the right rather than the wrong thing (not, perhaps, an infallible assumption) and that every such person can be expected to agree about disliking 'badness in people' and deploring moral stupidity. As George Eliot observed in a famous passage of *Middlemarch*, 'we are all born in moral stupidity'; Dorothea Brooke discovered that emerging from this state can be painful, if only because the likes of Casaubon have 'an equivalent centre of self' that cannot be ignored. As George Eliot knew, and as McGinn remarks, 'you have to work to get it right'.

* *Moral Literacy: or How to Do the Right Thing* (London: Duckworth, 1992).

Persons of comparably liberal tendencies will have little difficulty with most of what McGinn says. He dismisses 'taboo morality' as irrelevant, accepting only such constraints on individual freedom as can be provided with convincing reasons. Rational morality is his theme. He will have nothing to do with moral relativism, which is self-refuting. So is the notion that religion is the basis of moral behaviour – 'even God could not make murder right by judging it to be so'. He himself is an atheist; more than once he talks about the soul, but, if the matter isn't to become very complicated, he must suppose it to die with the body and certainly not to proceed to judgement, purgation, bliss or the fire.

Morality, then, 'is a set of rules for harmonizing what you want to do with what is good for others'. The application of these rules calls for some imaginative activity. McGinn provides some; he likes to illuminate problems by making up fictions. A chapter about animals contains a fantasy about a species of vampire bat that can live equally well on orange juice or human blood. Though law-abiding in most other respects, they traditionally prefer the blood, and farm humans to ensure the supply. They are said to be guilty of 'speciesism': *de nobis fabula*. They, and we, are also guilty of neglecting something that assumes great importance in this book, namely sentience. In considering our responsibility to other beings we need to ask how much they feel. Stones, even trees, have little or no sentience. Animals have; we know this but are able to ignore the knowledge when eating battery chickens and testing drugs on animals, just as our ancestors could switch off knowledge to which they undoubtedly had access when condoning slavery and child labour. Sure, the slave and the child mineworker and the whale suffer and exist, but we can act as if their pain is of no account, as if their existence is 'not an existence for us'.

Much of what is said here about animals, sex, violence, and so on will, as the author expects, seem uncontroversial, even if some of the consequences, for example vegetarianism, may remain unappealing. Since McGinn invites objections, I will offer a couple, doubtless cannon fodder for the professional philosopher. One concerns some of the exemplary (counterfactual) fictions. Thus: if it were the case that women were infallibly to induce conception by pulling their earlobes on a certain day of the month, and they chose not to pull their ears, so allowing the ova to die, could even pro-lifers hold them guilty of abortion? As things are, a rational morality will distinguish between legitimate abortion and infanticide by considering the degree of sentience in the living organism to be killed. Very early termination is what the use of condoms can ensure; very late abortion is infanticide. Sentience comes on by degrees. A rational argument, no doubt; but is it strengthened by the counterfactual fantasies?

If you, the ruler of a prosperous and peaceful country, believed devoutly in freedom of speech for all, how would you respond to the Devil if he visited you and demanded slots on prime-time television to persuade the people that they had a duty to be evil? The point of this one is that there have to be limits on free speech. But it hardly helps to make a point that arises in more credible forms in the ordinary course of things: rightly or wrongly, a ruler will sometimes have to inhibit what he or she regards as dangerous or immoral. The real difficulty is simply that some rulers hold views of which one may not approve and want to ban books or behaviour others think they should have no power over. A confrontation with the Pope would have been more to the point.

McGinn tells us that in morality there are no absolutes. To each case one applies reason. True, but he manages to make the application of rational morality a bit unreal. If somebody uses violence towards you, you are, he says, entitled to reply violently; but reason counsels that your violence must not be greater than the violence you have suffered; indeed it ought if possible to be less, and always exercised 'with a heavy heart'. But one would have thought that a rational moralist would need to allow for the fact that if somebody hits you on the nose you are less likely to have a heavy heart than to be shocked and angry, and almost certainly unable to measure your response so judiciously. Like Aristotle, McGinn thinks it possible to distinguish just from unjust anger. But rational morality should nevertheless allow for the fact that quite a lot of rationally unsound human behaviour results from people being shocked or angry, perhaps only momentarily unjust or intemperate.

The chapter on sex says what most of us would say – don't hurt people when pursuing your own satisfactions; always treat your sexual partner as a distinct, highly sentient person. Extreme promiscuity is simply irrational. The difficulty is that saying this, or explaining that what they are really interested in isn't sex but something else altogether, something they pitiably lack, will not deter extremely promiscuous persons, who often think their conduct 'natural' and therefore reasonable.

It is a difficulty also that few of the things one does can be thought to have no consequences for other persons; it is not true, for instance, that you can use crack or even pot or tobacco and absolutely confine the risks of doing so to yourself. Your behaviour may have consequences for other sentient beings. Moreover this problem of limit evokes different responses in different epochs. The controlled permissiveness of the McGinn moral scheme would have seemed immoral to most serious persons even a couple of generations ago. This is partly because they felt, perhaps presumptuously, that they had a duty to prevent others from destroying their lives or their souls – every man's death diminishes me – whereas nowadays one is rather inclined to think of self-destruction, of soul or body, as one's own affair if it can be achieved without harm to others, if it ever can. The ancestral reasons for interference, often associated with 'taboo morality', may no longer have general appeal; but our reasons for believing they don't may not hold either. Whether the problem is that reason is not strong enough to do the work, or that as applied here it is not reasonable enough, I do not know.

There are judicious, rational discriminations, for example on the freedom of the press and pornography. And there are some propositions not less likely to be true for being ancient, though always in need of qualification; for instance, that vicious people tend to be ugly, like Dorian Gray or Caliban, and virtuous people beautiful. But the differences between ancient and modern are more pronounced. In the old world the Cardinal Virtues were Justice,

Prudence, Temperance and Fortitude. Together with the three Theological Virtues – Faith, Hope and Charity – they formed the opposition to the Seven Deadly Sins. McGinn sets out his Cardinal Virtues as Kindness, Honesty, Justice and Independence (roughly speaking the avoidance of moral stupidity). Naturally McGinn includes no Theological Virtues. To balance the contest he has only four Deadly Sins – Prejudice, Ignorance, Narrowmindedness and Fear – which replace the old list of Pride, Covetousness, Lust, Envy, Gluttony, Anger and Sloth. It is not presupposed that these vices do not continue to exist, but as formerly stated they lack interest, and are presumably ruled out of contention by the consideration that the just, honest, kind and independent spirit will rationally and easily eschew them.

An admirable though arguable clause in McGinn's credo is that virtue, contrary to unexamined assumptions about it, is bold and attractive, nothing do with being dull grey, suburban. And it is so very unusual that the unvirtuous, the dark-souled, look shabby and commonplace by contrast with the beautiful virtuous 'maverick'. It is an idea that would have pleased, say, Milton. Why is it pleasant to see modern virtue cut from ancient cloth?

Moral Literacy is written with a certain colloquial dash; its sprightly prose and delight in fictive situations make it less surprising that McGinn should have simultaneously produced a novel. *The Space Trap** is indeed full of colloquial beans. It is also ambitious, literate and rationally moral. Its central character is a grey, flabby suburban insurance clerk with a taste for sci-fi fantasy. He chucks up everything, including wife and son, and swaggers the nut-strewn streets of New York on an extended and illicit vacation. He makes himself a new comely body (virtuous?) by frequenting the gym, jogging, and sleeping with a terrifically fit and honest Italian girl.

The metaphysician author is impressively streetwise New Yorkwise, with an easy command of the patois, mostly obscene, of Spanish Harlem and the Village. The New York of this novel is a lot more

* London: Duckworth, 1992.

gemütlich than Martin Amis's, and lacks that apocalyptic splendour, but it has some high-grade porn, harmless under the scrutiny of modern rational morality, though it might have run into trouble even thirty years back – no problem now if you keep it away from the children. The girl is fetching, especially after dropping LSD (same proviso), being free of Narrowmindedness, Prejudice, Ignorance and Fear. She shares the author's predilection for total honesty, a trait which gives the hero, Colin, some awkward moments, including a mildly embarrassing visit to a 'dick doctor'.

This ex-wimp Colin is encumbered with two other selves. One is said to be his 'phobic consciousness', and it regularly gives him a counterfactual bad time imagining the horrors underlying his currently pleasant course of life. They are of the order of imagining oneself to be a baby biting off the nipple of a haemophiliac mother; when her blood has drained away she dies, and so does baby, deprived of milk. This is a relatively mild example of the interspersed phobic fantasies, which are written with some intensity. The other self is a shadow brother, a New Yorker who flees to California to avoid Colin, and ends badly when Colin goes home. I had the feeling that, important as he was meant to be to the design of the piece, it would, like the world more generally, have been better off without him. A pleasing and, once you know what the expression means by reading *Moral Literacy*, a morally literate novel.

The Bible as It Was

The interpretation of scripture, as practised by learned rabbis from the first century of the present era, is called midrash. Midrash concerned with the Law is called Midrash Halacha; the other kind, which deals with non-legal parts of the Bible, is called Midrash Haggadah. The terms are properly used only of rabbinical interpretation after the destruction of the Temple in 70 CE, and the earliest extant examples date from the second century; but the Haggadic way of interpreting had roots in the past; some scholars refer to these earlier interpretative practices as 'proto-midrash'. Both midrash and proto-midrash were imaginative ways of updating, enhancing, augmenting, explaining and justifying the sacred text. What the passage of time had made unintelligible or offensive could be rewritten in conformity with later ethical standards and notions of plausibility. In one form or another midrash did much to shape the Bible, including the New Testament, as we have it.

Some years ago I was bold enough to take part in a discussion of midrash at the Hebrew University in Jerusalem. I wanted to understand how this fascinating and complex mode of biblical commentary might be related, in its methods and assumptions, to other types of exegesis and interpretation – whether it was possible to speak of some general conditions applying to them all. Was there, for example, anything in common between midrash and Hellenistic commentary, and, more important, was there any sort of resemblance between rabbinical and modern ingenuities, such as William Empson's analyses of ambiguities and complex words? But I was told right away, kindly but firmly, that midrash – and the concept can be extended to include Jewish interpretive methods that anticipated midrash as it was practised after 70 CE, or were in spirit like midrash without exactly answering the stricter definitions – was literally incomparable. It is like nothing else whatsoever. Its combination of imaginative freedom and pious restraint, its variety, even its humour, are unique. Midrash is 'an overwhelmingly broad field of inquiry, for at heart midrash is nothing less than the foundation stone of rabbinical Judaism, and it is as diverse as Jewish creativity itself'.*

James Kugel has dedicated his new book† to a study of the transformation of the Hebrew Bible by midrashic interventions, concentrating on the state of the Bible at a particular period, 'roughly speaking, from about 200 BCE through the first century or so CE'. He draws his evidence from many sources: the Septuagint (the third-century Greek version of the Hebrew Bible, which differs in many respects from the original and includes interpretations and additions); the Dead Sea Scrolls; some apocryphal works like Jubilees; the New Testament; the Jewish historian Josephus; and the Targums, or Aramaic versions of Scripture.

One gets a clear idea of his method from the earlier study I have just quoted. Kugel there offered a peculiarly neat instance of the midrashist at work. Psalm 145, a psalm in praise of the Lord, his glory, his kingdom and his mercy, is alphabetical – each line or group of lines begins with a new letter of the Hebrew alphabet; but the sequence is broken by the omission of the letter N. The reasonable explanation that a verse or group of verses simply got lost in transmission was not of the kind that the rabbis were likely to consider. Instead it was argued that the letter N was excluded from the psalm because it is the first letter of a very dark verse of the prophet Amos, which prophesies the fall of Israel, here represented as the Virgin

---

* James L. Kugel, 'Two Introductions to Midrash', in Geoffrey H. Hartman and Sanford Budick, eds., *Midrash and Literature* (New Haven: Yale University Press, 1986), pp. 77–103, p. 92.
† James L. Kugel, *The Bible as It Was* (Cambridge, Mass.: Cambridge University Press, 1997).

('The virgin of Israel is fallen; she shall no more rise . . . there is none to raise her up', Amos 5:2). David, it seems, had advance knowledge of this prophecy, and felt that it had no place in the context of his psalm; so he omitted the letter N, and in the next verse as it were cancelled Amos in advance by declaring that the Lord will lift up all that fall.

Kugel calls this 'wonderful midrash', not least because it presupposes the unity and timelessness of all Scripture, so allowing the verse to be read as applying directly to any present state of Judaism, a main object of midrash being this perpetual *aggiornamento* of the Scripture. He then describes another rabbinical way of dealing with Amos's pessimistic verse, namely resourceful punctuation. The texts under examination were not punctuated at all, so the prophecy of Amos, usually as 'She has fallen and will no more rise, the virgin of Israel', could be read as saying 'She has fallen and will no more; rise, O virgin of Israel.' This solution presented an apparent grammatical difficulty, in that the word meaning 'rise' could not properly be read as a Hebrew imperative, but the problem was got over by repronouncing the same words in such a way as to get them to say 'exactly the opposite of what Amos intended'. What Amos did intend is evident enough from the context, since he goes on to elaborate his lament; but this kind of interpretation is not about context, however plain and ostentatious; it is about something hidden between the lines or behind the words, something cryptic that must be there and has to be researched.

For here, as everywhere, the rabbis got at the truth by 'searching', which is the root sense of the word 'midrash'. There is a kind of humour in their procedures, as well as a desperate hope. 'Divine words have an existence independent of circumstance and immediate intention' and must be applicable to whatever the situation of Israel may be, rather than to the historical circumstances under which they were originally written.

Since the revised reading of Amos has a joke-like structure, Kugel is reminded of the old Latin teacher's trick sentence: '*Mea mater sus est mala*' may seem to mean 'My mother is a bad sow', but the right interpretation has to be 'Go, Mother, the pig is eating the apples.' At the heart of Benjamin Britten's opera *The Turn of the Screw* Miles offers a more tortured instance of the schoolroom Latin joke: '*Malo malo malo malo*', 'I would rather be/ Up an apple tree/ Than a naughty boy/ In adversity.' Of course the meaning of *malo* upmost in the mind is 'evil', as in the Lord's Prayer: '*libera nos a malo*', deliver us from evil'. But we can't avoid catching in this fundamentally trivial line the other associated senses of *malo*: 'I prefer' (the choosing of evil) and the apple tree which provided the fatally chosen fruit.

The point is that, as Kugel remarks, 'there is often something a bit joking about midrash', and the joking is founded on

the dissonance between the religion of the Rabbis and the Book from which it is supposed to be derived – and . . . more precisely the dissonance between that book's supposedly unitary and harmonious message and its actually fragmentary and inconsistent components. Midrash . . . is thus bound to be at the same time somewhat ironic and yet terribly in earnest. *Qum betulat yisra'el* [Rise, Virgin of Israel] is indeed amusing, the gallows humor of the prisoner of the Text; and it is the heartfelt hope of a people.

It might seem that only their precarious historical situation, their need for saving interpretations, however desperate, distinguishes the rabbis' manipulation of Hebrew from the manipulation of Latin in Britten's libretto, or from the ingenuities required by Empson's ambiguity types. But this is just the sort of inference that my mentors in Jerusalem declared irrelevant. I think I can infer from this new book that James Kugel, their equal in learning, might be more permissive. However, his concern is less with modern interpretative practices than with the progressive transformation of the Bible, by supplementary comment and revision, into what it became in the last centuries before, and the first century after, the change of eras.

The process, as I have suggested, had begun long before the text had reached its final form. Already in the post-Exilic period (late sixth and early fifth century BCE) the Scriptures had been revised and augmented. Interpretation involved not only the explanation of difficult words or apparently unacceptable senses, and the resolution of apparent contradictions, but also the addition of what might appear to have been suggested though for some reason omitted from the Bible as it had come down. These elaborations and explanations intruded, over the years, into the text of the Bible; some that did not do so survived in later writings that were not admitted into the canon but still influenced the interpretation of Scripture and continue even now to affect our notions of what the Bible is about. In other words, the sense of the Bible was continually changed by its expert readers. Since it was regarded as a whole, its interpretation might involve the bringing together of verses remote from one another in the text and in time (as in the collocation of Amos and the psalm). The assumption that the Bible was timeless, a seamless garment, persisted far into the Christian era, as one sees from George Herbert's poem 'The Holy Scriptures':

> This verse marks that, and both do make a motion
> Unto a third, that ten leaves off doth lie . . .

Certainly this idea was commonplace in the period Kugel is concerned with, approximately the centuries immediately before and after the change of eras. It has complex and sometimes apparently contradictory implications; for example, it was made consistent with the idea that earlier incidents could be prefigurative of later, a theory well known to the rabbis but intensively developed by the Christians in the same period and later, for example in the development of the Passion narratives from Old Testament types and prophecies. In the period Kugel is talking about there were natural affinities between Jewish and Christian hermeneutic assumptions.

'[I]t was this *interpreted* Bible – not just the stories, prophecies, and laws themselves, but these texts as they had, by now, been interpreted and explained for centuries – that came to stand at the very center of Judaism and Christianity.' Kugel's aim is to show what the interpreted Bible was at this critical period. As we have seen, the interpretative habits that shaped it had been formed long before, after the return in the sixth century from the Babylonian exile, but they were by now much developed. Both rabbinical and Christian interpretative lore, here reconstructed mostly from apocryphal writings (including the Dead Sea Scrolls), had achieved levels of extraordinary subtlety and freedom.

Much has been written by others, for instance Geza Vermes, in *Jesus the Jew* (1973) and *Jesus and the World of Judaism* (1983), about the initial family likeness of Christian and Judaic interpretation. The paths were later to diverge, but Kugel holds that in both traditions the interpretation of Scripture called for continuous rewriting, a view consistent with some modern Christian scholarship, such as that of Brevard Childs, author of *Introduction to the Old Testament as Scripture* (1979); Kugel agrees that to see the Bible in this light is more important than to try to get back to what it originally was or may have been before all the redactions and interpretations began. He has concentrated on a relatively brief period because it is reasonably accessible and because by that time the events of the Pentateuch called for more explanation than they might have done earlier. The world was different; old enemies – Assyria, Chaldea, Babylon, Syria – no longer threatened, and Palestine, like most of the world, was under Roman rule. Social and political institutions, and the language itself, had changed. In 70 CE Jerusalem and the Temple were destroyed, and Judaism was more than ever the religion of a book, its text more than ever passionately studied.

Scope for interpretation was increased by the character of the Hebrew language. Not only were the texts (as we saw in the example from the Psalms) lacking in word division and punctuation; they were originally also without vowels. The Hebrew system of triconsonantal roots means that differences of meaning are established by the choice of vowels to go with the three consonants. Consequently a word-stem might be the basis of a noun or a verb, passive or active; according to the vowels supplied, it could signify several different words, which opens playful possibilities for ambiguity or even of punning. Thus the Bible became a 'cryptic document', full of esoteric messages calling for professional decipherers. If necessary, the sage could explain that a word actually concealed or stood for its opposite, so that when Dinah's brothers speak deceitfully or 'with guile' to the men of Shechem (Genesis 34:13) the offensive word really means 'wisely'. 'This assertion reflects the belief not only that Scripture speaks or can speak, cryptically, but that Scripture's very nature is such that it would scarcely seek to present Jacob's sons as a bunch of liars. Something else *must* have been meant . . .' In the extreme form of interpretation practised at Qumran the old texts were applied with minute and fanatical particularity to the situation of the sect. Prophecies concerning earlier enemies of Israel were applied to the Romans, and allusions to the Last Days were found in the Scriptures in support of the view that those days were imminent, and that the Qumran community were the elect who alone would be saved. These sectaries were extremists, but their method was not essentially different from that of more orthodox contemporary sages.

The sages had taken over the job of the prophets; the word of God no longer came from divinely chosen messengers but from the repository of wisdom represented by Torah, which it was now the sage's job to explore. He was to do this work on the assumption that the Bible was never wrong, never wasted a detail or a repetition, was completely self-consistent, inerrantly prophetic. Of course this meant, whether or not he recognized the fact, that it accorded with the interpreter's own assumptions, religious, ethical or political. Such an interpreter would maintain that the prophet Obadiah, though he ostensibly speaks of the destruction of Edom, is actually foretelling the fall of Rome, which Edom prefigures. For Christians working in the same tradition the Crucifixion is prefigured in the sacrifice of Isaac. This matter of prefiguration, as I have already suggested, is especially important in the Christian tradition; Christianity, by extending what was originally a Jewish interpretative stratagem, eventually made the Torah over into what was quite a different book, since its prime significance was in its array of prefigurations of Christian history and belief.

Kugel calls such interpretations as these, in either religion, 'ideologically motivated' – but with the reservation that interpreters, though never absolutely free of conscious or unconscious presumptions, remained capable of a disinterested desire to establish the full sense of the biblical text and to account for all its apparent peculiarities. Modern fundamentalist readers of Scripture make much the same assumptions as the interpreters of Obadiah or even of the sectaries at Qumran, and since their books are often huge best-sellers it is reasonable to believe that there is a tradition of hermeneutic naivety still potent in the world, and not unconnected with strong ideological prejudices.

Even more sophisticated readers continue to assume that texts, especially poetic texts, are cryptic and require explanations that were probably not available even to their writers. It can be argued that an important point about *The Tempest* is that Shakespeare was dodging the strong colonialist implications of his story, and that Wordsworth's 'Tintern Abbey' should be read not as what it purports to be but as a cover-up for something more important that Wordsworth had reason to feel embarrassed about, namely the French Revolution, which the poem, with culpable craft, fails to mention. I take it that if we dismiss from consideration the sectaries who suppose they can explain Shakespeare in terms of ciphers or Masonic rituals, we still have to allow that in another and more respectable branch of interpretative tradition, strongly affected by Freud, it is still thought proper to seek occult or 'symptomatic' senses. The ingenuity with which this can be done remains one measure of critical achievement, especially among those who resist the reduction of highly wrought works of art to a degree-zero level of discourse, in the manner of some New Historicists, for whom a play by Shakespeare is entitled to the same kind of attention as a contemporary sermon or pamphlet. I mean that we continue to practise something like rabbinical ingenuity in the quest for the cryptic. It might be added that deconstruction, with its endless slither of signifiers, and its assumption that texts invariably somehow belie themselves, augments rather than limits the cryptic possibilities.

One difference between the modern and the ancient is that in the earliest instances the interpreter felt free to supplement or even replace the text on which he had fixed his attention, for instance writing conversations between Cain and Abel, who quarrel about the one woman available as a wife, which happens in a rabbinical commentary on Genesis; there was evidently a feeling that the original text, though sacred, was sometimes uncomfortably terse or reticent, or that there was something wrong with it that an alteration or augmentation could put right.

The establishment of a canon, and the development of the idea that every letter and every diacritical mark was sacred, meant that the interpreter had thenceforth to reconcile himself to commentary. This might explain away some difficulty, either by a manoeuvre of the sort performed on Amos 5:2 – by repunctuation or exploitation of the semantic structure of Hebrew words – or (possibly later on) by means of typology – treating an older text as prefiguring a later text or outcome – or allegory, means well known to the Christian evangelists and Paul, and, with due respect to the experts, not wholly dissimilar from the mode of Hellenistic allegory as applied to Homer. (Philo Judaeus, the great scriptural allegorist, was Alexandrian, wrote in Greek, and was familiar with pagan modes of allegory.)

Kugel has decided, in this book, to concentrate not on large blocks of text but on what he calls 'exegetical motifs' as the basis of expansions or alterations in the Bible as handed down. A small instance of the exegetical motif: Exodus says that the Lord overthrew the Egyptians in the midst of the Red Sea so that none remained (14:27); yet Israel then saw the Egyptians 'dead upon the sea shore'. The rather easy interpretation of this conflict of evidence was that the bodies sank and were then washed up on the beach; and thus was created what Kugel calls the exegetical motif 'Ups and Downs of the Egyptians', which recurs in other contexts.

The bulk of his book consists of twenty-five studies of such motifs, and of the changes their acceptance wrought in the understanding of the original text. By these means he hopes to explain what the Bible was in the period he is examining – a time when the ancient texts were on the point of becoming *the* Bible. Another of his objects is to show how, despite all the age-old polemics, 'rabbinical Judaism and Christianity emerged out of a common mentality'.

He begins at the beginning, with the Creation of the World, and carries on till the death of Moses, making his points clear by starting each entry with a plain account of the passage under inspection (say, the Adam and Eve story in Genesis 2:4–3:24) and ending it with another summary indicating the modifications of understanding introduced by commentary. For example, what might be called the plain facts of the story of Adam and Eve are that they were told they could eat the fruit of any tree but one, that a serpent tempted Eve to eat of it nevertheless, that she gave some to Adam, and that they were accordingly expelled from the garden, Adam being obliged to earn his bread in the sweat of his brow, while Eve was condemned to painful childbirth. Sample commentaries from various apocrypha and from Philo, Josephus and other sources add much to the story: the real punishment was loss of immortality (Adam and Eve, and indeed all created kinds, were to be made, as Milton richly expressed it, 'unimmortal'). This doom was passed on to the descendants of the original couple, probably because they inherited sinfulness. The Serpent became (and remained) Satan. Eve bore much of the blame for this outcome. The garden (a paradise) continued to exist, either on earth or transported to heaven, and entry to it would be the reward of the righteous.

One sees at once that the biblical tradition rests far more on this than on the plain version, and that 1,600 or so years later the learned Milton developed it in what might be thought, though probably not by the Jerusalem experts, a poem that is in effect an enormous midrash.* Kugel's point is that the elaborated version was basically the work of the commentators. They argued over the concept of what would later be called Original Sin and invented the idea that the transgression in the garden amounted to the Fall of Man. That Satan 'took the serpent as a garment' and that through his envy death entered the world was now established, though the plain text does not say so. The fault of Eve ('from a woman was sin's beginning, and

---

* Golda Werman, *Milton and Midrash* (Washington, DC: Catholic University of America Press, 1995), has argued that Milton was familiar with midrash, perhaps mostly from a 1644 Latin translation of the eighth-century UPiekei de-Rabbi Eliezer. '[H]is epic is much like a midrash . . .' (p. 1).

because of her we all die') may have been simply that she *was* a woman, as Philo supposed; without the stress of desire Adam would have given no offence (a persistent idea, echoed later by St Ambrose, and later still by Andrew Marvell, writing about 'that happy garden state/ While man there walked without a mate').

So serious doctrines grow out of exegetical finesse. Why does Adam, adding new words to those of God, tell Eve that God had prohibited not only eating of the tree but even touching it (Genesis 3:3)? She repeats these words to Satan. The moralizing Philo explains that the addition was necessary; since the senses operate by means of contact, the ban on touching would have kept Eve away from the fruit. More subtly, it was pointed out that Satan exploited the extra prohibition in order to show Eve he could touch the tree without dying, and in the course of doing so contrived to dislodge some fruit for use in the succeeding demonstration that he could also eat of the tree without fatal consequence. And so on.

To mention one or two more of Kugel's examples: Melchizedek is a mysterious figure in Genesis (14:17–20). After saving Lot from his captors, Abraham goes home and meets Melchizedek, king of Salem, 'a priest of God most High'. Melchizedek blesses Abraham, who gives him bread and wine and a tithe of his possessions. That is all we are told about Melchizedek until he is mentioned in Psalm 110 as the founder of a priestly line. Yet no interpreter could accept that the episode was as inconsequential as it looked. There were problems: how could Melchizedek be a priest before a priesthood had been established (incidentally on an hereditary basis that connected it with Abraham, not with this 'priest of God most High')?

Josephus, writing in the first century CE, says that not only Abraham but the whole army he had taken to liberate Lot were given food and wine, a kingly gesture. The name 'Melchizedek' could mean something like 'king of righteousness' – perhaps that is what he was. Perhaps 'king of Salem' meant he was king of Jerusalem, first of that line also. Josephus has him rename the city, build the temple, and serve there as priest. A Dead Sea Scrolls interpretation of the Psalm, which treats Melchizedek not as the subject of a transient allusion but as the figure set at God's right hand, makes him a heavenly figure charged with the punishment of the guilty, and possibly none other than the archangel Michael himself. Probably the most impressive and lasting interpretation is in the Christian Epistle to the Hebrews, where Jesus, sitting at the right hand of God, is a priest 'after the order of Melchizedek'. On this view it was not a problem that Melchizedek was not of the priestly line; neither was Jesus. So Melchizedek foreshadowed Christ, and his bread and wine the Eucharist. The Epistle to the Hebrews describes Melchizedek as 'without father, without mother, without descent, having neither beginning of days, nor end of life; but made like unto the Son of God; abideth a priest continually' (7:3).

Thus the vague figure of Abraham's host becomes not only the first king of Jerusalem but a perfect type of Christ. It would be hard to find a better example of the imaginative rewriting and transformation of a Torah text. Kugel, of course, produces many others, like the justification of Lot's daughters for their necessary and virtuous acts of incest; the demonstration of Jacob's probity in his dealings with Esau and Laban; the wisdom of Jacob's sons in taking revenge for the rape of Dinah; the conduct of Moses at many puzzling moments, and of the Israelites in making off with Egyptian property.

The passage of time created some ethical difficulties about the interpretation of some parts of the Law – for example with the Sabbath prohibition, the injunction 'an eye for an eye', and the apparently conflicting rules about divorce. These were not dry-as-dust scholarly inquiries, for they bore intimately upon the life and conduct of the entire nation. And the exposition of narrative and the exposition of Law were subjected to the same hermeneutic procedures.

'Ancient biblical interpretation', Kugel concludes, 'survives between the lines, as it were, of books like Jubilees, the Wisdom of Solomon, the Testaments of the Twelve Patriarchs, and other writings of the period', meaning roughly 200 BCE to 100 CE. Some interpretations did not catch on and were forgotten, but others survived, were assimilated, and without achieving incorporation into the text virtually became part of the substance of the Bible. Occasional contacts between Jewish and Christian interpreters in the Middle Ages served to reinforce them. The principles supporting them were questioned only with the onset of humanist scholarship at the time of the Renaissance, with its emphasis on *sola scriptura* – the text and nothing but the text – and a historicism which flourishes in much biblical scholarship to this day. But Kugel is attracted by a rival trend in modern scholarship which demands a new respect for the 'pre-scientific' interpreters and their part in establishing the Bible that remains a 'great, unitary, sacred corpus' still central to both Judaism and Christianity.

He is of course not the first to argue for a return to the Bible as the product of texts *plus* interpretation, and as a work that must be thought of as whole, contributed to by ages of readers, rather than an assemblage of books that needs to be broken up so that the parts may be studied separately and on strictly historical assumptions.

Unlike my ecumenical efforts, mentioned at the beginning of this review, his arguments would probably not be contested by the Jerusalem professors, yet I daresay he himself might allow one to argue that this development in biblical studies has certain secular implications. The tide of secular criticism is at present strongly set against the idea that there can, even though less rigidly than in religion, be canons, in which there is a relation between the parts (a relation perceived by educated readers) independent of the separate historical circumstances of those parts. Such assumptions are perhaps pre-scientific, but it may be that a new, post-scientific, theory of interpretation will turn out to resemble the older approach more closely than it does those which at present seek to exclude the kind of imaginative exegesis of canonical texts that Kugel's book handsomely illustrates. I mean, of course, those fashionable theories which condemn the study of integral works of art and instead break them down into historical documents that are no different from any other historical documents, interesting, if at all, because of what they reveal or conceal about historically located conflicts of power. So the kind of study represented by Kugel's book should be of some concern even to entirely secular critics and readers.

The Sexuality of Christ

In 1983 the magazine *October* devoted an entire issue to a remarkable study of genital display in some – indeed in a great many – Renaissance depictions of Christ. Publication in book form followed, and among the reviewers there were some who were embarrassed or shocked and some who were sceptical. The author, Leo Steinberg, kept watch on them and has now greatly expanded his original report.* He is agreeably discursive and writes informatively and exuberantly about all manner of marginal topics, but his revision has two main purposes: to multiply the visual evidence – seeking 'the cumulative impact of number' – and to rebut his critics. It seems to him that English reviewers in particular were inclined to be contemptuous or dismissive, so some venerable commentators – the late Lawrence Gowing, Michael Levey, Richard Wollheim, Marina Warner and, singled out for a special treatment, Charles Hope – are, in this new edition, keenly reprehended.

It should be said that Steinberg, a lively and resourceful writer, could not with any justice be charged with irreverence or lubricity. That he greatly enjoyed researching, writing and defending his thesis is clear enough, and fair enough; his satisfaction is of a legitimate, scholarly kind. He has achieved something original, and offered unignorable explanations of a body of rather mystifying evidence that has been almost entirely repressed for centuries (hence the 'Modern

* *The Sexuality of Christ in Renaissance Art and Modern Oblivion* (Chicago: University of Chicago Press, 1997).

Oblivion' of the title). His undertaking is so extraordinary, so adventurous, that one would expect him, at least now and again, to be wrong, and he must have foreseen opposition from professionally dissident art historians. He got it, and will doubtless expect it again on publication of this new version, though it must be a comfort that for a decade or more his arguments have also attracted much intelligent support. For my part I think he's right about the detail of the paintings, and his explanations of why they are as they are – why they attend so insistently to the genitalia of Jesus in infancy, during crucifixion, and in death – are very persuasive.

This revised edition is clumsy to use, for it simply tacks 200 pages on to the original, occasionally qualifying as well as augmenting it, and replying to its critics. (Steinberg says he was tempted to call it *Double or Nothing*.) It now contains many more illustrations, but of course doesn't repeat the ones that were already present in the first edition, although renewed discussions and refutations often make it necessary to refer to them. But the argument is so absorbing that these minor, probably inevitable, irritations are easily forgotten.

There is an immemorial taboo on the topic of the sexuality of Jesus, but it has sometimes been defied. Steinberg demonstrates that, from about 1260, painters (perhaps affected by the success of the Franciscans, who had a slogan *Nudus nudum Christum sequi*) departed from the hieratically clothed, unsexed Byzantine tradition and undressed the infant Jesus. Thereafter, for two centuries, they pictured him naked but without genital emphasis. But by the end of the fifteenth century they not only painted his penis but represented it as 'pointed to, garlanded, celebrated', stared at and venerated. In the following century it was touched and manipulated, and by the 1530s it was sometimes being shown in a state of infantile erection. This theme of erection, though under cover of a loincloth or other garment, was repeated in pictures of the Crucifixion and the dead Christ. There are some extremely fantasticated loincloths in paintings of the Man of Sorrows, as in two 'deeply shocking' pictures by Ludwig Krug (*c.* 1520) and Maerten van Heemskirk (1532). Some renderings of Crucifixion and Pietà are, I think one must agree, clearly intended to suggest large erections, which may have been intended to symbolize resurrection.

The purpose of these displays, it is conjectured, was to celebrate the Incarnation – though Steinberg prefers the obsolete term 'humanation'. God became an *entire* man, and therefore a sexual being; his sex, like his dependence on his mother's breast, is a pledge of that full humanity the doctrine asserts. And it will not do to offer naturalistic explanations of his infant behaviour; Jesus is entirely unlike other painted babies in his behaviour and the behaviour he elicits from others. There is no need to stress the humanity of ordinary babies or marvel at it.

In a woodcut by Hans Baldung Grien, dated 1511, St Anne is fondling the infant's genitalia, while he chucks the Virgin under the chin, an amorous gesture with a tradition going back to the Song of Songs (and here signifying their mystical marriage), while Joseph looks understandingly on. Steinberg (who throws in a catalogue of what he calls 'chin-chucks' stretching from antiquity to Proust and Nabokov) will have nothing to do with the notion that these images simply reflect the sort of thing that went on in the average household. They are first an affirmation of full humanity, with the reservation that the sexuality of Jesus was not like ours but like that of Adam and Eve before the Fall. He was 'like us in all things except sin'. His genitalia could therefore only with much impropriety be called pudenda. These pictures dwell on that paradox or oxymoron, the sinless generative organ.

Despite much bowdlerizing by overpainting there remain many hundreds of images which support this interpretation, some as striking as the Hans Baldung Grien. The practice of celebrating humanation eventually came to a halt as the taboo began to assert itself, in painting as elsewhere. But for a long stretch of time the sexual member had been an image of God's condescension, an image not of virility but of a voluntary divine abasement to humanity.

The member yielded not seed but, at the Circumcision, blood. The Circumcision was described by St Thomas Aquinas as 'a remedy for original sin, which is transmitted through the act of generation'. God further condescended when consenting to enact this sacramental admission of guilt, though of course free of it himself. Steinberg again and again illustrates the conjunction, or, as he calls it, the 'hyphen', formed by the blood from the spear wound in Christ's side and the blood of the Circumcision. The blood from the greater wound, it would seem by established convention, flows directly into the groin of the dead Christ. One bleeding is the type of the other: 'those first oozings guarantee Christ's humanity', and may be thought to foretell or even inaugurate the redemptive Passion.

Steinberg regards the insistent display of the penis, its potentially generative function and its wounds, as a silent counter to heresy, notably to Arianism but also to various forms of Docetism, which denied the humanity of Christ. In the first edition he was glad to find confirmation of this motive in Circumcision sermons of the relevant period, but in the new version he tends to disparage or even reject this extra-pictorial documentary support, perhaps because he wants to cast doubt on what he regards as the deplorable art-historical practice of depending more on documents than on pictures. He has to answer the objections of Charles Hope, whom he characterizes as a historian of that persuasion, and who is indeed sceptical of Steinberg's thesis precisely because it lacks documentary support. Hope believes that one needs to find out what Renaissance art meant to people at the time 'by reading what they said about paintings and about their faith'. Steinberg's rejoinder is that he would prefer to look at the paintings, and ask why the artists, of all people, felt it necessary to introduce these theological innovations and deal with the resulting representational problems.

In the course of a lengthy response to Hope's criticisms Steinberg considers his rival interpretation of the Adoration theme: the Magi, it is claimed, are primarily concerned not with Christ but with the Virgin; Renaissance babies are usually nude; the mage may seem to be staring reverently at the Child's genital area but is probably just checking its sex; the infant is at this moment only an adjunct to the Madonna; and so on. Hope particularly objected to the claim that in such pictures as Ghirlandaio's *Adoration of the Magi* in the Uffizi the mage is humbly contemplating the infant penis, unveiled by the Virgin, as proof of total humanation – as evidence that Jesus was born 'complete in all the parts of a man'. Yet similarly intent postures and gazes occur not only in a whole batch of Adorations, but in other Quattrocento pictures of the Holy Child with reverent donors. And it certainly looks as if the presence of the infant member was considered a particular miracle.

Since conversion or surrender tends to be rare in such disputes, Dr Hope will probably have his answers. But in certain matters of detail, such as the argument concerning what St Anne is really doing in the Hans Baldung Grien woodcut, I think Steinberg is the victor. In a sense this is the argument he needs to win if his thesis is to survive, so it is well that he wins it. We have the paintings, he says, and if we consent to look at them, rather than adopt the unimaginative, unseeing habits of art historians unhappy without the support of the written word, we shall better understand the motives of the artists.

I suppose this contest with Hope was crucial because it really does turn on what opponents might judge the most vulnerable point of the book – that the author deduces entirely from wordless pictorial imagery a complex religious mystery on which many thousands of words were written, though never, it seems, with reference to the unarticulated theology of painters. But the deduction turns out, I think, to be plausible as well as interesting.

The display of the sex of Jesus (*ostentatio genitalium*, he names it, on the analogy of *ostentatio vulnerum*, the showing forth of the wounds) is emphasized in all manner of ways. The *ostentatio* is sometimes made by the Virgin, holding aside the child's covering, sometimes by the infant himself, pictured with a hand on his penis, as in Veronese's *Holy Family with St Barbara and the Infant St John* in the Uffizi and in at least twenty other paintings of the Cinquecento – 'a gesture unknown to devotional art before or since', and later deplored.

Steinberg has a long and brilliant excursus on 'bowdlerism', the practice of eliminating or toning down such gestures for the sake of decency (and for other reasons no less reprehensible), citing Ruskin's destruction of Turner's erotic drawings as akin to the overpainting of the loins of naked Christs, or to the painting of a *cache-sexe* on Mantegna's *Madonna and Child with the Magdalen and St John the Baptist*, still on view in the National Gallery with the genitals cursorily covered, despite the cleaning of 1957.

A curious, recherché instance of bowdlerization was communicated to Steinberg by William Ravenhill, a geography professor at Exeter University, who read the first edition. In the course of his own unrelated researches Ravenhill had examined by beta radiography a watermark in an atlas by Christopher Saxton, printed about 1590. This watermark apparently shows the risen Christ bearing a cross above an eminently visible erect penis, emblem, doubtless, of resurrection; but even quite recent reproductions of it contrive to erase or conceal that member. Another English instance is an alabaster sculpture of the fourteenth century which had been buried under the chancel floor of a church at Long Melford in Suffolk, where it lay until it was discovered in the 1700s. A reason for its concealment may be that it shows the infant's phallus protruding from a knee-length robe – it was hidden, that is, out of modesty rather than to thwart sixteenth- or seventeenth-century iconoclasts. It is impossible to conjecture how many objects of this sort were destroyed or defaced, though the number is probably very large; but abundant evidence has nevertheless survived and is still being investigated, as Steinberg's second edition testifies.

He reproaches himself with having previously paid too little attention to what he calls the 'reactive modesty factor', a force which he thinks began, around 1500, to combat the representation of the genitals whether intended as evidence of humanation or for any other reason. The idea may have been that the pudency of Virgin and Child had been insulted and needed defence. This new trend eventually ended the fashion, if one may so call it, of the *ostentatio genitalium*. Perhaps this just went out of date; as Yeats observed, 'the painter's brush consumes his dreams'. But it may, for a long time, have seemed less a painterly fashion than a devotional necessity:

When the Apostle declares that God 'sent his own Son in the likeness of sinful flesh' (Romans, 8:3), and when Augustine speaks of the Word assuming 'the flesh of sin but without sin', we do not, we need not, suppose that they had the penis in mind. But Renaissance image makers? Those among them who were rethinking the God-man's physique had no choice but to mind it . . . The question before them was how to visualize sinlessness in the '*likeness* of sinful flesh'; and this is no writer's problem.

No doubt more and more recondite and relevant evidence will be accumulated on either side of the question. In an interesting disquisition on what he calls 'remote symbolism' – echoing the advice of Dionysius the Areopagite that symbols should not cleave too close to their referents – Steinberg cites the thirteenth-century sage Durandus, who said that one can represent the Church as a harlot 'because she is called out of many nations, and because she closeth not her bosom against any that return to her'. He can find no other instance of this symbolism, and supposes that Durandus must himself have invented this illustration of this thesis of the Pseudo-Dionysius, and 'judged it too good to drop'. Perhaps so, and there may be no earlier instances, but there is a familiar example of the Church as harlot in Donne's sonnet 'Show me, dear Christ, thy spouse', which ends:

> Betray, kind husband, thy spouse to our sights,
> And let mine amorous soul court thy mild dove,
> Who is most true and pleasing to thee, then
> When she is embraced and open to most men.

It may be worth noting that Counter-Reformation Catholicism, part of the tradition in which Donne was writing, believed not only in 'dissimilar symbols', as is evident from emblem books, but in the efficacy of a kind of sexual imagery which, though different from that which Steinberg attributes to Renaissance painters, is sometimes amazingly explicit; a famous instance is the orgasmic St Teresa of Bernini. In another religious sonnet Donne asks God to make him chaste by ravishing him.

Perhaps sex cannot be perpetually kept out of religion, if only by way of analogy; as in the old saw about nature, you may try to get rid of it but it always recurs. There is a modern manifestation of this recurrence in Steinberg's dispute with feminist theologians who found sexist reasons to quarrel with his original book.

What Steinberg does admirably is to relate technical practice in the painting of the period – the arrangement of figures, body parts, hands, drapery – to a theological and devotional position. He is very thorough; yet there is probably more work to be done. For example, some critics allege that typical patrons wouldn't be interested in enigmatic pictorial allusions to humanation. Is there anything to be said on that topic? How do we know, how can we be sure they wouldn't? Steinberg could argue that, while they might not experience, as the artists did, a pressing need to give visual expression to that doctrine, there seems to be little evidence that donors disliked or complained about the representations, which could have been explained to them as in perfect conformity with a doctrine to which the pious should assent. As for us, we can dissent all we like, but the religious art of the Renaissance will never look quite the same again.

The Other Yeats

We attach the epithet 'great' rather loosely to artists, but there is probably some tacit agreement about which ones deserve it. It doesn't seem wrong to call W. B. Yeats a great poet, and in certain contexts he may be called a great Irish poet, though most of the time it might seem odd to insist that Dante was a great Italian poet, or Shakespeare a great English one, partly because we vaguely think of them as transcending nationality. But Yeats was the necessary great poet of the national cultural renaissance that accompanied a struggle for political independence with which he was inevitably and willingly associated; he would have been a great Irish poet even if he had not become supranational, more universal than that description suggests.

The new nation also needed a great Irish painter, and Jack Yeats, brother of the more famous W. B., was seen to supply the need. The question whether he was a great painter or just a great Irish painter haunts this book.* If you think of him as a gifted artist with an inextinguishable interest in depicting the posture and movement of horses, donkeys, droll Irish characters and Sligo scenes – everybody has seen those pictures of horse races on the sands of Rosses Point; reproductions are widely available – you may be content to leave him to the nationalists, who in any case wouldn't accept that a great Irish painter isn't a great painter *tout court*. But it is a virtue of this book that you cannot honestly avoid the issue. It raises with urgency

* Bruce Arnold, *Jack Yeats* (New Haven and London: Yale University Press, 1998).

the question whether Jack Yeats did not deserve, like his brother, to be hailed, even by the non-Irish, as great in the more absolute sense.

That Bruce Arnold has a profound admiration for his subject is evident from the minute care of his research, but he avoids idolatry, and this measure of reserve lends credibility to his estimate of the painter's stature. His text may be too long, too conscientious in recording details of exhibitions, banquets and committee meetings, but these rather tedious passages testify to a determination to be a biographer on whom nothing is lost.

Yeats was a private man, seemingly incapable of the usual excesses and vanities, and to know a lot about him is to admire a life of prodigiously hard work made tolerable by innocent diversions like making model boats and then helping Masefield to sink them, and collecting vast quantities of ephemera. He also enjoyed violent and exotic action, but always as an observer rather than as a participant.

The publisher has done the author proud, for this is a great slab of a book, on heavy paper, with over 200 black-and-white illustrations, mostly disposed in wide margins, and there are seventeen colour plates. The book is carefully designed, though less carefully copy-edited and proof-read; perhaps having it set in Hong Kong and printed in Singapore created problems. Still, the volume has an appropriately monumental air, and the author will surely be forgiven for ignoring the painter's frequently reasserted ban on reproductions. The instruction in his will is clear enough: he required that 'no photographs or reproductions of any kind be made of any of my paintings or drawings, and that [of] photographs or other reproductions of any of my paintings or drawings already made there shall be no publication and no further copies shall be made'. During his life he reluctantly permitted very small, imperfect reproductions in catalogues, but believed they put a screen between the work and the viewer; 'the better they are the worse they are'. A painting was an event, and these images turned an event into a reference and deflected attention from the works themselves.

Observance of Yeats's austere interdict would of course make books of this kind impossible. Once the decision to ignore it has been taken the possibilities are without obvious limit, for in the course of a long life (1871–1957) Yeats produced 1,100 oils and thousands of drawings, many of the latter intended for reproduction in the first place, though admittedly in ephemeral or trivial circumstances. He must have known that his wishes would be politely ignored, even that they were incompatible with his estimate of his own merit; but although he was generally a quiet, amiable man he rarely preferred the opinions of others to his own, which he expressed with great clarity.

This independence of mind was an enduring characteristic, evidenced, for example, in his polite, rather distant responses to the views of his remarkable but notoriously unsatisfactory father, the painter J. B. Yeats, whose irresponsibilities and financial dependence on his children did not prevent him from harrying them with advice. The elder brother, W. B., was far more easily disturbed than Jack by his father's conduct. J. B. couldn't understand why his gifted painter son seemed to have learned nothing in the London art schools; he simply followed his nose and never even bothered to learn the rules about painting in oils and other useful technical tips. The charge that he didn't understand oils was repeated in his later years, when he painted a great many of them, but he didn't care; and his refusal to be associated with any school or movement was lifelong, though Arnold is willing to link some late works with the Surrealists. He admired artists who, like himself, went their own way without regard to such matters – Oskar Kokoschka, who greatly admired him; Joyce, who owned one of his pictures; and Beckett, who was to be his champion in old age.

Despite this Bartlebian attitude – 'I would prefer not to' – Yeats couldn't avoid being buffeted by rival claims and clamours. Born into a remarkable family, with a famous elder brother and two talented sisters, his early life was divided between west London and Sligo. He had to join in the family scramble for money, but unlike the rest of the tribe he found making it easy enough. Still in his teens, he found plenty of work in the newspapers, for these were the days before they began to use photographs and instead employed artists to illustrate horse races, prizefights, circuses and entertainments like those provided by Buffalo Bill Cody. Long after he gave up those early assignments he went on, pseudonymously, doing cartoons for *Punch*, though he kept as quiet as he could about them. Once a *Punch* cheque was sent in error to W. B., and Jack was cross to think his brother thus knew about this apparently rather good source of income. His skill in these activities was much admired, although Arnold, in his judicious way, ranks Yeats below such masters of the craft as Ralph Caldecott and Phil May.

In the early years there can have seemed little reason why Yeats should not have made a successful career in this kind of journey work, and he energetically produced drawings for visiting cards, bookplates and doilies, as well as producing all those bluff depictions of horses and clowns. But he was clearly determined to give himself time to decide what to do next; he was remarkably self-reliant.

He married young and distanced himself a little from his exigent family, living for a while in Chertsey and then moving to Devon, with frequent visits to the west of Ireland. Much later he moved his household to Ireland. One fate he shared with his brother the poet: he was always balanced on the hyphen in 'Anglo-Irish'. He disliked the term, remarking that it 'means, to my ear, one brother planting tea in Ceylon, Ethel married to a rubber planter in Siam, and Doreen, married to a decent chap who has tried sheep farming in New Zealand. Or perhaps it means, the Big House or the Little Big House at the back of my mind.' He wondered if the term could properly be applied to a family like his, for whom connection with the Big House was a remote fact of history; they belonged to the Protestant merchant class, and neither the Yeatses nor, on the maternal side, the Pollexfens, who were fairly rich, had genuine aristocratic pretensions. In the midst of Catholic Sligo they were bourgeois and Protestant, but also Irish and proud of it.

Yet Yeats declined to think of himself as an Irish painter. Lady Gregory wanted him for her renaissance (to a considerable extent an Anglo-Irish affair). Later on his not altogether helpful champion

Thomas MacGreevy loudly claimed him for Ireland, but Samuel Beckett, deploring this claim as he deplored attempts to exaggerate his own Irishness, claimed Yeats as an international master. That, as it happens, was Yeats's own view. In all modesty he declared himself 'the first living painter in the world', adding that the next best was 'so far away that I am only able to make him out'.

This estimate would not have been endorsed by brother William. Relations between them were generally cool, and Jack was never pleased to be mistaken for the great poet or thought of as his talented brother. They were temperamentally quite different, the painter a one-man school, with no cronies, no pupils, no public panache. Yet there were, inevitably, resemblances. Over long years the poet worked his way, with great effort and discipline, towards what we recognize as his modern style, reaching full power in the volumes of the 1920s, when he was already a Nobel prizewinner. The painter became modern at much the same time, but in a rather sudden, revolutionary move. He had, rather surprisingly, figured in the great American Armory show of 1913, probably at the instance of John Quinn, the New York lawyer to whose patronage the Yeats family, as well as T. S. Eliot and Ezra Pound, owed so much. Yeats mistrusted 'the New', although he knew well enough what was going on; and after what seems to have been a quite serious nervous breakdown in 1915, which held him up for some years, he suddenly began to be serious about oil painting. Making this switch from line to tone in the teeth of those who said he was ignorant about this kind of work, he painted vast numbers of canvases, 500 of them between the ages of seventy and eighty-five. It seems very characteristic that, following his own bent, he took a virtual holiday to write seven novels and nine plays, none of which struck his brother as worth staging. It was in later years that his painting was more wildly 'modern'.

It was not universally well received, and sometimes it was described as 'paint run amuck', or paint 'dragged about'. It belongs to no school (Yeats remarked that Picasso might have been a better painter if he had skipped Paris altogether), and Arnold speaks of 'the problem of emptiness or diffusion of effort' in the larger canvases, of 'technical

limitation', and, quite simply, of 'bad painting', with excessive impasto, a wild palette, and 'relative ignorance in the use of oil paints'.
It was the mere act of painting, the determination to follow his own
nose and ignore criticism, that propelled this self-made artist into the
extraordinary feats of his last quarter-century. The break was quite
sudden; gone were the days when Masefield was his close friend or,
having toured the west of Ireland with John Synge, he illustrated in
his sketches that author's reports for the *Manchester Guardian*.

Some of the results of his conversion are to be seen in the colour
plates of Arnold's book, though of course they do not convey the
depth of his impasto. And since so many of these paintings are in
private collections Arnold, in publishing these reproductions, has
done him the service he would have declined on principle.

It might be that the slower self-modernizing of his brother had
some part in the painter's change of direction. And, again like William, he could not quite avoid the political implications of Irishness
in the years after the Easter Rising. He stood apart as much as
possible, always amiable and pacific, but taking De Valera's side
after the Civil War, when his brother went with Cosgrave and became
a Free State senator. Meanwhile he remained confident in his own
idea of himself, and, although he was, almost inevitably, a guest of
Lady Gregory's at Coole, he continued to choose his own friends.
His most ardent admirers among painters were Kokoschka and
Sickert, and among artists more generally Samuel Beckett, at first a
shy visitor, later a close friend. It is quite reasonably claimed that
Yeats, who loved solitary figures and clown-like pairs, influenced
Beckett's work, and that Gogo and Didi are Yeatsian characters
immersed by Beckett in 'the mystique de la merde.'

Despite the apparent violence of his switch to oils Yeats never
quite lost contact with his old themes or with his Irishness. His
brother found himself, in his last years, once more haunted by
Cuchulain, but now as a feature of universal rather than national
myth. There may be nothing in Jack's work to compare with the
dark splendour of 'Cuchulain Comforted', or the violent rant of the
Old Man in *The Death of Cuchulain* ('I spit upon the dancers of

Degas', etc.) but there is still great energy and some enumeration of old themes. Above all there is that serene assurance: there was only one way for him, and that was the way he had chosen.

Yeats was always a competent manager and, without achieving anything spectacular, his work sold well enough to keep him in comfort in his old age. In his last years he spent part of his time, whenever he felt like it, in a nursing home. He remained faithful to his Church, and regularly went to services in St Patrick's because he enjoyed the singing. After the death of W. B. he became friendly with his niece and nephew, whom previously he had hardly known.

In an epilogue Arnold tells of the prices now being paid for the paintings. The 'seriously wealthy Irish business tycoon . . . with more money than understanding' has moved into the market, and the Million Pound Yeats may not be far in the future. Such purchasers disregard Arnold's point that some of what they buy is 'overblown and boring . . . without much sense of structure and form', and presenting, by the 'exuberance of [the painter's] thick impasto, problems for posterity which are far from resolved'. While he is busy deploring these facts, Arnold goes on to complain that the Irish National Gallery has favoured Yeats at the expense of other artists – a tribute to the success of the campaign to establish him as *the* painter of the national renaissance. Another consequence of this apotheosis is the abundance of 'general bric-a-brac', the books, record covers, calendars, and so on, bearing Yeatsian images and offering a vulgarly diminished idea of the artist himself.

One good motive for the writing of this book may have been to correct these distortions. It avoids falling into a different fault; that of making its counter-claims too unreservedly. Like his subject, the author cannot altogether escape the pressure of nationalism: whether or not he is a great painter, Yeats is a great Irish painter. Arnold has a deep respect for a remarkable career, and would presumably endorse the higher estimate, but still wants to make some quite severe qualifications. His is a judicious book, and entirely worthy of its subject.

Howard Hodgkin

Faced with such a book as this,* it is hard not to regret the passing of an age when it seemed easy to write about painting and painters. The grapes of Zeuxis, as Pliny admiringly observed, were so real that birds came and pecked at them. Vasari, a painter himself, believed that in his day art had rediscovered those lost antique skills, had built on them, and was now close to perfection. To make representations look deceptively real, and remain untroubled by considerations of what 'real' could possibly mean, was the aim of the artist, and the function of the critic was simply to admire the technical accomplishments that made the illusion credible.

You could also express an admiring or even a disgusted interest in the personal life of the painter. Writing about Piero di Cosimo, Vasari does more than comment on the strange works of this artist. He adds that Piero lived more like a brute than a man, subsisted on boiled eggs, cooking fifty at a time while he was boiling his glue, and studied a wall on which sick persons had used to spit, imagining that he saw there fantastic cities and combats of horses. Moreover he would never suffer the fruit trees of his garden to be pruned or trained; and so on. Vasari improves the story by arguing that there was method in Piero's madness: he was so eccentric that people mistakenly thought him a fool, and this assumption prevented other artists from

* Michael Auping, John Elderfield and Susan Sontag, *Howard Hodgkin: Paintings*, with a catalogue raisonné by Maria Price (London: Thames and Hudson, 1995).

profiting by his example. George Eliot remembered Piero's eggs and reclusive habits in *Romola*, improving the story yet again; why she has the eggs delivered ready-boiled is a question for Victorianists.

Vasari had got on to something important when he perceived that the lives of painters are likely to be of considerable general interest, as well as being rather easier to write about than their productions. He does describe certain works in detail, for example Piero's *Car of Death*, with tombs from which emerged figures with skeletons painted on their black body-socks. He can remark that Piero drew well from life, that he painted St Antony wearing spectacles and reading an excellently represented parchment book, that he displayed to perfection the art of colouring in oils. He was clearly aware that biographical information, gossip indeed, was seductive; as to technique, it was enough to say, without going into great detail, that Piero had lots of it. The excellence of his colouring in oils could be remarked without further analysis. So with Leonardo's 'great and marvellous art' in the representation of the rotundity of the dates on a palm tree, and the wonderful texture of the table cloth in the *Last Supper*. If virtually the whole art of painting was perfect representation there was no need to strain for a vocabulary appropriate to anything other than skilled and diligent workmanship.

Everything was bound to get harder when painting found other tasks than mimesis. Picasso said that painters no longer live in a tradition but need to 're-create an entire language . . . from A to Z'. This development could, he admitted, be called a liberation, 'but what the artist gains in the way of liberty he loses in the way of order'.* The writer about painting is in an even greater difficulty than the painter himself, for he must learn the elements of that new language and seek for himself yet a matching other, which has to consist of words. The problem of translation now looks insuperable.

Despite the endlessly quoted and variously interpreted opinion of

* Quoted in Andrew Graham-Dixon's *Howard Hodgkin* (London: Thames and Hudson, 1994), a splendidly illustrated work, and an indispensable companion to the book under review.

Horace, *ut pictura poesis*, the match between painting and what can be said about it has grown more and more strained. Proust's Bergotte, a writer, contemplates the 'little patch of yellow wall' in Vermeer's *View of Delft*: 'that's how I ought to have written', he says, and, after weighing his own works against that patch, falls over and dies. Only a life of perfect writing, made of language 'precious in itself', could equal the beauty of that passage of paint; and yet to equal it, even by such hopelessly arduous effort, would still not be to match it or describe it.

Here is a final surrender of words to paint. There is a long tradition of poems about paintings, but there is really never a contest; the poem is always talking more or less vainly to an interlocutor using sign language – at best offering an oblique and unsolicited tribute. There is evidence of this persistent dialogue of the deaf in John Hollander's excellent book *The Gazer's Spirit: Poems Speaking to Silent Works of Art*,* a learned study of the tradition of *ecphrasis* – poetic description of paintings – illustrated by a 'gallery' of paintings and their tributary poems – Aretino on Titian, Rossetti on Leonardo, Baudelaire on Callot, Donald Hall on Munch, Hollander on Monet, and dozens more, including Richard Wilbur's exquisitely meditative imitation of a baroque wall fountain, a poem that sounds more like the work of art it imitates than any other I know.

The painting of Howard Hodgkin is a first-rate example of the vivid muteness that resists critical attempts at conversation. Vasari himself, after praising Hodgkin's power as a colourist, would have had trouble explaining the relationship of the paintings to their titles, which often suggest scenes, persons and ideas that were perhaps the points of origin of the works but have more or less entirely disappeared from the finished product. There are, for example, a number of portraits of husbands and wives in which not even the couple who commissioned the works could be sure which figure was which. Sometimes the human shapes have virtually disappeared under the paint or, as in *Mr and Mrs Stephen Buckley*, are converted into

---

* Chicago: University of Chicago Press, 1995.

geometric forms; which doesn't prevent the artist from saying 'the subject of the painting is simply a family group sitting round the fire in the evening'. Other titles seem to promise that the picture will tell a story: *When did we go to Morocco?* or *It can't be true* or *Haven't we met?*.

Of *It can't be true* Michael Auping of Fort Worth, who certainly knows his Hodgkin, says 'it is echo-like in its composition. It is composed of a series of tilting frames jostling each other for position within the whole. The eye is teased back to a bright yellow frame in the center of the painting and stopped short by a series of abrupt strokes that violate its containment.' So far, fair enough; after all a critic needs to say *something* about this dazzling production, and the words seem not entirely unrelated to the painting. But Auping continues, 'What "can't be true" is not altogether clear, unless it is Hodgkin's hesitant acknowledgement that the voyeuristic tendencies that inspired an early work like *Memoirs* [a small gouache done when Hodgkin was seventeen] have for a number of years been turning increasingly inward.' A despairing lunge at a biographical interpretation; a likely story. If you can believe that you can believe anything, which could be said of many desperate interpretations, many words addressed to the questioner that sits so sly, so mute.

The gap between title and work is often remarked on by the contributors to this gorgeously illustrated volume. It is really the catalogue of an exhibition organized at Fort Worth, Texas, by Maria Price, who also edited the book and provided a more than useful catalogue raisonné, which offers, among much else, information as to how ostensible subjects are eroded, sometimes after much repainting. When the picture has been exhibited in more than one state it can be seen that its originating subject was at first more readily discernible. In *Large Staff Room*, for instance, we are told it was once possible to detect human presences at the table, and possibly even to relate the image to a particular staff room; but in later reworking about 70 per cent of the picture surface was reduced to 'a vast expanse of cadmium red', leaving only a small image of a knee under the table. One is inevitably reminded of Balzac's story 'Le

Chef-d'œuvre inconnu', in which a perfectly executed foot alone
survived the mad, obsessive onslaught of paint. Art critics contrive
to say fairly solemn things about the much reduced *Large Staff Room*
(the expanse of colour suggests 'a kind of mind-space in which the
memory – a knee under a table – exists') and, if some prefer to call it
a leg-pull or visual pun, they don't mean by that to disparage the
work – leg-pulls have an honoured place in modern art, and to
suspect one may be a move intellectually preferable to a flight into
allegory. Like Picasso, Hodgkin has his own technical alphabet and
can do exactly as he pleases, as his brush pleases, according to his
humour; it is, after all, the biggest of leg-pulls to kid us into believing
that words can be found to explain the beauty of these patches of
paint.

What can be done instead, and what convention permits, is to
perform certain art-historical rituals: to divide the artist's career
into phases (voyeuristic, post-voyeuristic, etc.), and to identify the
painters who influenced him, a long list: Seurat, Pasmore, Bonnard,
Morandi, Bacon, Matisse, Vuillard, Degas, Stella, Johns, Pollock,
and so on. All this Auping does. On other topics, such as Graham-
Dixon's proposition that 'there are a lot of pictures about fucking',
he judges it best to be non-committal; yes and no, certainly many of
these works are about bodily pleasures, he says, but they 'may or
may not refer to intercourse'. 'Refer' is anyway too strong a word.
Graham-Dixon quotes Hodgkin as saying that he is a representational painter, but at once adds firmly 'he is nothing of the kind'.
It's an issue that comes up again and again, but Graham-Dixon seems
to get it about right when he remarks that 'the passage of forms
across these bright surfaces is of no more consequence than the
passage of clouds across the sky at sunset. They are as insignificant
as weather.' Yet among the strange gaudy forms, some distinct, some
vague as clouds or weather, it cannot be denied that a good few bear
some resemblance to the male organ.

To write as Auping does is perfectly reasonable in view of the sheer
difficulty of finding anything really susceptible to being written about.
As Susan Sontag remarks in her essay, 'the thoughtful – as distinct

from the inarticulate – may have good reason to be wary, anxious, at a loss (for words)'. She endorses Valéry's *obiter dicta* 'One must always apologize for talking about painting' and 'A work of art, if it does not leave us mute, is of little value.' 'Of course,' she adds, 'we do not *stay* mute.' The implication is that the necessity of saying something about art reduces its value. This is one of those aporias Paul de Man likened to getting trapped in a revolving door, but Sontag, as it were noticing the normal exit usually available at the side, emerges to say several valuable things about Hodgkin; for example, 'having renounced painting's other primary resource, drawing, Hodgkin has fielded the most inventive, sensuously affecting color repertory of any contemporary painter – as if, in taking up the ancient quarrel between *disegno* and *colore*, he had wanted to give *colore* its most sumptuous exclusive victory'. She dwells convincingly on Hodgkin's hesitations between revelation and concealment, and comes close to explaining the obviously intense pleasure she gets from these works; which is an achievement.

Yet the best writing in this book is to be found in a correspondence between the painter and John Elderfield of the Museum of Modern Art, New York. Hodgkin complains of 'the tyranny of words in England' but submits with elegance to this epistolary conversation. Elderfield, an expatriate Englishman, so still under that tyranny, puzzles over the way his correspondent's works 'attach to the external world', finding that they both afford and deny narrative readings. Hodgkin affirms, as he always does, that the subject matter of his paintings 'is of primary importance – I couldn't make a picture that was not "about" anything' – and is irritated when people describe his pictures as 'beautiful', so suggesting that because 'they look "pretty" they cannot have any content'. He thinks that in England richness of colour is thought to denote 'a fundamental lack of seriousness'. In these letters he says many revealing things about concealment and other matters, repeating in his own terms the lament of Picasso quoted earlier: 'Never underestimate the heroism demanded of the artist . . . at a time when no one tells the artist what to do, except himself . . .' He writes about Vuillard and, with the greatest admiration, about Degas – 'a classical artist, something I have always wanted to be . . . As for being tied to the past, what other home have we got?' Together with his remarks on his own techniques, for example his preference for wood over canvas, he makes one feel, with deep ingratitude to the critics, that if painting has to be talked about, and it does, the painters may do it best. Yet they may need critics to make them talk, as David Sylvester, that master of interviewing discipline, has induced Hodgkin to talk in the past.

When all is said, the paintings do the real talking in their own tongue, but we still need to have our attention directed to them, our possible blindnesses cleaned, our sensitivity to their weathers refined. Reproductions are one aid; Hodgkin is understandably sceptical about their value, and nobody will take them as adequate substitutes for the real thing, but I find that on the images abundantly presented in this book, and in Graham-Dixon's, one dwells with increasing pleasure. The actual paintings now provide an extra delight, an enhanced shock of recognition, as if what had been seen through a glass, darkly, though not too darkly, were now seen face to face. The real thing can now thrive without further articulate description.

Having been made ready for the experience, no one will care that Hodgkin's Venice is hardly a place, that *Waking up in Naples* may have something to do with waking up but not, as far as one can see, particularly in Naples, that *Egyptian Night* contains an identifiable pyramid yet looks like a sumptuous carpet, or that *Sunset* is a sunset belonging to Hodgkin's private meteorology – though if told it's a sunset you might just recognize it as such, which is more than you can do when searching for Patrick Caulfield in *Patrick Caulfield in Italy*. But if you don't *have* to say anything about these paintings your pleasure will be the greater, and so, if we are to believe Valéry, will the paintings.

Sylvester on Modern Art

In a preliminary chapter called 'Curriculum Vitae' David Sylvester explains that he became interested in art when, at seventeen, he was fascinated by a black-and-white reproduction of a Matisse.* He at once began to paint in oils, but soon discovered that he lacked talent and began to write about art instead, devoting himself thenceforth to the black and white of the page. A left-wing journal here inaccurately called *The Tribute* accepted an article he wrote about a London exhibition. Now eighteen, he was launched on a career for which he was, on his own account, but insecurely qualified. It was wartime, and he had seen very few foreign pictures; the National Gallery exposed only one old master a month. But, then as now, he was almost as interested in artists as he was in art, and met many examples of the species in Soho clubs. Being at home with painters and intellectuals considerably his seniors seems to have come naturally to him, and soon we find him in Paris on familiar terms with Michel and Louise Leiris, Jacques Lacan, Sylvia Bataille, André Masson and Alberto Giacometti, the last of whom was to be enduringly important to his career.

For almost half a century he has practised not art, a strenuous and competitive business, but what he calls 'the sham heroics of the game of criticism'. This carefully chosen collection is proof that he has a genius for the game. Rather like that Matisse reproduction, it is

---

* David Sylvester, *About Modern Art: Critical Essays 1948–1996* (London: Chatto & Windus, 1996).

impressive without the aid of colour; not even Sylvester's favourite painters are honoured with reproductions of their work, and I take this to have been an aesthetic rather than a financial decision, for such photographs would add nothing to the author's prose.

Although he was unavoidably ignorant when he started out, the excellence of Sylvester's writing has come to depend on easy access to files of learned information. There are gaps – he says he can't handle the work of painters born since 1945, and regrets that he has written so little about old masters, seeming, a shade implausibly, to blame this omission on lack of nerve. Occasionally he worries that his writing about painting could be an intrusion on the painting, and for that reason he has refrained from writing anything in the catalogues of some of the innumerable shows he has curated. But he must be well aware that looking at pictures and then writing about them, representing them about as well as they can be in such reports, is his true business. One understands his regret at the long gap (visible in this book) between 1970 and 1986, when he was preoccupied with the huge catalogue raisonné of Magritte, and with a monograph on that artist. 'I still love the work,' he says, 'but the fact remains that I spent years of my life, like Swann, on someone who was not my type.'

Which artists are his type? One of his favoured rhetorical modes is eulogy, and high claims are made for a good many artists, including of course Giacometti and Bacon, but he exalts several others, including Auerbach, Dubuffet and Newman. He tentatively withdraws his estimate of Bomberg as 'the finest English painter of the century', and repents some early limiting judgements on Picasso: 'The young critic cuts his teeth on Picasso. He proves his manhood by putting down Picasso, which is quite easy because he is so flawed an artist, is such a colossal figure that he has several parts that are clay, probably including his feet, but not his balls.' He treats the last works of Picasso, very old and thought to be impotent, with reverence: the painter can no longer affirm his manhood, but is still the one to beat. There are some other medal winners, including de Kooning, who gets more space in the book than any other artist and is called 'the supreme painterly painter of the second half of the century and the greatest painter of the human figure since Picasso'.

Among Sylvester's preoccupations are a need to specify the differences between modern and pre-modern art, and a need to predict the future of painting. The latter interest is less interesting, for it is not his foresight but the intensity of his gaze and the rapture of his report on what is there at the present moment that give him his peculiar distinction; and anyway he might have known from his first surprised (and hostile) response to Jackson Pollock that the future of an art is predictable only by hindsight. His meditations on the characteristics of modernity are more considerable. Writing admiringly about a print by Barnett Newman, he remarks in a parenthesis, 'I'm no Modernist by persuasion: Michelangelo and Poussin are my cup of tea.' This may be a joke. He does cite with approval a remark of Adrian Stokes to the effect that 'modern art, the art typical of our day, is the slang, so to speak, of art as whole, standing in relation to the Old Masters as does slang to ordinary language', adding that Picasso's last works are an apotheosis of that slang. But despite these qualifications he seems to sense that the gulf between the modern and the old is very deep. He surveys it from the modern side and, unlike Ernst Gombrich, for instance, finds it, on the whole, to be a good thing.

Although pre-modern art is often a presence in his writing, it is usually there not for its own sake but because some modern painter seems to have been looking at or alluding to it. He dwells rather on the individualism of painting since Expressionism and Surrealism. From them the modern painter has learned the value of his own gestures. 'It is precisely his desire for freedom to find his way as he goes along, creating his own values as he goes, that impels the artist today to create works which are a complex of traces of his acts. The work itself renders visible his process of exploration.' So Sylvester in 1955, near the beginning of his acquaintance with action painting. On occasion he will think of this development as the historical consequence of the earlier discoveries of Cézanne and Monet. But in 1957 he is still holding back from Abstract Expressionism, and there is nearly always a sense of discontinuity, of disparate epochs.

In the same year, writing of English abstract art, he reminds us that whatever a picture depicts it is 'essentially a plane surface covered by paints arranged in a certain order'. And he continues:

The basic assumption of modern art – I speak of the major trends, those related to Matisse, Bonnard, Braque, Picasso, Soutine, Klee, Mondrian – is that the first concern of a work of art is to present a configuration of shape and colours and marks which in and of itself stimulates and satisfies, and that only after that condition has been fulfilled can the subtlety of observation, the depth of human feeling and insight, the moral grandeur, expressed in the work, have validity: before the work conveys reality it must achieve its own reality.

This is not, in itself, a satisfactory account of the differentia of the modern, since much the same may be said of the art of any period, and Sylvester here means more than he is actually saying. Elsewhere he tells the story of Mondrian asking to change his seat if given one from which he could see real trees, as Cézanne might not have thought to do; and it is this sort of rejection of or flight from one idea of the real that he wants to talk about. And so he does, when contemplating paintings rather than sketching theories. It is hard to imagine a better introduction to the self-involvement of Klee's pictures than a very early essay collected here; and the same power of explanation, augmented but not radically altered by experience, animates his later studies of Giacometti and Jasper Johns. He is most at home with the art of the world he grew up in, with the painters as well as with their work.

Given his belief that modern art is gesture – gesture expressing individuality – it isn't surprising that he has no inhibitions about providing biographical detail, often derived from acquaintance or from the many interviews he has conducted over the years. He will devote space to the extraordinary life of Soutine and interest himself in the amours of Picasso. And how could one celebrate Gilbert and George without specifying that they are rather unusual human beings? Even the Establishment figure of Sir William Coldstream is treated with a certain wry intimacy, his career recorded, and all the business that kept him out of his studio. 'Before he became Sir William, before he became Professor, he was unaccountably known as Captain Coldstream . . . No doubt the surname encouraged the usage, but there must have been something about him which made it difficult for others to think of him as Mister.'

This was a tease, written when Coldstream was alive and thriving. The painter was undoubtedly a devoted though idiosyncratic committee man. When the idea of moving the opera company from Sadler's Wells to the Coliseum came up it was seriously debated by the Arts Council, of which Coldstream was then vice-chairman. The chairman, Lord Goodman, was all for the move, and as usual he got his way. There were some doubts expressed about the financial prudence of such a change, but the keenest opposition came from Sir William. Afterwards he told me that he was unmoved by considerations of finance, and that the real reason he wanted the opera to stay in Islington was that he lived conveniently near Sadler's Wells. On the other hand he was willing to take on some of the most laborious jobs that came our way. Sylvester asks whether the work 'done in odd hours between committee meetings' suggests that there would have been more than a quantitative gain if he'd painted more. The nudes of 1953–4 suggest that there might have been: they were 'the highest fulfilment yet of [Coldstream's] dream of a kind of painting in which the subject would be starkly itself'. And perhaps all the holding back was a necessary phase in his work. Anyway, Sylvester thinks about this possibility, accepts it, and decides, with characteristic generosity, that Coldstream is 'one of the two or three finest painters working in this country today'. This is merely awarding a bronze or a silver; but what is then said about the artist's work is subtle and sympathetic. In fact this author rarely writes about anything or anybody he unequivocally dislikes; the only rough treatment meted out is reserved for a realist rival, John Berger.

Sylvester is a lover and always seeking to make his reader understand his passion, whether it is for the turds in Gilbert and George's 'Naked Shit Pictures' or Cy Twombly's 'scribbling and scattering': 'Such a painting is surely the paradigm of an "arena in which to act".

The action over, the canvas is like a soiled sheet after a wild night.'
This may explain his admiration for Twombly, but it also explains the
bewilderment of more sober citizens in the new Twombly permanent
collection at Houston, where such souvenirs are exhibited in a context of chaste splendour.

Mostly the passion works, borne along by a prose that is always
stretching itself, always impressive, sometimes tortuous, though
often witty. One's reverence for the old Third Programme increases
as one reads some of the talks he gave on it. And it is real pleasure to
follow him thinking on the page, for example about Claes Oldenburg:

But is a collapsed typewriter like the setting sun? [The artist had more or
less said it was.] Is it how nature is? A relaxed typewriter is not a typewriter
by night, it is a useless typewriter. On the other hand, why should it, when
soft, be called useless? It is a sculpture, not a typewriter, and unlike a
typewriter is not rendered ineffectual by being soft. On the contrary, its
pliability gives it ways in which it can be used which it could not have if it
were rigid. It can be pressed, caressed, squeezed, like a woman's body: it
has the springy softness of a woman's body to the touch. Or rather, it has
the springy softness which is sought in a woman's body. That is to say, it is
not soft merely by default of being hard: its softness is positive, proposes an
alternative norm. If tautness in sculpture corresponds to an ideal of male
desirabilty, perhaps the softness of Oldenburg's sculptures corresponds to
an ideal of female desirabilty?

Here you can observe him in the process of falling in love with
Oldenburg's sculptures, and getting the reader to do the same by
writing so delightfully and not supposing that he mustn't be funny
when being serious. It is not part of his intention to avoid this tone.
He admires Richard Long, but allows himself to wonder about the
size of that artist's reputation. 'His solitary walks through the deserts
of the world have come to have a scriptural resonance. To start
singing his praises now is like taking a food parcel to someone who
is in the middle of eating his dinner at the Ritz, or his manna in the
desert.' This was written as the introduction to the catalogue of a
Long exhibition. It went on to praise him, but Long ungratefully

though understandably requested that it be left out, and it was published later in the *London Review of Books*.

Much as one values the jokes, the real achievement of Sylvester is, as hindsight informs us, much as his rather prodigious early work suggested it would be. It consists of an almost unrivalled power to gaze, and to find language to express the rewards of intensive contemplation. He says he was glad when John Berger turned away from the gazing business and wrote fiction instead. It is impossible to imagine Sylvester doing anything of the kind; his art of prose depends on Art, a state of affairs prefigured in his abrupt abandonment, at seventeen, of painting for writing. It seems that he knew at once what he must do from then on, and, to the great benefit of the ignorant, he has gone on doing it into his seventies.

The Meaning of Money: Frozen Desire

'I have no life except in poetry,' runs an aphorism of Wallace Stevens; but in another he says, 'Money is a kind of poetry', so the fact that he spent his working life as vice-president of a large insurance company did not invalidate the first claim. It is plausible enough that money, with all its promises of pleasure, the anxieties it brings by being elsewhere when needed, the care one is expected to take to prevent it being so, and, I suppose, the delight to be had in simply making it, has a certain relationship with poetry. And, in so far as it is believed, whether sensibly or not, that money is somehow real and credit merely imaginary money, we, who largely live on credit (mortgages, credit cards, etc.), could claim with Wallace Stevens that our whole life, whether we are reading or writing poetry or applying for life insurance, is an affair of the imagination. As a certain Richard Price explained in 1778, paper money must be thought of as the sign of a sign. If coin represented real value, paper, 'owing its currency to opinion, [had] only a local and imaginary value'.* We have no choice but to re-imagine it daily.

I looked forward to this book† because my attempts to understand its subject, interesting as I find it, have hitherto always failed. If it had an affinity to poetry, which I can sometimes handle reasonably

---

* I borrow this quotation from Peter de Bolla's grippingly difficult chapter 'The Discourse of Debt' in his book *The Discourse of the Sublime* (Oxford: Blackwell, 1989), pp. 103–45.
† James Buchan, *Frozen Desire: An Inquiry into the Meaning of Money* (London: Picador, 1997).

well, I was missing it. In particular it was puzzling that it was precisely when one needed money that it was always hard to find; I remember I was once suddenly switched from monthly to quarterly pay, and filling the gap was a huge problem, greater in those days (when the bank manager wrote sternly if you overdrew by four or five pounds) than it would be now, when banks implore one to borrow as if there were no tomorrow. Much later, if you're lucky, you find yourself not particularly needing anything though within reason able, if you choose, to have it. Money may be Frozen Desire, but when it thaws out Desire may emerge less lively than one had hoped.

James Buchan would agree that it isn't much use talking to economists about these money mysteries, for they will all tell you different things, with little in common except their unintelligibility. He himself clearly does know a lot about all these matters and is pleasantly and even passionately involved in them, though admitting that they are 'diabolically hard to write about'. Apart from a few excited passages in which he has failed to gauge the ignorance of such a reader as myself, he is willing to explain the mysteries in reasonably ordinary language.

There are moments when he becomes poetic about money, calling it an invention at least as great as language, and agreeing with Stevens that you can produce poetry from both. And, just as we are willing or even eager to admire some wicked poets, he has a certain regard for operators who have learned how to manage money on what might properly be called an epic scale. On the whole, though, he decides that money is bad for us, that it can be blamed for much, even most, if not all, our woe. It is the forbidden tree, and that is itself an epic theme. Moreover he dares to hope that in some fortunate future we'll regain paradise and find the tree gone.

In fact it is one of the more enriching aspects of the book that, although the author has a horrified apprehension of the mischief money causes, he cannot help admiring people who have a practical understanding of how it works and a vision of the extraordinary things that can be done with it. This is not just a matter of knowing that to have money is always to be on the point of having more money, because of unstoppable interest, for that is something every small person understands. You have to be great enough to see that once you get the hang of money not mere comfort, security and luxury but the entire world can be yours. People who have mastered that skill can defrost all their desires, and, for a while at any rate, have anything they like, though often this turns out, disappointingly, to be just a desire to have even more money.

Buchan offers a fascinated sketch of John Law, who for 500 days or so 'ruled France more completely than its absolute monarchs'. During this period, in the early eighteenth century, he controlled the country's foreign trade and its national debt, as well as about half of what is now the United States. In his personal possession were a third of the Place Vendôme, most of the Faubourg Saint-Honoré, and the land on which the Bibliothèque Nationale and the Bourse now stand, to say nothing of the American territories, millions in cash, and fifteen country estates. In principle there seems to have been nothing to prevent his owning everything he took a fancy to. He was a gambler, a duellist and, according to Marx, a 'pleasant character, mixture of swindler and prophet'. Buchan shares Marx's admiration. Law thought he could manipulate credit to create a just and prosperous society, and 'he damn near pulled it off'. He had a System, which, to put it much too simply, involved transferring the vast accumulated debts of France from the past to the future. For a time the state, like Law himself, had absolutely no credit limit. The System collapsed in 1720, the year, as it happened, of the British South Sea Bubble, which, though its bursting was a major disaster, was no more than a faint echo of the French experience.

Law was taken up again at the time of the Revolution, when the System resulted in the mother of all inflations, but the principal long-term effect of his dealings was to ruin the monarchy, and pass the wealth of the nation into the hands of the bourgeoisie, thereby making possible, among many other things, the Paris of Balzac and Baudelaire. He had a vogue also in America, where Franklin, for one, understood an important element of his system and could therefore explain how the Americans sustained a four-year revolutionary war without having any secured money – by printing it, and waiting for the inevitable depreciation, which meant that in the long run everybody was compelled to redeem its value.

However, Article I of the US Constitution is not in the spirit of Law, for it insists on gold and silver coin as legal tender for the payment of debts. Buchan thinks that this article had far-reaching and on the whole harmful effects on future American civilization. Since the French dependence on paper also proved disastrous, it seems that, whether you believed Law or didn't, money in whatever form did you little good. No doubt the careers of Trollope's Melmotte and Dickens's Merdle, based as they were on those of gigantic Victorian speculators, pointed much the same moral.

J. M. Keynes, we are told, had apparently never heard of Law, here described as 'the greatest of all Scots', so there is some excuse for me. On the other hand most of us have heard of Michael Milken, of whose Law-like career Buchan offers a vivid sketch. He could 'create money with a single sentence', his salary in 1986 was $550 million, which, on the Buchan-approved capitalization model of Sir William Petty (twenty times one's annual income), made his personal worth about $11,000 million. Just as we are deciding that this is an achievement to wonder at, Buchan adds with some severity that 'fortunes made in finance . . . require little intelligence and energy to administer'. Nevertheless, they provide those who bother to have them with 'an ineradicable sense of election'. Milken, for instance, imagined he could without too much difficulty refinance the debts of the Latin American states and 'become sole creditor to a hemisphere'. For money enables you to 'wish the world'. But Milken was hounded out of the markets and sent to prison. Buchan calls him not a tragic hero but an *idiot savant*. Yet there seems to have been no substantial difference between the way he ran his affairs and the way nations fund their debts and wars. If credit is imaginary you might as well imagine a great deal of it.

The accumulation of money for its own sake, beyond any conceivable need, strikes Buchan as a pathology we all now share; money has displaced 'all other psychological goals', including 'duty, religion, public service, liberty, equality, justice or aristocracy'. Only money is now to be trusted. It is no longer an instrument but an absolute end, 'the God of our Times'. He seems to date this transformation from 1974 and the inflation caused by the quadrupling of the oil price, though many moralists would date it a lot earlier. I admit I am not clear why the debasement of money that occurred in 1974 should make us trust it even more than we did before that date, but, as this author agrees, about some of these matters it is not easy to be clear.

Along the way Buchan offers some very weird examples of what money can be and do: for instance, the currency instituted by Jews, apparently with Nazi connivance, at the Theresienstadt concentration camp in 1943, which is now a collector's item (Buchan has some). Then there is the fact that money can be anything (it is only a sign), from axes, skins, iron, tobacco or gin, to gold bars and electronic impulses. It has no intrinsic value; while barter annuls two wishes, money survives a sale but ceases to be money until it is used again. So it circulates incessantly, creating cities, satellites, populations, millennial domes. It is completely unheroic. Homeric warriors knew nothing about it; they might have saved themselves trouble by using it, but at a considerable cost, for money replaces trust and honour, qualities they valued highly.

Schopenhauer observed that 'other goods can satisfy only *one* wish and *one* need' – food satisfies hunger, sex the needs of youth; these are goods which serve a specific purpose. But money 'confronts not just *one* concrete need, but Need *itself* in the abstract'. Thus it becomes a universal, inhuman answer to what Sartre called *besoin*; or it may even have created that generalized need, which makes it even more hateful. One ancient way of demonizing money was to accuse it of breeding like a sentient being. Aristotle in the *Politics* noted this indecency, the birth of money from money. His word for 'interest' is *tokos*, which means offspring – money out at interest offers a demonic parody of natural reproduction. A couple of millennia later Shakespeare is writing harsh speeches about the breed of barren metal. Usury was condemned throughout the intervening centuries, and often compared to homosexuality, also regarded as a perversion of the act of breeding; but it was practised, as it had to be, under other names. Some methods of money-making were called virtuous, for instance adventuring, which entailed genuine risk; Shylock, who made money breed, and Antonio, who risked his wealth in cargo vessels, argue quite schematically about this in *The Merchant of Venice*. The Church, knowing that credit is necessary and that it cannot be had without interest, made the necessary accommodations.

In a feudal society money had not been important, since that arrangement entailed a fundamentally simple exchange of services or obligations. But in came money, and bonds, bills of exchange, and so on, to corrupt such simplicities. Buchan offers many lively illustrations of the sort of freedom that came with a money economy, and of the cost of that freedom. He is quite impassioned about some of the inventions that made capital supreme, for instance double-entry bookkeeping, which Goethe called 'one of the loveliest inventions of the human spirit'. Its discovery has been compared with those of Newton and Galileo, and Buchan himself, though professing to keep his head, compares it with Hegel's theory of the duality of historical events and Marx's *Eighteenth Brumaire*. It seems that modern capitalism is unthinkable without double-entry bookkeeping. I wonder if this will be as great a revelation to others as it is to me. Equally surprising is the information that the overdraft, or cash credit, was invented by the Royal Bank of Scotland in 1728, previous loans having been secured by land. It is hard to imagine overdrafts having to be *invented*, but they were. And without cash credit there could have been (except perhaps in aristocratic circles which still went in for sumptuary display) no civilization of conspicuous expenditure, no beaux or dandies; and later no middle-class mortgages and credit cards.

What was the position of women in this world of money? Not good in England, which introduced the Married Women's Property Act only in 1882; better in Islam, where a woman retains her property on marriage. Women had to rely on other resources – 'prostitution would seem to be the exemplary form of sexual love in the age of money . . . In taking payment for sex, women free themselves from the authority of home and husband and gain the imaginative liberty of money.'

Buchan can't help loving this imaginative liberty, despite its high price. He is a radical romantic, despising Adam Smith for his selfish bourgeois certainties, cross with Mill for neglecting the imagination, and contemptuous of Keynes for being, at moments, tiresomely ethical about the proper use of money, while admitting that 'the money-motive ... does its job well'. He prefers Dostoevsky, who saw that the true consequence of money was 'the world reduced to a scorching slum, its women to whores, its men to murderers'. And he identifies as 'the great sadness of our civilization' the fact 'that by using money, we convert our world into it. Humanity ... is estranged by money from its natural habitat, without any hope of appeal.'

It isn't quite clear whether this remark is in the full voice of the author or, more obliquely, the expression of a strong anti-money tradition; but in the end he seems to agree with this sentiment. It is, appropriately, expounded in a chapter on Marx, incidentally discovered by Buchan to have been a distant relation of Law's. Here, one feels, is the ultimate source of Buchan's own sombre belief that 'the physical and intellectual senses have been replaced by ... the sense of *having*'. And his book, without losing its sparkle or its power to amuse, grows more and more apocalyptic as its end approaches. There is a very interesting chapter about how the Cold War and other wars were won by money and how the Germans financed their war from 1939 to 1945. But after that he starts opening the seals, and stars fall from their places.

The great change in sentiment, from thinking money bad to thinking it good, even the only good, is described as a catastrophic inversion in the moral sentiments of the West. Money is the expression of our profound unhappiness. It is the great destroyer, the dragon of the Nibelungen. 'Only when we recognize it for what it is and allow interest and profit to fall away can we be at peace with the world.' And the book ends with an allegorical dream: 'Honour pushes Credit away with an indescribable grimace of disgust, etc.' It is a dream on the epic scale:

the Tempter foild
In all his wiles, defeated and repulst,
And *Eden* rais'd in the waste Wilderness . . .

If money is a kind of poetry, a book about money can decently be poetic, too. Wallace Stevens thought that the natural condition of the world was poverty, and that poetry is what we have to make that condition bearable. And, of course, money is a kind of poetry. So, in the end, Buchan deviates from the Stevens position; for he thinks that money, far from being a consolation in our poverty, is precisely what has destroyed the natural condition of the world. Here is Buchan, a lively spirit who in his unregenerate youth has loved money as a means to the satisfaction of desire, turning against it in the manner of Marx in Dean Street, hating and fearing it as Augustine feared the sins of Carthage, writing poetically against it, hoping that at the imminent great turn of time it will somehow disappear and leave us to enjoy the happiness to which our nature entitles us. Meanwhile, however, he seems to be really enjoying these last days, and his pleasure is communicated in this almost inappropriately amusing book.

Darwin's Worms

William Sherlock's *Practical Discourse concerning Death*, published in 1689 and known familiarly as *Sherlock on Death*, was a best-seller in its day and long after. Dr Johnson commended Sherlock's style as 'very elegant'. There was a long tradition of 'How to' books about dying, and, as his fuller title suggests, Sherlock was offering an approach suitable to his own time. I thought of Sherlock when reading this brief new book by Adam Phillips, which might well be entitled *Phillips on Death*, and could also justly be described as very elegant.*

Like Sherlock, Phillips thinks something should be done about death. We need to start thinking about it in a wholly different way, and with the help of Darwin and Freud he can get us started. He weaves the counsel of these sages together with much art, for it is part of his plan to make the contemplation of death an enjoyable, even a sublime, experience.

At the lowest practical level Phillips advises us to regard death as a satisfactory as well as an inevitable terminus, and to stop wanting it to be other than it is, either by supposing it isn't the end or by regarding it as something for which in one way or another we should live; as if lives were the material of fictions dependent on that end. He is keenly pro-life, and quotes, ultimately with approval, what John Cage said in response to a complaint that there was too much suffering in the world, namely that on the contrary there was just the

* *Darwin's Worms* (London: Faber, 1999).

right amount. This is theodicy with God left out, or replaced by 'Nature'. The argument here is that Darwin and Freud so redescribed nature that we ought to be able to forget the old regrets about transience and accept an ephemeral existence, suffering and all, as a source of joy.

For Freud the neurotic's project (and 'neurotic is his jargon for an ordinary person') is 'to have the right amount of suffering'; neurotics provide it themselves by feeling inescapable guilt on account of repressed desires. For Darwin existence is a losing struggle against scarcity and extinction. But in the end these wise men tell us to be glad about this situation, to value existence though haunted by a knowledge of loss. They make life more bearable by redescribing its conditions, finding the sublime in the impermanent, and abolishing the idea of immortality as an enemy of life. Phillips wants as much as anything to acknowledge, even more fully and subtly than Freud himself did, the true force of that belated fiction the death instinct, and to accept death as an 'organizing principle'.

This is to make the book more preachy than it is, but it does have a homiletic aspect, masked by the subtlety and force of the prose. Phillips has always liked to offer readers the chance to watch him thinking things over in his own stylish and epigrammatic way, and can often surprise them by making original a perception they know not to be as new as it sounds. Why do we expend so much of ourselves on lamentation, on whining about our condition? 'After all, nothing else in nature seems so grief-stricken, or impressed by its own dismay.' This is well said, the last phrase new and memorable, though the point is really the one Whitman made in more homely terms by contrasting people with animals, not one of which 'is respectable or unhappy over the whole earth'. Here it sounds new partly because it is freshly, elegantly expressed, more because we are uncomfortable without some dismay and find it a strain to do without it. As Phillips puts it, we have 'misconstrued our needs'.

His sages will help us to think of death as the exemplary fact, 'the fact that lures us into fictions' which we should not need since, rightly considered, the fact, unadorned, simply makes life intelligible.

Darwin and Freud make death count in a new way by keeping it secular and finding a wholly secular, this-world language for it. We can be more than half in love with easeful death; correct thinking makes it an object of desire.

The chapter on Darwin concentrates on his studies, early and late, of the earthworm, his celebration of the incessant labour of the millions of creatures who make the earth inhabitable, 'contingently hospitable', by sustaining its fertility. This is the stuff of a new kind of epic, in which the gods and heroes have been levelled with worms: 'Darwin', says Phillips, 'wants to justify the ways of worms to Man.' His delight in the worm is like that of an anthropologist discovering a new tribe.

Worms make possible the agricultural efforts of humanity. Through the bodies of worms the earth is reborn again and again. What difference would it make to our lives if we were to think seriously about worms? Darwin hints that we should have to revise our assumptions of hierarchy, our relation to God as well as to the worm, and we might be tempted to reconsider ideas of political and social order that reflect those assumptions. We should have to think again about our natural status, about how lucky we are that nature is 'contingently hospitable', even though there is nothing contingent about our inevitable extinction. What we have – and as it is the only thing to be glad of we should be glad of it – is the kind of life that the inevitability of extinction makes possible. As Wordsworth remarked, quite in the Phillips mode, we are called on to exercise our skill in living not while situated in some utopia

> But in the very world, which is the world
> Of all of us – the place where, in the end,
> We find our happiness, or not at all.

That very world is the world of the contingently hospitable, and also of the earthworm, to whom, presumably, it is also hospitable in the same mode.

The second of Phillips's this-worldly arguments concerns Freud. It starts out not from Oedipus but from Freud's distaste for biography.

He destroyed his early notes, years of work, in order, he said, to frustrate future biographers. He wanted to be enigmatic, the Sphinx not Oedipus. Moreover he believed that biographers get everything wrong. He wanted to watch them going astray as they tackled his life without a hope of telling the truth about it, though the destruction of the papers suggests that he silently feared they might, with the aid of such evidence, get closer than he would like. Above all he wanted to be the sole possessor of his life story, the secret truth about how he came to be what he was or became. No one else but the subject can tell that story, and only the teller should have the right to tamper with it, which is something everybody does. In any case the truth cannot be told except obliquely, as on the couch, and biographers are not in the business of obliquity.

What tampers most successfully with the truth, by spoiling or stopping the story, is the death instinct – 'that part of ourselves that determinedly wishes not to know'. Biography, for Freud, was 'a monument to the belief that lives were there to be known and understood, rather than endlessly redescribed'. Phillips redescribes the death instinct; contesting Freud's too nihilistic account of it, he describes it as an agent of happiness. In *Beyond the Pleasure Principle*, Freud observed that in earlier times it was as easy as it was necessary to die; but we now have to reach death by what he calls 'complicated detours', denying that it is the simple aim and end of life, wanting it to be coherent with the idiosyncratic story one tells of one's history. It is in this sense that death is, to the unconscious, an object of desire.

Here there seem to be two distinct historical perspectives, one very long term, reaching back to a primitive desire of the animate to relapse into a primal inanimateness, the other quite short and requiring the invention of myths to explain what consciousness fears, even thinks unfair: survival beyond the conditions of survival imposed by nature. 'Inexplicable thy justice seems,' complains Milton's Adam, still in the 'delicious garden' he must shortly leave, still not knowing what death means. But he says he would not fear insensibility: 'how glad would lay me down/ As in my mother's lap' – a curious remark, since he is imagined to have had neither mother nor childhood, not at all an apt analysand. What he dreads is 'deathless pain', 'a living death'.

Milton's Adam is worth mentioning here as evidence that a strong pre-Freudian imagination could present a version of the death wish in a man inhabiting, for the moment, a garden offering total, licit, sensuous pleasure, about to be lost for the sake of inexplicable justice, for the sake of a legalistic contract ostensibly drawn up by God but really by the guilt that necessitates all the complicated detours of our stories about life and death.

These include the stories of loss told by Freud and Darwin, stories made necessary by fossils, worms and coral, and by the denial of primitive desires. Death makes us sad, but maybe this sadness is, as Phillips suggests, merely a bad old habit, arising out of a refusal to live in the world as it is. His sages offer ways of breaking the habit, so we have the machinery to do so. And we are directed to the famous passage in *Beyond the Pleasure Principle* about the baby's game of *Fort–Da*. The baby manages by inventing a game to get pleasure from having renounced his protest against the departure of his mother. Without the mother's departure there would have been no game, no new pleasure. The child is finding not a substitute but an alternative. There is a difficult parallel in the process of mourning, which gives us an experience of transience with which we normally learn to deal. These absences give us pleasure, like the baby's, and also allow us practice for our own absence.

To write about that absence without writing about despair, 'without the refuge of optimism', without assuming that transience is intolerable, was what Darwin and Freud contrived to do. Phillips is forced to the philosophical conclusion that for them and also for him the only world that is possible must be the best of all possible worlds – Leibniz's conclusion, though arrived at by another route. Leibniz made up the word 'theodicy' from the Greek words for 'God' and 'Justice', and the point of this book is that we have no legitimate concern with either.

So this, in the end, is not even a modified theodicy; it is a Darwinian/ Freudian naturalism. It belongs to a world in which reason establishes the facts of natural transience on the one hand and on the other urges us to believe that human conduct is motivated by desires and privations about which we tell ourselves lifetimes of lies. They deny us our happiness. This brave and subtle essay is a declaration of faith in the naturalist notion that we find that happiness here or nowhere, and will not find it here if we carry on being so wrong about death. We are left with the serious question whether this distinguished essay could, like Sherlock's, be called a practical discourse.

The Search for a Perfect Language

This book* is published in a series called 'The Making of Europe', of which the general editor is the eminent medieval historian Jacques Le Goff. Other volumes are by Peter Brown (*The Rise of Western Christendom*), Aaron Gurevich (*The Origins of European Individualism*), Ulrich Im Hof (*The Enlightenment*). Some nine volumes have so far been published or are on the point of publication, and there are many more on the way, all by distinguished authors. The series is published in five languages. It may be unfair to say so, and it doesn't appear that there is subvention from Brussels, but the augustly institutional air of such enterprises can be rather chilling, and some Eurosceptics may suspect this one of being high-class cultural propaganda for such projects as the single currency and other malign Eurocratic plots. Yet Professor Eco's book, though it naturally has something to say about the problem of a common language, says nothing whatever about common money. A few pious pages near the end are devoted to the desirability of achieving a Europe 'where differences of language are no longer barriers to communication, where people can meet each other and speak together, each in his or her own tongue, understanding, as best they can, the speech of others'.

There is no sign here that the Professor considers a common language as even a remote possibility. The five publishers associated with these books were evidently equally sceptical about the possibility

* Umberto Eco, *The Search for a Perfect Language* (Oxford: Blackwell, 1999).

of issuing them in some supranational dialect, and sensibly decided to risk the well-known difficulty of accurate translation rather than commission works in Latin or Esperanto. As it happens, James Fentress has translated Eco's book into English of remarkable elegance and resource, though it is true that readers without French and a smattering at least of Latin, and maybe some elementary Greek vocabulary, may find it hard going. Translation of passages and titles in these languages is sporadic, and Eco, like some of the very dead scholars he discusses, is very fond of unusual words like 'pasigraphy', 'pasilaly', 'pansemiotism' and 'steganography'.

Again like those dead scholars, Eco is polymathic to an extent most will regard as practically inhuman, and he has never seemed more so than in this well-organized, sprightly and exhaustingly informative book. He would hardly mind being compared with one predecessor in particular, the encyclopedic and fluent seventeenth-century Jesuit Athanasius Kircher, who wrote huge books on virtually everything – the Tower of Babel, Egypt and universal music, as well as the treatise on Universal Polygraphy that is part of Eco's present concern. Kircher was very famous in his day, and so were many other scholars here considered, but unless, like Leibniz, they achieved distinction in studies less vulnerable to the action of time they are now forgotten except by scholars interested in forgotten scholars.

The reason why is simple: unlike the calculus, a demonstration that Hebrew or Dutch or French is the closest surviving relative of an original universal and perfect language is unsustainable and useless; and so, in the end, is the rival notion that language can be reduced to a kind of algebra. But Eco is writing history of ideas, and since dead ideas can have interesting histories he loves to explain just why it was that the work of Kircher and other laborious researchers was rubbish in the end. If, as occasionally happened, some benefit quite fortuitously and unexpectedly accrued, he rejoices to tell us what it was. As I read I found myself thinking of some lines John Donne wrote about futile alchemical experiments:

> . . . no chemic yet the elixir got,
>> But glorifies his pregnant pot,
>> If by the way to him befall
> Some odoriferous thing or med'cinal . . .

Kircher, writing before alchemy was quite discredited, would have had no trouble understanding this point, but the pregnancy of his own pot was a false one, as Eco demonstrates, and nothing medicinal ever came out of it. What one feels after examining Eco's own pot, which is for the most part and necessarily a history of failure, is that it contains many interesting materials but was in any case never meant to arrive at the elixir – a solution to the polyglottism of Europe in particular and of the world more generally – and moreover that it produces, by the way, nothing very medicinal. That doesn't mean it isn't a virtuoso performance; so was Kircher's.

For all manner of reasons, generations of scholars and visionaries have wanted to overcome the confusion of tongues that prevents fruitful understanding and promotes distrust between peoples. One line of inquiry was devoted to the recovery of the language used by Adam and his descendants up to the catastrophe of Babel – a language presumably perfect, because it was communicated directly to Adam from God. Hebrew was an obvious contender, but Egyptian, Irish and Chinese also had their supporters.

The quest for a necessarily perfect ur-language being more and more obviously a wild-goose chase, some preferred other ways of tackling the problem of communication across language difference. The most notable of such projects were the artificial languages devised in the seventeenth century – attempts at a philosophical language 'designed to express ideas perfectly'. Efforts of this sort persisted through the years, and Eco places under the same description such nineteenth-century artificial languages as Esperanto and Volapük. Since these languages were put together from already existing words, Eco calls them a-posteriori constructs, to distinguish them from the earlier a-priori 'philosophical' languages of such writers as Wilkins and Leibniz. He also has a category of 'magic languages', which claimed 'mystic effability' but were available only to initiates, as were steganographies or secret languages, of which the descendants are modern codes and ciphers. As a sort of appendix to all this Eco scrupulously lists various kinds of invented languages that on this occasion he declines to discuss: oneiric and fictitious languages (invented by Rabelais, Orwell, Tolkien, and presumably by Anthony Burgess in *A Clockwork Orange*), jargons, formal constructions like the language of chemistry, and sundry mad inventions by glottomaniacs. He feels, understandably, that he has enough to do without getting into these, though he might have said more about pidgins, which admittedly have nothing to do with the idea of perfection but are particularly good examples of languages providing efficient communication between people not sharing a common language; in fact Esperanto, which he does discuss, has been authoritatively described as 'glorified Pidgin European'.

Eco begins at the beginning with Genesis, and makes the point that the Babel story (Genesis 11) contradicts the tale of the posterity of Noah in Genesis 10, where the sons of Japheth scattered, and spoke 'every one after his own tongue'. So exactly when did humanity lose the divinely acquired language with which Adam named the beasts and presumably everything else that needed naming? When did the fatal multiplication of tongues occur? After Eden, rather than after Babel? The need to know arose from a desire to find a language which, like Adam's, had a direct relationship to things.

The scholars who pondered such questions had copious evidence of the irresistibly fissile nature of language. Writing a version of classical Latin, itself corrupted by age and unnatural use, they, like the sons of Japheth, spoke every one after his own tongue, and among those tongues were the widely divergent versions of Latin developed in Italy, France and Spain. Could one get behind this linguistic diversity to the perfect language that preceded it? We are told that the earliest attempt to make out of contemporary material a new language closer to the original was the work of medieval Irish monks, but it had many successors, and they would show an understandable preference for the languages deriving from Latin rather than Irish.

Eco is of course clear that dreams of a perfect language will always take colour from the culture and politics of their moment. They were frequently associated with a longing for universal peace. Scholars were careful about the timing of their requests for financial support, choosing rare moments when their rulers, the potential backers, were not fighting expensive wars. But, however honourable their intentions, their work could not escape the constraints and prejudices of contemporary learning. For this and doubtless for other reasons, most of the appallingly arduous and virtuously ambitious studies Eco discusses are hopelessly stranded in their own epochs. From where we stand their limitations are easy to see: for instance, belief in the literal inspiration of the Bible was an enormous handicap to linguistic as to other kinds of research, and so was the primitive character of the available semiotics. This, of course, is not a reason to feel superior, since we are equally unable to see our own limitations. But there is no denying that this book contains large amounts of palpable nonsense, briskly and serenely exposed, as well as evidence of great if useless ingenuity.

The cabbalistic writings, founded on a view of the Torah as having originally been a mass not of words but of letters, are an example of this, and Eco devotes an interesting chapter to what he calls 'The Kabbalistic Pansemioticism'. But it is with Dante's exaltation of the vernaculars that we enter a world more like our own. We regularly face the problem that perfect translation from one language to another is impossible. One's own language shapes and is shaped by one's own world, and the differences between languages and worlds are hard to reduce – witness the case of near neighbours like Britain and France. Yet it is only common sense to remember that, despite philosophical and linguistic arguments that suggest the hopelessness of the situation, we have every day evidence that good communication is always possible.

How can this be? We can, if we like, imagine that there presides over the act of translation a virtual superlanguage, which mediates between the source and target languages. Walter Benjamin had something like this in mind when he talked about a 'pure language' that lies behind the impure ones we use. Dante's notion is somewhat different, but it seems to belong to the same family. Deferring to learned convention, he wrote his treatise *De Vulgare Eloquentia* in Latin, but its subject was 'the illustrious vernacular', a virtual language standing above the common vernaculars, though incarnated in the Tuscan Italian in which he wrote his poetry. It is hardly too much to say that Dante is here inaugurating modern European culture. Most of us derive our sense of literary value from the constantly changing vernacular we speak; though we accept its relation to what Dante called the *grammatica*, the relatively unchanging Latin of the civilization from which we descend, we are most at home in the mutability of our own language. Erich Auerbach, in *Literary Language and its Public*, described the formation of a reading public as occurring when a high vernacular – what he called, Germanizing Dante, a 'Hochsprache' – made one reading public of aristocrat and bourgeois, and ultimately made for a literature dominated by the bourgeoisie. Auerbach's point is primarily sociological, but he does have in mind a language constructed from existing vernaculars, and argues that 'even the most oppressed bourgeoisie, the German . . . awoke from the depths of its national amorphousness and, precisely because Germany was not a nation, was able to create a genuine universality, the European internationalism of national diversity and historical perspectivism'.* This new public spoke many different languages but acquired something like a common European spirit. It began to demonstrate the possibility of achieving something rather like the conditions of language and spirit Eco recommends for polyglot modern Europe.

Not that there is a straight road from Dante to our own time. There were many dark byways. Soon after Dante's day there came from Majorca the influential Ramón Lull, a vastly learned friar. He was working on a universal language primarily required for the conversion of infidels; Eco reports that he tried it out on the Saracens

* 'The Western Public and its Language', in *Literary Language and its Public* (London: Routledge & Kegan Paul, 1965).

with so little success that they murdered him. He enthusiastically expounds the combinatorial mathematics of Lull's system, which I admit I don't understand; but over some centuries it interested great men, among them the Platonist Nicholas de Cusa, the mystical heretic Giordano Bruno, and the polymath G. W. Leibniz. In our own time Frances Yates has more than once reminded us of Lull's existence, and of his importance in the history of ideas.

Lull, however, did not prevail, and new-minted languages were eventually to occupy more learned time than the quest for the original Adamic. Yet the old idea that all languages descend from a single mother tongue – what Eco calls 'The Monogenetic Hypothesis' – lurks behind many perfect-language schemes, even those of more recent times. The assumption was that to find such a language would be tantamount to solving the problem that also exercised the makers of artificial languages, namely the need to have at one's disposal words that truly matched the world. Among those who believed that such a language had originally existed, in which case there was no need to make one up, Hebrew was a favoured candidate, but it was known by few non-Jews until the Renaissance, at which time the vernaculars, having acquired national dignity, could be proposed as rivals. By the seventeenth century the goyim had largely given up their advocacy of Hebrew, and eventually the idea of a possibly recoverable primitive ancestor itself began to fade, though the 'nationalistic' hypotheses lingered on; as late as 1868 a Belgian baron was proclaiming that 'Flemish is the only language spoken in the cradle of humanity.' One unexpected but lasting outcome – the equivalent of Donne's medicinal accident – was the Indo-European or 'Aryan' hypothesis of nineteenth-century German philologists. Their claim was not that Aryan was the original or perfect language, merely the notional mother of a whole family of languages, from Sanskrit on. There are of course no records of Indo-European, and philologists who invent Indo-European words scrupulously mark them with an asterisk; this virtual language was a pure scholarly invention, but by a further and less happy accident it fostered the development of a destructive racial myth.

Leibniz had thought Celtic was the probable ancestor language but did not seek his answer there, having other ideas about ensuring universal mutual intelligibility. Abandoning a heritage of magical speculations, languages founded on occult imagery, the fake ancient Egyptian of Horapollo, the almost universal cult of emblems and symbolic icons, he went to work as a philosophical mathematician, though still with a touch, it seems, of Lullian mysticism and even of the *I Ching*. Leibniz's invention, a faint anticipation of the computer languages, is an attempt not so much at a universal language (his monadological philosophy encouraged him to enjoy variety) as at the provision of 'a lexicon of real characters upon which the speaker might perform calculations that would automatically lead to the formulation of true propositions'. Eco has much admiration for Leibniz: he failed, but only because projects for a philosophical language always will, since they must always reflect the limitations of the stage of linguistic development that has been reached at the time of the project.

At much the same time, in Restoration England the scientists of the newly constituted Royal Society were also conscious of an urgent need for a rational language. Eco has a good deal to say about John Wilkins, whose *Essay towards a Real Character, and a Philosophical Language* (1668) was the most complete attempt so far at an artificial language. Wilkins was a polymath, an important Fellow of the Royal Society, a man of exceptional and various ability, with a serious interest in all aspects of the new philosophy, but Eco has no difficulty in showing that his vast linguistic project was deeply flawed. In any case the need of the Society was not so much for a universal all-purpose new language as for a new way of writing, plain and un-rhetorical, appropriate to scientific reports.

One logical but farcical outcome of this passion for establishing an exact equivalence between words and things was the language of the Academy in Swift's Laputa, where the virtuosi have decided that 'since words are only names for things, it would be more convenient for all men to carry about them such things as were necessary to express the particular business they are to discourse on'. So Laputans would load themselves and their servants with every object foreseen as a possible requirement for an expected scientific conversation, producing each item at need. Yet despite Swift's mockery the plain prose advocated by the Society contributed to the development of an easy and accessible English style which, in the very long run, became, as they had wished, the lingua franca of international science.

After the seventeenth century we are in a more familiar world. 'The Enlightenment was less concerned with the search for perfect languages than with the provision of therapies for already existing ones.' Nevertheless the old dream refused to die altogether. Eco records the claim of the late-eighteenth-century Count Antoine de Ravarol that the perfect language already existed and that it was, obviously, French, with its sweetness and harmony, its logical word order, and the grandeur of its literature. Eco cites other interestingly foolish claims of the kind, but he also quotes the Italian poet Leopardi as remarking, half a century or so later, that a universal language must necessarily be 'the most enslaved, impoverished, timid, monotonous, uniform, arid and ugly language ever'.

The descendants of the a-priori artificial languages are such as BASIC and Pascal, perfect indeed within their severe limits (they reflect only Indo-European grammar and lack 'effability'). Of course they do nothing to ease the problem of interlingual communication outside their limits. The problem remains; and if one thing is sure it is that nobody would endorse the choice of any one existing language as an agreed auxiliary international language. Eventually it began to appear that a new language, based on and resembling as closely as possible all the others, would be the only answer; and it was also sensibly conjectured that it would need to be heavily promoted by some international authority.

Many such languages have been proposed, and Eco gives several examples of their enjoyable absurdity, like '*Con gran satisfaction mi ha lect tei letter . . . Le possibilità de un universal lingue pro la civilisat nations ne esse dubitabil*', which is Mondolingue, 1888. Some sound a little like *Finnegans Wake*, but Joyce was looking for maximum resonance from natural language, whereas these attempts seek on the contrary to reduce ambiguity. The Italian mathematician and logician Giuseppe Peano proposed in 1903 a language that was Latin without declensions; it didn't work, and for all the eminence of its maker became one more curiosity in the history of such ideas.

Esperanto gets some serious and mostly admiring attention from Eco, for it is still thriving and has even acquired its own literature. It is an old point that any universal language would itself be changed and diversified by its users, as all language is; but Esperanto, suggests Eco, might partially escape this fate by remaining obstinately an *auxiliary* language. Yet it has been around for over a century and does not seem likely to gain universal support and acceptance. That English is the nearest thing we have at present to a universal auxiliary language is due to historical accident rather than inherent suitability; had the other side won the Second World War we might, Eco speculates, be having our international conversations in German.

Oddly enough, he has nothing to say about Basic English, though it looked extremely promising to many intelligent people in the pre-war years. It is, or was, an experiment in an English tradition stretching back to the early days of the Royal Society; it was well propagandized and supported by men of the calibre of I. A. Richards, who worked with C. K. Ogden to devise it, and William Empson, who spent a lot of time on it. Churchill and Roosevelt gave it some wartime backing. The main object was to reduce the lexicon of English to 'a scientifically selected vocabulary of 850 words'. Ogden, who thought this could be done, allowed that short additional vocabularies could be added to cater for minority interests and specialist fields of study. The Chinese showed interest, urged on by Richards, who remained an intellectual hero to them long after he had passed the peak of his celebrity in the West. But the chances of the whole world agreeing to use a modified form of one national language must always have been small, and the post-war explosion of nationalistic sentiment diminished them further. Yet English, in unsystematically reduced forms, has had considerable post-war success, and BASIC (an acronym: British, American, Scientific, International, Commercial) might have been more useful. One would have liked to have

Eco's comments on this failure. At a guess, he would find BASIC tainted by nationalism, and rather clumsy in use, for it makes a few verbs like 'get', 'make' and 'do' work much too hard, and the scanty permitted vocabulary must often be under strain. According to the *Oxford Companion to the English Language*, the *Oxford English Dictionary* records 18,416 senses for the 850 words of the BASIC vocabulary, almost 18,000 of them undesirable in an avowedly minimalist language.

However, this admirable book records enough failures already, and, as Eco remarks in his introduction, the subject is so close to inexhaustible that he repeatedly finds in antiquarian catalogues and bookshops works hitherto neglected in the colossal bibliographies of existing books on the subject; so he felt obliged to 'proceed by a campaign of deliberate decimation'. Most readers, fully convinced by him that further search for a perfect language, of whatever kind, would be futile, will add to their expressions of gratitude for that demonstration another congratulating him on the decision to discuss not all the failures but only a selection that struck him as exemplary.

The Sea, the Sea

Alain Corbin is a prolific new-style French historian, and these books* are notable contributions to an interesting genre he describes as 'the history of sensibilities'. *The Foul and the Fragrant* created something of a stir some years ago when the translation appeared in hardback, partly, I suppose, because no respected historian had ever before written so much, and so explicitly, about shit, which, as more sanitized historians had omitted to specify, occupied in former times the worry-space now claimed by nuclear waste. And by reason of its natural properties it had much greater power to compel contemporary attention.

Corbin's documentation, collected from a huge variety of sources, the academic equivalents of Dickens's dustheaps, is impressive as well as disgusting. Even the pages on perfumes tend to dwell on their excremental origins, though part of the story is the adoption, by persons of refined taste, of fragrances derived from flowers rather than civet cats. The malodorous effluvia of human 'excretory ducts' – 'the hairy area of the head, the armpits, intestines, bladder, spermatic passages, groins, the gaps between the toes' – also came to be deprecated by the upper classes. Since the activity of these ducts was used as a measure of individual and racial vitality, doctors could at one time maintain that dirt was good for patients deficient in animal

* *The Lure of the Sea*, trans. Jocelyn Phelps (London: Polity Press, 1994), and *The Foul and the Fragrant: Odour and the French Social Imagination*, trans. M. Koshan (London: Picador, 1994).

vigour. They condemned 'the thoughtless use of water', warning against 'the luxury of cleanliness', especially pernicious to women in childbirth. It is impossible to read this book without marvelling at the rich blend of credulity and chicanery that characterized medical practice, and at the docility with which patients submitted to manifestly absurd and even injurious 'cures'. The doctors, as we learn from *The Lure of the Sea*, were just as crazed and just as authoritarian when they decided that the sea, like filth, had therapeutic possibilities, preferably to be exploited with the maximum degree of discomfort to the patient.

The Foul and the Fragrant has chapter headings like 'Air and the Threat of the Putrid', 'Redefining the Intolerable' and 'The New Calculus of Olfactory Pleasure', so one may expect few concessions to the hilarity that sometimes marks lay responses to disorderly ordure. Freud was unusual in devoting some attention to the relatively feeble olfactory powers of human beings; and philosophers, as Corbin remarks, have tended to ignore the sense of smell on the grounds that it has little to do with thinking, and smell when strong is associated with animality. Kant excluded it from aesthetics. Yet there were those who, shrewdly noting the proximity of the nose to the brain, emphasized its power to warn of 'the presence of miasmas', and to enable man alone to value the fragrance of flowers. Discursive contradictions of this kind are meat and drink, or offal and stagnant pools, to Corbin, and by describing the evolution of social attitudes to olfaction he is carrying out a plan to give smell some of the authority so long usurped by seeing and hearing.

He chooses a time when there was a lot of it about. Corpses, tanneries, serried banks of latrines, vast and leaky urban cesspits contributed their dangerous miasmas. The corridors and courtyards of Versailles were 'full of urine and faeces'. Unlucky Montfaucon was 'the epicenter of stench in Paris'. Corbin's gusto as he piles it all on is an indication of his pride and pleasure in the historian's craft, and of his hands-on approach to the subject. Like the doctors whose bizarreries he describes so fully, he has taught himself 'to smell reflectively'. Much in the manner of their ancestors, the scientists of

Swift's Laputa, they devised experimental methods of collecting and analysing farts; with a philological ingenuity worthy of Molière's physicians they invented the male *aura seminalis*, of which the smell stimulates women, while affirming that the sweaty garments of women enchanted men.

This professional interest in smells was natural enough in an age when the stink of hospitals, ships and prisons could knock you down as you passed by. But the pampered modern reader may feel a certain relief on arriving at the point, in the middle of the eighteenth century, when 'odors ... began to be more keenly smelled'; thresholds of tolerance were lowered, and it became self-evident that something needed to be done about improving the situation. Corbin attributes this change in perception, in part at any rate, to the influence of scientific theory, but without suggesting that scientific theory was correct. Most of it was Laputan; but, as he remarks, historians of science, interested in success, have largely neglected the history of scientific error.

The demands for improvement came not from the masses, who long remained indifferent to the quality of their air, uninhibitedly doing their shopping or churchgoing in the fetid atmosphere of rotting bodies. But their betters were developing a 'new sensibility', so the commonplace horror of cesspool-emptying was regulated, and there were other improvements initiated by the authorities. The best people used more delicate scents in their rooms and on their bodies; and cautious washing with soap was now recommended, although wholesale bathing was still under suspicion. Of course working people did not need to wash, as sweat cleansed their pores. No doubt human beings still made their personal contributions to the general miasma, but city parks were provided for their inoffensive release.

Finding an enlarged market, parfumiers vied to make their scents ever more sensually subtle, and their customers grew ever more susceptible. So, in sympathy, does Professor Corbin, who maintains that a woman smelling a flower wears the facial expression appropriate to lovemaking, and that prolonged indulgence in flower-smelling could even result in orgasm. Alexander Pope had thought it providential that humans were not so made that 'sweet effluvia darting through the brain' could cause them to 'die of a rose in aromatic pain', but the advance of civilization was proving him naive.

However, the main impulse in this modified smell discourse (as one might now be encouraged to put it) was towards the practice of deodorization, of both the body and the city. As to the latter, Corbin knows all about new systems of ventilation ('powder was exploded inside the church of Saint-Etienne at Dijon to drive out the stench of corpses'). Individual beds and tombs were newly in demand; hospitals henceforth required patients to use the privies provided. Later, utilitarian considerations advanced the cause, and schemes were devised for the commercial exploitation of excrement and corpses. Somehow this splendid idea of exposing excrement to the play of market forces, possibly of privatizing privies, has dropped out of the discourse of democratic capitalism.

The introduction of chlorine had revolutionary effects, and greatly speeded progress towards 'the bourgeois control of the sense of smell'. That the poor were unable to join in simply emphasized their difference and their undesirability; the 'secretions of poverty' were blamed for the cholera epidemic of 1832, which had several very distinguished non-poor victims, including Hegel.

Progress was still only by fits and starts, and by no means uniform across the whole spectrum of smells. The upper classes were more tolerant of farting than of smoking, about which there was medical as well as class-based disagreement; for some regarded tobacco as a disinfectant, while others, who, as things turned out, have had a more numerous progeny, thought it the origin 'of every disorder'. Despite these disagreements, progress was undoubtedly in progress. It was reflected in domestic architecture and in innumerable enactments controlling public health. A French law of 1848 required that every citizen should have fourteen cubic metres of fresh air. As in so much else, the English led the field in the provision of taps and water closets. Baths and bidets slowly caught on. Meanwhile the pleasures of olfaction reached the heights of super-refinement we associate with Huysmans. Yet the crowd remained obstinately 'loyal to filth'. Corbin enjoys reporting that medical nonsense continued to flourish as these benefits accrued. At bottom the doctors had of course got it right, bad smells are correctly associated with bad health; but the reasons they gave for the connection were usually wrong, and the cures they proposed were wrong almost always. It took a Pasteur to set them on the right track.

Stench was a wonderful idea for a book, and Corbin carried it out with tact as well as zest. Could he keep it up when dealing with the relatively odourless ocean? In fact he does so admirably, digging in new dustheaps of information and detecting at the sea's edge sensual excitements and provocations almost equal to those of the scented boudoir.

The French title of the book is *Le Territoire du vide: L'Occident et le désir du rivage (1750–1840)* and the English title, at once vague and 'popular', somewhat belies the original: Corbin's method and manner are appropriate to serious history. The book has a continuous argument, its exposition diversified by hundreds of illustrative citations and supported by a large body of notes. The detail is not always absolutely correct; for example, Corbin situates the Giants' Causeway in Wales, quotes a remark supposed to have been made by Francis Bacon years after he was dead, and claims that King Lear tried to throw himself off the cliff at Dover. Such are the problems that arise in works of broader scope; the smells, good and bad, of the earlier book are mostly French, but the *désir du rivage* was to a great extent of English origin and nurture. Incidentally I hope and believe he is wrong in stating that the phenomenon of marine phosphorescence no longer occurs; it was still around and beautiful in my seagoing days in the 1940s, and I can't think why it should have stopped.

The book begins with a section called in English 'Unconsciousness and the First Premises of Desire', and it is worth pointing out that this is a translation of '*L'ignorance et les balbutiements du désir*'; the translation is often odd, sometimes extremely literal ('*en tout cas*' = 'in every case') and sometimes perverse. When women began to bathe in the sea at Brighton, we are told, men lined the promenade watching them through lorgnettes. This makes a pleasant enough picture, as of a row of Regency gallants all looking like the archetypal cover picture of *The New Yorker* and staring lasciviously out to sea, but of course the usual translation would be 'opera glasses' or 'binoculars' – the translator uses 'field-glasses' in another passage – though the *OED* does just about endorse 'lorgnettes'. Sometimes the original, itself somewhat pretentious on occasion, is distorted into scholarly babble: 'this [the North] was precisely where a new type of recourse took shape, fanned by the temptation to return sincerely to nature' renders *'c'est au nord que se dessine un nouveau recours, que gonfle la tentation du retour à l'authentique nature'*. Where the French speaks of the importance to the ruling classes of their genetic capital (*'leur capital génétique'*) the English says they were concerned about 'the valve of their genes', and even if there's a misprint here the interesting notion of genetic *capital* is obscured. The translator also ventures some rather inappropriate colloquialisms ('the flipside of enlightened despotism' (*'l'envers'*)) and is fond of the verb 'to rehash', which suits rather ill with Corbin's lively but thoroughly academic manner. At Palermo the orchestra at the Marina played popular music for the lower classes until 6 p.m. and then played again, presumably selecting more elegant music, for the quality; but the translation says the orchestra 'tuned up' for the better class of people, with an unwanted implication that they hadn't bothered to play in tune for hoi polloi; the French merely says *'joue alors pour les grands'*. It hardly matters that 'minuscule' is invariably misspelt, or that 'vascillate' (*sic*) is not a good translation of *'osciller'*. But many little botches of this sort amount to a considerable distortion of the whole.

Still, bumpy and awkward as the translation often is, the virtues of the book shine through. Once again Corbin scores by using material other historians neglect: 'a prolific literature including medical case-studies, travel accounts, and descriptions of cure stays [*sic* – *'séjours thérapeutiques'*], abundant correspondence, and constant word-of-mouth publicity all testify to the intense appeal of the seaside'. In a last word on method he attacks what he calls 'Braudelian temporality'. The need, he feels, is to study the ways in which people of the chosen epoch reinterpreted ancient representations and incorporated them in a new ensemble of their own. So we begin with an ancient 'system' that regarded the sea as the consequence of the Flood, a repulsive indication of the partial ruin of the world (there was no sea in Eden, and Revelation promises that there won't be one after Apocalypse). The shore was where the sea was providentially halted. In Classical literature the sea was usually very treacherous, as Horace and Lucretius attest, and of course Odysseus took a long time to get home because of its enmity. It was also, rather vaguely, full of monsters. Ages elapsed before people began to think of it as other than a hostile void, something that made them sick if they ventured on to it.

Corbin attributes the change of view partly to the rise of natural theology and the discrediting of Genesis. The sea, no longer a *vide*, could now be a spectacle; towns like Rotterdam, with their blend of city, sea and countryside, domesticated the alien element, and the bristling masts meant money as well as adventure. Great navies contested control of the sea, and painters celebrated its splendours. Their seaside scenes foreshadowed the later cult of the beach as a place of pleasure.

Before the 'invention' of the seaside holiday there was a long therapeutic prelude, and the doctors flourished on the sea's edge. There they cured, among other things, melancholia and the spleen; and the cure could be nasty. Medical wisdom emphasized the value of shock, so bathing took place in the winter months, and preferably in cold northern waters. Since the fear of drowning was an essential part of the cure, the patients – whether suffering from hypochondria or nymphomania – were violently thrown in. Women and children and old folks were spared to the extent of being allowed into water at the tepid, unmanly temperature of 10° Celsius (50° Fahrenheit). But that was the only concession to frailty. The bathing attendants 'would plunge female patients into the water just as the wave broke, taking care to hold their heads down so as to increase the impression of suffocation'; this should have been good for at any rate a temporary remission of nymphomania. However, Fanny Burney, staying at Brighton, found it pleasant and stimulating to bathe at dawn (20 November 1782). And Corbin suggests that the whole business became rather sexy: 'the mere contact of a bare foot on the sand was already a sensual invitation and a barely conscious substitute for masturbation', he says, though we are not told, in any of the very numerous notes, where this information comes from. He observes other stimuli – there were half-clad women around to be *leered* at through one's lorgnette – and explains that 'the virile exaltation . . . a man experienced just before jumping into the water was like that of an erection'.

All this hyperaesthesia was manipulated by the doctors, who professed to know the exact number of immersions necessary for a cure of whatever it was. The bathers, believing them, carefully counted their dips, 'just as others count their orgasms' and yet others their rosaries. Scores were competitively and boastfully advertised, as by boys at conkers.

The virtues of sea air and sea water were now well established. Corbin devotes several pages to a Richard Townley who in 1789 went to the Isle of Man for his health. He explored the island Crusoe-fashion, and without bathing himself commended its splendid beaches. This reminded me of the bathing machines I observed, though without lorgnette, in my Manx childhood. Horses towed them a few yards into the water, and female bathers, shrieking faintly, descended their steps into the ocean. Of course by that time Douglas – modelled on Blackpool as Blackpool was modelled on Brighton, but having the advantage, or disadvantage, that you had to undergo a rather thrilling sea voyage to get there – was already a proletarian resort; but there was a residual beach decorum, soon to be abandoned, as it may have been already by the ruder masses elsewhere.

Corbin somehow missed those extraordinary late-Victorian photographs of beach behaviour, taken by Frank Sutcliffe with concealed cameras. They might have helped him to illustrate what went on after the seaside holiday was invented by the toffs, and then democratized. No doubt there are lots of scenes in Victorian novels which give an idea of the mixture of manners on Victorian beaches; there is one in Trollope's *The Way We Live Now*.

Meanwhile the ocean offered images of the fashionable sublime to some, and erotic satisfaction to others, with whom, as we have seen, Corbin amiably sympathizes ('the dream of vanishing into the waves like an act of slow penetration'). The beach was now both an 'erotic site' and a mothering one, at any rate for francophones (*la mère = la mer*). Occasionally one is left to wonder how the Professor knows all these things, but for the most part evidence is abundantly provided, as for the peculiar pleasure to be had from watching sailors drowning as their ships sank near the shore. This gratification might be supplied by paintings, but with a bit of luck a holidaymaker might be in just the right place to enjoy the real thing. The chance of a good wreck within view of the beach was regarded as 'one of the tourist attractions of a coast'. Corbin mentions several shipwrecks known to have given keen pleasure at Ostend and Weymouth.

So the beach moved out of the therapeutic into the hedonist mode. The move was led by the aristocracy, or '*les grands*' as Corbin calls them, but the people soon followed, and to spend some time at the seaside became a necessary part of even the millworker's life. The phenomenon of the English 'wakes' he doesn't discuss, yet it was an interesting bit of industrial history: whole populations transferred themselves homogeneously to crowded beaches and lodgings with postcard landladies, their factories closed behind them – surely one of those 'practices' which arise from the altering 'discourse' of an epoch, though perhaps not in France.

As the author knows well, there are many aspects of his topic that he has not been able to consider – the importance, for example, of new forms of transport, the trains and boats that brought the masses to their favourite beaches, which have in turn lost favour because the airlines can now get the masses to those Mediterranean *plages* which, as we learn from this book, were in the early days of the seaside holiday despised as less bracing than the colder waters of the North. He may well think he has done enough for the moment, even if the sea, despite his best efforts, proves slightly less thrilling than the filth of the earlier book.

The Lure of the Sea made me consider the elements of my own marine discourse, which seems to contain various vestiges of the historical process: a touch of sublimity, a recognition of amplitude, a vague sense of the *vide* left over from cruising for weeks in an apparently shoreless Pacific; a soupçon of voyeurism; a childhood familiarity with sand and seaweed, tide and storm; above all a sense of being both at home with it and rather frightened by it. Not very sexy, I'm afraid, but even the Flying Dutchman had his Senta, and M. Corbin is sure that there are similar consolations for all who go down to the sea in bathing machines and have their pleasures on the edge of great waters.

A Sea and Its Meanings

Jonathan Raban is afraid of the sea, saying it is not his element, which is probably why he spends so much time on it. He does not claim to be a world-class sailor, though he is obviously a competent one. One good reason for sailing is that, being a writer, he likes to write about having sailed. It is guaranteed to provide alarms and achievements for his pen to celebrate.

In this book* he regretfully parts from his wife and daughter in Seattle and makes his solitary way up the Inner Passage to Juneau in Alaska. The Inner Sea is 'an extraordinarily complicated sea route . . . In continuous use for several thousand years, it is now a buoyed and lighted marine freeway, 1,000 miles long', sometimes as narrow as a modest river, sometimes open ocean. Bits of it sound like hell for a small craft; Raban both fears and relishes 'the brushfire crackle of the breaking wave as it topples into foam; the inward suck of the tidal whirlpool; the loom of a big ocean swell . . . the rip, the eddy, the race'. Controlled insecurity provides the thrill: 'The three-step waltzing motion of the boat, the throbbing strings-and-percussion sound of wind and water on the move, came back to me as an old, deep pleasure. But a pleasure tinged, as always, with an edge of incipient panic.'

One of Raban's epigraphs comes from Conrad's *The Shadow Line*: '"That's a funny piece of water," said Captain Hamilton.' He has many other matters to occupy him, sailing a thirty-seven-foot boat

* *The Passage to Juneau: A Sea and Its Meanings* (London: Picador, 1999).

alone, but he still has an eye for a funny piece of water. Speaking as one who has occasionally seen some funny water, I can say that I have rarely if ever seen its funniness so accurately described as it is here – not by Conrad, not by anybody in Raban's own *Oxford Book of the Sea*. For spectacular accounts of extreme conditions (such that Raban's boat could not possibly have survived to let him tell the tale) I might choose Richard Hughes on hurricanes, but for all less overwhelming though still astonishing manifestations of troubled water Raban must surely be the man.

Auden wrote about 'the pluck and knock of the tide', which is a good but tersely elementary way of talking about water in action. Raban, voyaging on this strange sea, encounters on the one hand ocean conditions, the vast Pacific swell underlying whatever may be the disturbances brought by local weather or current, and on the other the extreme turbulence of water in narrow gorges, of deadly whirlpools in straits. There are huge submerged dead logs that would tear the boat asunder, and whales suddenly surfacing, with shock waves that could nonchalantly capsize a craft like Raban's, far frailer than the *Pequod*. This water, beautiful and full of menace, is here rendered in exact prose.

To show that the writer knows more about these matters than mere ignorant observation of surfaces could supply, one might consider this elegant little disquisition on waves:

In the making of waves, first the air 'deforms' the water, which then begins to 'perturb' the flow of air across it; and it is out of this delicate intercourse between the elements that the wave is born. As the ripple turns into a wavelet, its slight convexity gives the wind something to shove against, and soon the wavelet develops a leeward face and a windward back, with a growing differential between the weak air pressure in front and the strong air pressure behind. The unstable air, given these sudden inequalities of pressure, helps the wave (as it now is) to climb: the water's line of least resistance is to go upward as the energy of the wind is transferred to the sea . . . Seen from the cliffs, the sea might have looked as evenly arranged as the strings on a harp – the lines of white-caps running parallel at intervals of sixty feet or so. Seen from the wheel of a small boat, it presented quite a different aspect. Each wave in the train carried a multitude of smaller deformities – nascent waves bulging, heaping, trying to break as they rode the back of senior waves in the system. Many-angled, climbing every which way, they turned each square yard of water into an unruly brew of shifting planes and collapsing hillocks. Wherever the wind found an exposed surface, it raised tiny wrinkles of waves awaiting birth.

This is unaffected, accurate poetry. Sometimes the style is more conceited but still elegant: 'The boat sauntered ... through ... a scene of spent turmoil, like the tumbled sheets of an empty bed, with an appropriately salty, post-coital smell of bladderwrack drying on the rocks.'

There is a minimum of jargon. Raban rarely uses landlubber-baffling language, though some may find they have to guess or look up what is meant by 'scandalizing' a sail, or by terms like 'the cabin sole' and 'advection'. Such is the language of sailors, even sailors with other cultural attainments firmly associated with dry land, like a love for Mozart as played by Gervase de Peyer, a taste for painting and for wine, an ability to do the *Times* crossword in thirty minutes. An unusually large library accompanies him to sea. Being in no particular hurry to commit himself to the deep, he leads the reader seawards with talk of tackle and the chat of Seattle fishermen lounging at noon. Then he writes about his books. All in good time he ventures on to the 'magnificently eventful' sea.

So this book is in some respects rather superbly self-indulgent. It has a curious structure: Raban's voyage has a sort of ghostly double, the voyage of *Discovery*, commanded by Captain Vancouver, which sailed from Falmouth in April 1791. *Discovery* proceeded via Cape Town, Australia and New Zealand, Tahiti and Hawaii, to the north-west coast of America, where Vancouver was to chart the coast and the Inside Passage, for the most part unnecessarily, for the job had in large part already been done, though Vancouver did have the pleasant job of assigning good British-imperial names to geographical features. In due course he was to achieve that nominal immortality himself, and his lieutenant is remembered in Puget Sound. Raban has researched this expedition and counterpoints it with his own. The result is a vivid imagining of life in a man-of-war at the period: always uncomfortable and nearly always boring, with tension constantly increasing between the rather low-bred, ugly, choleric captain and his patrician midshipmen, for whom the cruise seems to have been a sort of substitute for the old Grand Tour.

Vancouver, lacking aristocratic ease and natural authority, felt obliged to assert himself in other ways, as he did when, disastrously, he had one of his midshipmen, a cheeky young nobleman, flogged. He was to suffer for this mistake much later. His was an unhappy ship, made so by personal incompatibilities compounded by cultural differences. The young men, influenced by Burke's fashionable treatise on the Sublime, were in search of rugged scenery and 'delightful horror': Vancouver was interested in filling his pockets (not unusual in the Navy of the time and indeed later), and, more virtuously, in the search for the secret of longitude.

He favoured the method of lunar distance, and since it involved difficult observations and complicated mathematics this discipline was not to the taste of his young officers. The method will be familiar, at least in principle, to readers of Dava Sobel's *Longitude*, in which John Harrison the clockmaker is the hero of the urgent but endlessly protracted quest for a method of accurately determining longitude (so essential to expanding maritime power). Sobel casts the Astronomer Royal, Nevil Maskelyne, firm believer in the lunar method, as Harrison's rather treacherous opponent. Vancouver, however, was on Maskelyne's side, and so, on the whole, is Raban, who doesn't think much of Harrison's chronometers; apparently they worked only a few weeks before getting out of sync with Greenwich. None of this now matters; chronometers and sextants are no longer really necessary, and even Raban's little boat carries an electronic device, the Global Positioning System, that instantly gives mariners their position within yards anywhere on the earth's surface.

Strongly as he approves of this instrument, there is more than a touch of primitivism in Raban's attitude to other seafaring aids. He thinks the invention of the compass was a disaster, causing 'a fundamental rift in the relationship between man and sea'. Since it came into use, perhaps a thousand years ago, it has become the main object of the steersman's gaze; he concerns himself with a geometrical abstraction and no longer has to study the waves and *feel* the sea. And the ocean, once a *place*, with all sorts of things going on in it, is now reduced to a mere space. Since his job is merely to keep steady on a course, the helmsman can be replaced for long stretches by an autopilot, which may be why Raban had time to look so carefully at the waves.

The small ports at which he puts in on his voyage are mostly sad dumps, or Raban makes them sound as if they are. The indigenous 'Indians' do interest him, not least because of their easy and intimate relationship, as it were pre-compass, with the sea. The canoe is not merely a means of transport but a dominant symbol, so that the tribe itself is mythologically thought of as a sort of canoe. Their sea-stories reflect their basic social rules, and their art, on which this book is always interesting, is canoe-based, too. But their lives have been damaged beyond repair by white intruders, to the degree that they have adopted soft white versions of their culture. According to Raban they were never soft primitivists, believing that in the past, before the whites arrived, they had lived in conditions of paradisial natural abundance. On the contrary, they have always treated nature as unremittingly hostile. Versions of the past that seem to suggest friendly intimacy with it are sentimental white inventions they have unfortunately taken over. Watching a 'spirit-dance', Raban finds that the whole show is a mixture of 'animist tribal custom, Shakerism, and Pentecostalism, all refurbished for service in the late twentieth century by white American anthros'. (He is sceptical about anthropologists.) The process of corruption is continued by the big cruise ships, and the swarms of gaping tourists, buying toy totem poles in the sad ports. Meanwhile the loggers, apparently uncontrolled by distant Ottawa, ravage the first-growth forests. There is a lot of disgust and contempt in this book.

As one might gather from these meditations on compasses and Indian culture, Raban's book contains a great many digressions. The main structure, within the outer autobiographical frame, consists of the two parallel voyages, his and the *Discovery*'s, but there are many opportunities to talk about other matters, so we have leisurely passages on Burke, Wordsworth, Turner and Shelley, on a television painting programme, on the maze at Hampton Court. One excursus leads to another, as when the recovery of a drowned woman brings to mind another woman found drowned years ago in the Thames near Chiswick, and a speculation as to what Shelley's body must have looked like when washed ashore at Viaréggio.

Not least because of these often diverting digressions, the book, like the voyage it describes, is longer than it might have been. Raban the sailor is teased for taking so long to make his passage to Juneau. It is tempting but it would be unfair to redirect the criticism to Raban's account of his trip. In fact the voyage was interrupted and delayed by non-nautical considerations; certain disturbances occurred in the life of the author. He had to return home; his father was dying, and he remained in England until the old man died. The funeral is described in detail. It is an occasion for an appropriate piece of writing, like everything else.

Whenever he could, Raban, on his boat or in port, tried to reach his adored small daughter by telephone. Occasionally he also spoke to his busy wife. As his journey ended she joined him in Juneau as planned, but told him she had discovered during his absence at sea that she wanted to leave him. By hindsight one sees that this catastrophe has, in a literary sense, been prepared for, and the terminal conversation is a convincing stretch of dialogue.

The sailor's solo return trip from Juneau is disposed of in a page or two, and the last words, apt and literary as always, show the writer finding his shore legs but now facing 'the rougher sea'. Even this allusion to Cowper's 'The Cast-away' is prepared for by an earlier digression about the poet and his poem, which is certainly a great one, and appropriately both nautical and tragic. So the story of the sailor's personal loss is finally wrapped round the whole story of his achievements as lone voyager, all the fine perceptions, the history, the learned digressions. The sailing stops, but not the writing, which goes on, skilful and resourceful as ever, to the end.

Sylvia Townsend Warner

Sylvia Townsend Warner died in 1978, aged eighty-four. Her first novel, *Lolly Willowes*, appeared in 1926, and none of her later works quite matched its success. In her later years she was probably better known to most people as a name that appeared (as the custom was, and until recently remained) under rather than above story after story in *The New Yorker*; that journal published about fifty over a period of some forty years. She was a copious, elegant and witty writer, and, since she produced these stories rather easily, she came to think of *The New Yorker*, for a long time an indispensable financial support, as a generous old admirer whom she could please fairly easily when she needed to.

In addition to the stories and novels she wrote poetry, and a biography of T. H. White. She also translated Proust's *Contre Sainte-Beuve*, was a devoted correspondent, and kept a diary running to thirty-eight volumes. More surprisingly, she was a musicologist of considerable importance, as well as a knowledgeable gardener and a resourceful cook. Since she also seems to have been a good and sensitive friend, it is fair to conclude that she was altogether a rare and admirable person.

Many pages of the diaries now published* are about her love for Valentine Ackland, the woman with whom she lived for forty years. She had in youth a long unimpassioned affair with an eminent

* *The Diaries of Sylvia Townsend Warner*, ed. Claire Harman (London: Chatto & Windus, 1994).

married musician, whom she gave up when Ackland appeared. They had their ups and downs, of course, and Warner's intelligent devotion to this partner is impressive.

She has been posthumously fortunate; her 'first-wave' feminism has proved of interest to the second wave, and much of her work has been republished. William Maxwell, a friend and correspondent who was for years her editor at *The New Yorker*, published a selection of her letters in 1982, and Claire Harman, having edited the *Collected Poems* in 1983, published a good biography in 1989. A lively study by Wendy Mulford gives a fuller account of the political activities of the 1930s, when Ackland and Warner joined the Communist Party and visited Spain.* So in one way or another it is now possible to know quite a lot about them. Their politics, and the ways in which they put their beliefs into practice, have a special interest to anybody who is baffled by the behaviour of the 1930s intelligentsia.

Yet, despite this rush of information, Sylvia Townsend Warner remains rather mysterious, possibly because she thought women in general were or ought to be so. Candid and high-spirited in male company, she didn't seem to feel, as a woman, deprived, but *Lolly Willowes*, which got her off to such a good start, is about a downtrodden middle-class woman who escapes her male oppressors and becomes a witch. This reminds one of Keith Thomas's observation in *Religion and the Decline of Magic* (1971) that medieval women, if they wanted a hearing, had to become prophetesses ('the best hope of gaining an ear for female utterances was to represent them as the result of divine revelation'), though doubtless at some risk of being taken for a witch. The last publication of Warner's lifetime was, appropriately, a collection of stories called *Kingdoms of Elfin* (1977).

---

* Sylvia Townsend Warner, *Letters*, ed. William Maxwell (London: Chatto & Windus, 1982); Sylvia Townsend Warner, *Collected Poems*, ed. Claire Harman (Manchester: Carcanet, 1983); Claire Harman, *Sylvia Townsend Warner* (London: Chatto & Windus, 1989); Wendy Mulford, *This Narrow Place: Sylvia Townsend Warner and Valentine Ackland, Life, Letters and Politics 1930–1951* (London: Pandora, 1988).

Many of these had appeared in *The New Yorker*, though eventually Mr Shawn, the editor in unelfish Manhattan, called a halt.

She was devoted to the Powys brothers, especially Theodore, who devised such dark and perverse quasi-Christian myths; she even chose to live near him, and so could testify that his descriptions of the Dorset peasantry were 'exceedingly just and clear-sighted'. In the 1920s Powys was still little known, though that was to change when *Mr Weston's Good Wine* won enough esteem to become one of the first sixpenny Penguins. (It even got a perceptible nod of approval from Downing College.)

Warner had a hand in Powys's rise to fame, having recommended him to David Garnett, another fantasist, whose *Lady into Fox* had been a great success in 1922. There seems to have been a market in those years for a peculiarly English brand of fantasy, but any imputation of parochialism must fail: Garnett was a man of wide interests, who wrote poems in French as well as fantasies in English; he was a friend of D. H. Lawrence, and of course his Bloomsbury connection was hereditary. Warner was in touch with that world yet independent of it; she knew Virginia Woolf but condescended to what she regarded as the over-selfconscious *Mrs Dalloway*, and indeed one suspects that she thought of herself, though without vanity, which was not one of her vices, as simply a better writer than Woolf.

Her father was a housemaster at Harrow, and her education – highly privileged, as we may now think – was curiously similar to Woolf's, for it was undertaken, more or less alone, in her father's library. She was prodigiously literate and seems to have acquired the kind of social assurance that allows the possessor the privileges of candour as well as the popularity of complaisance. Her first professional steps were in music; she was an expert on Tudor church music and occasionally comments on performances, some of them made possible by her scholarly labours. She wrote music of her own, and at one point considered becoming a pupil of Schoenberg's, but she gave it up. If Schoenberg doesn't sound quite right for her, the reason may be that one tends to think of her as *echt* English, which is not strictly relevant, since although she was certainly that she was not at all insular, and was familiar not only with the great Tudor composers but with the canon of Western music. She could be critical: Bruckner's Eighth Symphony as conducted by Klemperer 'was like being in a slow train with so many stops that one becomes convinced one has passed one's station'; but she was good also at admiring, as when she writes thus of Stravinsky's *Oedipus Rex*: 'A great deal of the choral writing was almost pure Taverner, the construction that of an early passion. It is really impressive music, it sounds old and cold, a chilly shadow that has never lifted from man's mind.'

Much later she admired Britten, who set some of her poems, and in the days of their widowhood grew close to Peter Pears. She also admired Vaughan Williams (detecting a physical resemblance to T. F. Powys, also to Arthur Machen) and records a significant conversation she had with him while his wife and Gerald Finzi's were buying things in Valentine Ackland's antique shop. He asked her why she had given up composing. She said she had found she was doing nothing of her own. He told her originality was

stuff & nonsense. The essential thing is to go on composing, never mind who it's like. Authenticity, I said, not originality. He gave me a long look, & said, against the grain, Well, you showed unusual strength of mind. But [she said] in my next incarnation I think I shall be a painter. What about you? Music, said he, music. But in that world I shan't be doing it, I shall be being it.

What makes this chat of interest is the composer's bluff unmarked allusion to Donne's 'Hymn to God, my God, in my sickness' ('I shall be made thy music'). Here one senses an almost obsolete culture, or subculture. It is characterized by an easy affection for the Anglican pieties which Warner accepted only as part of a sociolect. Intellectually she had no time for Christianity. She remarks that to her it is the emptiness of a church that is holy, and she writes with much feeling about hearing church music in an unlit King's College Chapel. (On the other hand she might well have been delighted at the news that female parsons have been dancing in Hereford Cathedral and stroking the effigies of bishops.)

Her second novel, *Mr Fortune's Maggot*, catches the religious tone. Mr Fortune is a missionary who goes to an unknown island with the object of bringing Christianity to the hitherto happy natives. He makes only one convert, a boy with whom he falls in love. Having built an altar and ecstatically celebrated the Eucharist, he finally comes to and finds the naked boy kneeling beside him:

He gave no sign of surprise, he did not even appear to have noticed the newcomer. With steadfast demeanour he took from the dish a piece of bread and ate it, and drank from the cup. Then, rising and turning to the boy who still knelt before him, he laid his hand upon his head and looked down on him with a long look of greeting. Slowly and unhesitatingly, like one who hears and accepts and obeys the voice of the spirit, he took the cup once more and with the forefinger of his right hand he wrote the sign of the cross upon the boy's forehead with the last drops of the wine. The boy did not flinch, he trembled a little, that was all. Mr Fortune bent down and welcomed him with a kiss.

Here the rite is removed from religion to magic. Warner's attitude to the supernatural seems usually to be of this kind, the Christian merging with witchcraft and magic, as, in different ways, she let medicine merge into faith healing and astronomy into astrology. There is something rather vaguely upper-class English about this gentle antinomianism, with its nostalgia for the old ways, and its little jokes about religion ('my theory why St. Paul speaks as he does of women: that he knew only church workers'). A diary entry speaks of 'that English mixture of the genteel and the raffish'; another of 'lovely Suffolk, how it combines amplitude with modesty, a model to the English mind'. A sort of cosy grandeur pleases that mind. 'Leaving outer London, seeing the dusk, the clusters of houses lighting up, the rambling line of street lamps, I thought how evening descends like a tea-cosy over Southern England.'

In almost every word she writes one discerns a sort of easy, unconventional correctness, the quality she recognized admiringly as 'breeding'. 'I read *The Winter's Tale* and *wept* for joy. *Breed* coming out in Perdita the moment she's threatened.' Or, nearer home:

Janet ... came in the morning, having done some shopping for us in
D[orchester] & looking, in an old weatherproof jacket, a fisherman's jersey,
black watch trews of much hard wearing, and a pair of short rubber boots,
more elegant, more nymphlike and better dressed than I have ever seen her
look before. It is odd how English breeding blazes as soon as it is wrapped
in clothes of this kind.

The origin of this idea is deep in romance – most handily in Spenser
and Shakespeare (Perdita, Miranda, the boys in *Cymbeline*) – but it
clearly still has a place in this later world of well-bred ladies, doubtless
a little snobbish, though quite unconsciously, who make jam, adore
exotic cats, garden, cook, clean, write letters, and in their leisure
hours frequent Boulestin's or apply themselves to the labours of
literature and music.

It might even be an indication of breeding to have a well-bred
lesbian partner. Warner's was tall, distinguished and boyishly hand-
some; wore masculine clothes and, habitually, a tie. She had been a
London beauty in her youth, and was now a rather disappointed
poet; she drank too much and was often ill. In general she strikes one
as a somewhat formidable companion (celebrating an anniversary
she says, 'I thought we would be vulgar and have champagne'). She
was converted to Roman Catholicism, which Sylvia disliked ('I went
into Valentine's bedroom before she was up, and my eye fell on a
small rosary by her bed, curled up and neat as a snake'), and she
caused Warner, notionally quite permissive in such matters, much
torment by a protracted and agonized affair with another woman.
She was extravagantly loved and, when the time came, deeply
mourned. 'Grief, my sole comfort, do not go,' says one diary entry.

That Warner and Ackland should have joined the Communist
Party is not surprising: it was what almost all intellectuals of their
class and kind were doing or feeling they should do, for what seemed
the best of reasons. The diaries have little to say about Spain, which
Warner fell heavily in love with, though she refused to go back as
long as Franco lived. She had worked in a munitions factory in the
first war, and was ready for militant action in the 1930s. Neither the

243

diaries nor the Garnett letters* have much to say about this period; she was probably too busy to attend to the diaries, and the correspondence lapsed for twenty-three years (1933–55), apparently because Ackland objected to it. Warner worked energetically for the Party, writing for Edgell Rickword's *Left Review*, the *Daily Worker*, the *New Statesman* and other left-wing papers, and running a book-lending scheme for the working class of her Dorset district, thus enabling them to read the works of Engels and the Hammonds. Ackland, for her part, took a break from poetry and wrote a serious study of the condition of agricultural labourers (*Country Conditions*, 1936). They seem to have been rather neglected in studies of the period – Valentine Cunningham's *Writers of the Thirties*, for example, merely includes Warner in various lists of names, without detailed comment.

At the time, though, she attracted more notice, and made herself heard at the famous Madrid Writers' Congress (she and Ackland were the only women in the British delegation). Stephen Spender represented her in his autobiography as 'a Communist lady novelist' with a 'lady poet' friend; she resembled 'a vicar's wife . . . graciously forbidding . . . She insisted on calling everybody comrade.' Wendy Mulford improbably attributes Spender's attitude to 'homophobia'. Since Warner had proposed his expulsion from the Party he had cause to feel aggrieved and may have been getting back at her; but there is nevertheless a certain plausibility in his description.

Nevertheless she was not in Spain merely to play the English lady-Communist, and her novel *After the Death of Don Juan* (1939) is, as she said, 'a parable . . . of the political chemistry of the Spanish War'. A more impressive book, *Summer Will Show* (1936), is also a kind of parable, a story set in Paris in 1848, but with Spain in mind; it has a lesbian element, and ends with the heroine reading a passage from a fresh copy of the *Communist Manifesto*.

No labours on behalf of the Popular Front could quite expunge privilege, or do much to modify cultural assumptions. The Warner–

* *Sylvia and David: The Townsend Warner/Garnett Letters*, ed. Richard Garnett (London: Sinclair-Stevenson, 1994).

Garnett letters are testimony to the culture they shared. They had intellectual as well as social intimacy. This is Warner on writing novels or stories:

First we build our houses of air and geometry. The stairs that no foot can tread go up undeviatingly, and underneath there is a convenient cupboard in which we can house darkness (or coats and hats, just as we please). Then we begin to write and build them of brick. The horror is, not that the bricks are square and solid, but that they are an insult to geometry, not a pure right angle among them, and no more solid than a crumpled mosquito net.

I wonder if writers still write to one another so interestingly. Of course there is also a lot of talk about publishers, but a lot also about recipes, bereavements, cats and why they make love to their owners, the weather, sometimes superbly described. The correspondents are in some ways remarkably alike, distinguished inhabitants of the same distinguished literary parish. Whatever one quoted the other would already know; so Garnett could no doubt identify the source of the lines 'Earth, that grew with joyful ease/Hemlock for Socrates' – which I can't. Altogether one could say of this book what Warner said of the letters of Garnett and T. H. White: 'a splendid record of how two superior mid-twentieth-century minds exchanged experiences and opinions, and were candid with each other . . . you were obviously designed by natural selection to correspond with each other'. Only from time to time may less superior onlookers feel a bit left out; but, after all, our privilege is merely to eavesdrop.

Golding's Last Novel

A publisher's note explains that when William Golding died he had written two drafts of this novel,* and was about to begin a third. The signs are that this might have been longer than the second, but not substantially different. Some necessary editing has been done, on the basis of notes made by Golding in his journal, and there is a page of typescript missing in the middle of the book. It sounds as if the novel is in a form less close to the final than, say, Virginia Woolf's *Between the Acts*, but still close enough for readers to feel confident that they have before them what they need to make a reasonable guess at what Golding was up to; for they will assume that he was, as usual, up to something.

It should prove possible to come up with a better title than *The Double Tongue*, something less suggestive of oral technique in the brass section, or the forked tongue that wicked white men were sometimes said to speak with. The allusion, however, is to the forked tongue of the Python which Apollo inherited when he killed the beast, and so to the phenomenon of oracular ambiguity. Macbeth, having at last rumbled his oracles, says they palter with him in a double sense, and early Christian writers believed something like this of the pagan oracles; to them the old gods and their communications were simply demonic. The pagans themselves were of course aware that oracles spoke ambiguously, though not, as a rule, with the object of harming the questioner.

* *The Double Tongue* (London: Faber, 1995).

The name Pythia was given to the priestesses chosen to relay the oracles of Apollo at Delphi. The Pythia sat on the sacred tripod, suffered violent quasi-rape by the god, and prophesied. As a matter of business she might be required not only to convey the messages she received in her trance but also to satisfy the requirements of important people who might have come a long way to benefit by the divine predictions and were willing to pay the agents well for the service.

Golding always thought strenuously and accurately about detail, but behind its screen he is often obscurely allusive. He is sometimes keen to create a subtext that turns out in the end to have concealed the main point of the narrative, hitherto no more than hinted at. Sometimes he took pride in making this point by a revelation on the very last page. In his earlier work this could take the form of a surprising allusion to some book in which he had found the seed of his fiction, and generally the effect was to reverse the assumptions of that source. Ballantyne's *The Coral Island* is explicitly mentioned on the last page of *Lord of the Flies*. A story by 'Taffrail' called *Pincher Martin, O.D.* makes possible the ingenious final sentence of *Pincher Martin* (Golding's Martin, unlike his more honourable namesake, never even got his seaboots off before he drowned). H. G. Wells's story 'The Grisly Folk', as well as *The Outline of History* as quoted in an epigraph, prompted the remarkable switch of perspective at the end of *The Inheritors*, by means of which, after for so long looking, hearing and feeling with the Neanderthals, we are suddenly obliged to see them from the point of view of their evil successors, us. Endgames like this remind one that Golding was a good chess player.

These ingenuities and the terminal *coups de théâtre* they provide can be seen as hallmarks of the earlier Golding; the later novels also have elaborately contrived endings, but this particular combination was not used again. Of course he still often has some earlier book in mind, though without using it in quite this way, literally as a means to an end that snaps down satisfactorily on the narrative like a lid on a good wooden box. Not, that is, until now; for in this last novel we come on the last page to the shock of an ending very much in the old style.

The story is set in Greece at the end of the first century BCE and the beginning of the new era. Golding, a keen classicist, preferred Greek to Latin. He once asked me if I was keeping up my Greek, and when I confessed that I wasn't asked what I would do all day in retirement if I couldn't read Homer. But he liked the tragedians even more than Homer, and Euripides above the others. One can see why *The Bacchae* appealed to him; he was obviously fascinated by ecstasies, whether in the individual or in the mass, and the plot of that play is quite like some of Golding's, the rationalist bully Pentheus standing little chance against the whole female population of Thebes on a Dionysiac rampage, and none at all against the god himself. However, this book, perhaps surprisingly the only one set in ancient Greece, is about the Delphic oracle, so the more appropriate play is the *Ion*.

It's never quite clear where Golding stops being scholarly and where he is just, by intelligent speculation, making things up; if he could build a cathedral spire in his head he might not flinch from the Delphic oracle. But of course he had a lot of useful prior information, and probably did some reading as well, in such authorities as E. R. Dodds's *The Greeks and the Irrational* and very likely in other learned sources. He would hardly need to take down his Bible and freshen his acquaintance with Acts, here his most surprising, most decisive, source.

Whatever scholars may dig up (and scholars have more or less appropriated him since *Lord of the Flies*, after running its fantastic popular course, ended up in the classrooms of the world), Golding had almost to excess that qualification that epic poets were once urged to acquire, and which modern novelists can to some extent ignore if they choose: the ability to see or to figure out how complicated things work. *Pincher Martin* could hardly have been written by somebody who had not been a watch-keeping officer on a warship on North Atlantic convoy duty. This is not merely a matter of knowing about steering zigzag courses, about withdrawal from the convoy to break wireless silence, about the feel of the thing, the dark bridge and the small binnacle light, and so on; but also of being able plausibly to invent the critical moment at which Martin's intentions encounter an interfering external force he couldn't possibly have taken into account. It may be remembered that, having been questioned by his captain on a recent lapse of attention (he deals with this, characteristically, by telling a plausible lie), Martin invents an emergency and gives the sudden, correct helm order for dealing with it, but too late to avoid the real torpedo that is already, unnoticed, on its way. This enables the author to elaborate one of his metaphysical or ethical cruces: Martin actually gave the order with the intention of murdering his friend Nathaniel, who liked to perch in a precarious position from which a violent change of course at high speed would dislodge him; had Martin given the order a few seconds earlier, as he might have done if he'd been attending to his business and spotted the approaching torpedo, he could have saved his ship and killed his friend in the most innocent-looking way. As it is, though *in extremis* and indeed beyond, he is able to deceive himself by claiming to have given the right order.

Golding knew this sort of thing at first hand; he was a seaman during the war and went on being one afterwards. In this new book we learn as it were incidentally why the javelins of Roman legionaries had points of soft iron, which would pierce flesh but bend on a shield, so that they couldn't be thrown back. Golding wasn't a Roman legionary, but this is nevertheless the sort of thing he can be relied on to know. He was not a Neanderthal man, either, and yet in what may have been his most perfect book, *The Inheritors*, he seemed to know pretty well what it must have been like to be one, to be in all respects alien and vulnerable to *Homo sapiens*, 'not wicked enough to survive'. Having such a point to make entails knowing or imagining in detail how it can plausibly emerge.

Literary intellectuals, who as a rule know nothing in quite this way, have actually counted it against Golding that he did, and let it be known that he did; as if knowing such things must prevent him from knowing others they take to be of greater importance. He can thus be thought of as a sort of minor Wells, or perhaps a minor Kipling. But whatever else he believed – and he had strong, sad views on the world – Golding believed that he knew as well as anybody how the world worked, and also how its workings could best be represented in fiction.

When *The Spire* came out one's first reaction was to be astonished that he seemed to have found out how such a spire could have been built; what the risks were (considering the lack of foundations); what would happen if the absurdly colossal burden of the spire should prove too much, and so on. All this must have been known, or at any rate the risks of partial knowledge on the part of the builder and of the novelist calculated, before the story of the spire, like the spire itself, could be constructed and supported. As a bookish person in an entirely different style of bookishness from Golding's, and one who knows little about how anything works, including of course not only spires but the world, I reviewed the book on its appearance. Pondering the question where had he got all this information about medieval building techniques, I suggested some possible learned sources. Golding wrote cheerily to say that he had done no such reading; instead he had stood at the crossing asking himself how, if he had been charged with erecting the spire, presumably without modern building equipment, he would go about it. It all came out of his head, and inevitably out of his whole body, as in a sense it all came out of Jocelin's.

The importance of all this is that the physical facts as reported conform neatly to the metaphysical agenda; they proceed from the same initial impetus. Consequently one expects that Golding, arriving at last in Greece, after a *bon voyage* longer than that of Odysseus, will know, or seem to know, all about it – know what there is to be known about the oracle in its declining years – and also its place in world history. He will choose an improbable point of departure, as he generally does: the Pythia will tell her own life story. He will then think the story through (knowing its terminus) and, while he will use his knowledge to prevent anachronism (except when it is judged desirable), he will do it on his own.

*

250

Socrates, in the *Phaedrus*, says that our greatest blessings come to us from madness, provided that the madness is of divine origin. One form of madness is prophetic, and issues from Apollo; another madness is of a ritual character and proceeds from Dionysus. The Pythia has little to do with the mad goings-on of the Bacchae; the god who enters her is Apollo. She is thus 'possessed', an 'enthusiast' – and, as Dodds puts it, the god uses her vocal organs as if they were his own. When she speaks she is hoarse, unlike a woman, unlike herself.

Before settling into the sacred tripod and prophesying she bathes in Castalia and drinks from a sacred spring. A Pythia may hold a branch of laurel, sacred to Apollo, or she may inhale the fumes of burnt laurel leaves, or even chew them. This last expedient was judged dangerous, for the laurel was held to be very poisonous; but Dodds says that 'Professor Oesterreich once chewed a large quantity of laurel leaves in the interests of science, and was disappointed to find himself no more inspired than usual.' But laurel, or its fumes, work for the Pythia. Plutarch records that her responses were unpredictably various, that sometimes things went wrong; she might, instead of prophesying, scream, collapse or run away, causing terror among the onlookers. His remarks are remembered in this book.

Lacking any convincing explanation of the Pythia's inspiration, some scholars have treated the whole show as a fraud, the answers written in advance with material derived from what Dodds calls 'an excellent intelligence service' run by her priests or managers. These would also, if necessary, relay the prophecy in hexameters. Dodds himself thought the truth was that the oracle depended on both the Pythia's genuinely mediumistic performance and the manipulations of her staff. He stresses the durability of the oracle, pointing out that faith in it survived a number of discreditable episodes, and waned only when 'other forms of religious reassurance' became available.

This position provides something like the groundwork of Golding's novel. His Pythia, writing in old age, tells how, as a young girl, she showed signs of having paranormal powers, however trivial their early manifestations. They seem to be associated with the menarche. It is not known how the Pythias were chosen, but it could be that such pubescent powers were taken into account. Plutarch says that one Pythia, in his admittedly late day, was the respectable daughter of a poor farmer. Golding's Pythia is also a farmer's daughter, but her father is rich, as well as cold and unsympathetic. He lives near Delphi and has benefited from the 'appropriation' of some of the riches of the oracle. The girl has been taught to read and loves Homer, but is so plain that suitors can be attracted only by the offer of a large dowry, begrudged by her father. A visit from the chief priest of the shrine ensures that this dowry, and the girl, go to Delphi, where she becomes a trainee Pythia, second in succession to the tripod, wielding the sacred besom we have seen in the hands of Euripides' Ion.

The priest is called Ionides – a name which relates him to that earlier tale of oracular deceptions and accommodations ('he wasn't my ancestor but he filled the same position as I do here'). He is even able to show his Pythia the prompt copy of the ancient play in the Delphic library, calling it 'a cruel story'; and later she attends a performance. He is keen that she should use the poetry library as a means to training herself to speak in hexameters. Ionides also arranges lessons in how to make her voice carry. She continues her education by learning the cursive script.

Ionides is another in the procession of Golding's gay men, a civilized Athenian, totally without belief in the oracle he tends, but with a keen interest in its present and future profits. He has one disinterested aim: to exploit the oracle in a bid to free Greece from the Roman yoke, an enterprise known in advance to be hopeless. He has developed a messenger-pigeon service which covers most of the eastern Mediterranean – the intelligence service mentioned by Dodds – and is anxious to encourage tourism. He conceals his nationalistic ambitions, but otherwise is candid though respectful in his dealings with his Pythia. On formal occasions, sometimes with irony, he addresses her as Young Lady; more privately he uses her original name, Arieka. These distinctions are important; Ionides is her instructor but also, when she is in formal or prophetic mode, her servant.

What is about to happen is a confrontation, not at all unusual in this author, between religion and rationalism. The deaths of both the first and second Pythias ensure Arieka's sudden promotion. Unlike Ionides (or Ion, as he is often called) she believes in the gods, though she fears that they have turned their backs on her. She is a more intelligent, less weird devotee than Matty in *Darkness Visible*, an ordinarily gifted young woman, but, especially when menstruating, sensitive to the numen of the oracle. And the numen persists in spite of the fraud and commercialism condoned by Ionides, even when he is cheating by giving prepared, politically adapted answers. But, although he doesn't believe that the god speaks through the Pythia, Ionides cannot finally gainsay the evidence. There has to be this sort of climax: the godhead enters into the female prophet, and the sceptic has somehow to deal with the irrefutable fact of the holy.

So, amid all the cynicisms and deceptions of 'modern' corruption, 'there was something connected with the hidden centre of existence that lay there and sometimes spoke'. The new Pythia gives a startling performance. Later the act grows more routine, though still on occasion inspired: 'perhaps the truth of life and living lies in the strange things women do and say when they are hysterical'. She remembers the cry of the raped Creusa in Euripides' *Ion*: 'O my soul, how can I keep silence?' Meanwhile Ionides is being educated out of total cynicism: 'we must not take our modern wisdom for granted as the final thing'.

When the whole shrine is falling into ruin, and repairs are under consideration, Ionides takes the Pythia to Athens to raise money. Stopping at Corinth on their way, they encounter 'a rowdy element' which can nevertheless be called 'the salt of the earth'. The rowdy element are the early Christians. This is the first move in Golding's endgame. In Athens they do badly at fund-raising, but on the way home they stop again at Corinth and get a major donation. Their pleasure in this windfall is dimmed by well-informed threats from the Roman propraetor Lucius Galba, who knows all about Ionides' intelligence service. And then the gods definitively turn their backs. Henceforth the oracles are dumb, replaced by Christianity; a new age begins; a shame culture yields to a guilt culture. The next phase in the history of holiness is commemorated in the last sentence of the book: the Athenians raise an altar 'to the unknown God'.

This ingenious tale has all the qualities for which Golding has been admired and condemned. He is the laureate of a guilt culture. All the troubles of Sammy Mountjoy in *Free Fall* stem from his seduction and desertion of Beatrice. All the desperate posthumous inventions of Pincher Martin stem from his callous adulteries and his intention to murder. As Jocelin demonstrates in *The Spire*, the most heroic achievements of the spirit are built on a foundation of human filth. *Homo sapiens* is born to guilt as the sparks fly upwards; man is always fallen man. In *Darkness Visible*, Golding's most obscure and impassioned novel, the twin girls are variously dedicated to evil, which as usual includes sexual evil; the hideous millennialist Matty, who emerges from the holocaust of the Blitz and in the end departs into apocalyptic fire, is excluded from sex and is an almost inhuman representative of the holy. Saints, Golding once remarked, are 'the most interesting thing in the world'. 'I don't mean very good people,' he went on; 'I mean people round whom miracles happen.' Here and there, perhaps in reality, perhaps only in art, there are irruptions of the holy, more or less weird agents of holiness: Simon in the first novel, Nathaniel in *Free Fall*, Matty above all. They may suffer and live apart, but they can affect the indifferent and even the condemned – such characters as the child abuser Mr Pedigree in *Darkness Visible*, and the painter Mountjoy in *Free Fall*.

These epiphanies happen, regardless of cruelty, of commerce, of politics, of ordinariness. To make them happen requires both a grasp on fact and a dangerous rhetorical effort. Rereading Golding's novels one is repeatedly struck by the violence of that effort, its defiance of comfortable and conventional literary opinion. Yet for moments at least it seems amazing that work of such force and integrity can be so slightly regarded. Perhaps, as people say, the Nobel Prize is a kiss of death. Perhaps the ambition of these books seems to put them a bit over the top, a bit out of their time. It may be that *Lord of the Flies*, the novel everybody knows, came to seem too easy, and by contrast the rest of the work too hard or too hectic (though that could hardly be said of *The Pyramid* or *The Paper Men* or the long-maturing trilogy that began with *Rites of Passage*). Or possibly Golding's fate has been to become the property of aspiring assistant professors, who have teased out allegories and pestered the amiable author with questionnaires. Their books, however virtuous in intent or accomplished in performance, stand in a battered row on library shelves, unable to avoid looking second-rate, and communicating some of that sadness to their subject.

But it may be that the worst of our impediments is a general unwillingness or incapacity to think about guilt or indeed shame except in terms that minimize individual responsibility. And as for holiness, well, the sight of Matty transfigured, all golden, as he appears to Mr Pedigree, is certainly over the top as far as we are concerned; it belongs, if anywhere, to another epoch or another culture. Dostoevsky is also over the top, but interestingly, safely, crazily exotic. Graham Greene could do saints as well as sinners, and even include miracles, for example in *The End of the Affair*, but he keeps reasonably cool, Catholic and sad about it. Golding had Quakerism in his background, and occasionally he makes us think of the prophet James Nayler running naked through the streets of Bristol: embarrassing, even though nowadays we don't think such conduct deserves the punishment of protracted torture. We can more easily accept Ionides than the growling Pythia, drunk on the fumes of burning laurel, possessed by the god, as she herself remarks, through her other mouth. We have lost the idea of the holy, or retain only the idea that it happens, if at all, somewhere else. So for some or all of these perfectly understandable reasons we are uneasy when this bold writer declares himself. Ionides, whom in so many ways we resemble, nevertheless knew better: he did not believe in the holy, did not believe that the Pythia was inspired, but honoured her all the same.

Philip Roth

Checking through the old Roth paperbacks, one notices how many of them make the same bid for attention: 'His most erotic novel since *Portnoy's Complaint*', or 'His best since *Portnoy's Complaint*', or 'His best and most erotic since *Portnoy's Complaint*'. These claims are understandable, as is the assumption that Roth is likely to be at his best when most 'erotic', but that word is not really adequate to the occasion. There's no shortage of erotic fiction; what distinguishes Roth's is outrageousness. In a world where it is increasingly difficult to be 'erotically' shocking, considerable feats of imagination are required to produce a charge of outrage adequate to his purposes. It is therefore not easy to understand why people complain and say things like 'this time he's gone over the top' – by being *too* outrageous about women, the Japanese, the British, his friends and acquaintances, and so forth. For if nobody feels outraged the whole strategy has failed.

It seems essential to understand the seriousness of Roth's transgressive imaginings. He is hilariously serious about life and death. In this new book* life is represented as anarchic horniness on the rampage against death and its harbingers, old age and impotence. There is only one possible outcome: life can't win against the last enemy; it can at best put on a scandalously good show. So there is really only one way to tell the story – defiantly, facing the outrage of death with outraged phallic energy.

* *Sabbath's Theater* (Boston: Houghton Mifflin, 1995).

D. H. Lawrence, complaining about Arnold Bennett's 'resignation' or 'acceptance' in *Anna of the Five Towns*, said that tragedy ought to be a great kick at misery. Simply to accept misery, resign oneself to the inevitable, is merely pathetic; the kick of tragedy can convert misery into something magnificent, worthier of the living. Such is the kick delivered by *Sabbath's Theater*, not only the adman's 'best' and 'most erotic' but – as a reviewer might on rare occasions be allowed to say – among the most remarkable novels of the age. With his Rabelaisian range and fluency, his deep resources of obscenity, his sense that suffering and dying can be seen as unacceptable though inevitable aberrations from some huge possible happiness, Roth is equipped for his great subject – one that was treated in their own rather different ways by the authors of Genesis and *Paradise Lost*.

We are disposed to think well of some novels because they have the power to make social subversion attractive. Hence the *picaro* of early fiction, or Defoe's Moll Flanders, or the Smollett heroes who 'take to the highway by way of a frolic', or even Lovelace's fatal assault on the virtue of Clarissa. They all, in their measure, provide a touch of the diabolic, in Blake's sense – hell is energy; the energy of the anarch is hellish. Georg Lukács called Thomas Mann's *Felix Krull* a 'satyr play', meaning that it inherits the force of its antecedent tragedies but uses it for comic subversion. Whereas Christian Buddenbrook, however reckless, could not escape the bounds of middle-class propriety, Krull was, from his beginnings as a child thief, a breaker of those bounds – he has to be a confidence trickster in order to live a life appropriate to his imagination. In his impersonation of a young aristocrat, as in all his deceptions, Felix is more 'genuine' than his original, just as Falstaff, with all his lies and all his fake pretensions to gallantry, is more 'genuine' than the Machiavellian royal princes Henry and John.

That such tragicomic or satyr-play outrageousness has, in recent American fiction, taken predominantly sexual forms is largely due, as Norman Mailer remarked in his *Genius and Lust*, to 'the irrigation Henry Miller gave to American prose'. Mailer cites *Portnoy's*

Complaint along with *Naked Lunch, Fear of Flying, Why Are We in Vietnam?*, and even *Augie March* as instances. They all came out of Miller's *Tropic of Cancer*.* But that book was in its early days contraband fiction, passed around in secrecy and not, like its successors, sold in every bookshop. After 1961 it was more generally, and legally, available, and it might be thought that if Miller first irrigated the prose of novelists he later did the same service to the conversation of a larger constituency. For nowadays anybody can say or write almost anything, even in prim Sunday newspapers or in what used to be called 'mixed company'. And consequently the requirement of outrage becomes more difficult to meet. Yet *Sabbath's Theater* meets it. It is essential to Roth's achievement that he can startle hardened readers, make them pause to remark that they cannot remember having seen such language in print before; and to reflect that further outrage now seems close to impossible, the future charges on Roth's imagination almost unthinkably high.

Sabbath is a con man and a thief, inevitably, but cheating and thieving are the least interesting of his antisocial habits, merely incidental to his principal occupation. He has dedicated himself to fucking 'the way a monk devotes himself to God . . . Most men have to fit fucking in around the edges of what they define as more pressing concerns . . . But Sabbath had simplified his life and fit the other concerns in around fucking.' Practising most of the perversions listed in the textbooks, he exploits women (what else are they for?) and despises most people who assume that decent behaviour is a valuable activity. He is wonderfully loquacious, and that makes him more dangerous and seductive, even as a fat old man. In certain respects he resembles the subman Moosbrugger in Musil's *Man without Qualities*, a kind of id on the loose, a threat to society. 'If mankind could dream collectively,' says Musil, 'it would dream Moosbrugger.' Sabbath

---

* A valuable study of the influence of *The Tropic of Cancer* forms the coda of Warner Berthoff's *A Literature Without Qualities: American Writing Since 1945* (Berkeley: University of California Press, 1979).

has a Croatian mistress, whom he has trained to be joyously and insatiably promiscuous; he loves to hear of her sexual adventures, and is delighted when she tells him she has had four men, not including him, in a single day. When she shows signs of conventionality and asks him to be faithful to her he is deeply shocked: 'As a self-imposed challenge repressive puritanism is fine with me, but it is Titoism, Drenka, *inhuman Titoism*, when it seeks to impose its norms on others by self-righteously suppressing the satanic side of sex.' But normally she is his exact female counterpart, the other half of what mankind and womankind might dream if they could dream collectively.

The immediate action of the novel takes place after Drenka's demise, so she is an old man's randy flashback. He continued to desire her desperately after her death from cancer, regularly masturbating on her grave; 'he had learned to stand with his back to the north so that the icy wind did not blow directly on his dick'. And he observed other lovers of hers, bereaved and inconsolable, doing likewise. Some vestige of civility, hardly understandable, prevents him from insulting her bountifully cuckolded and grieving husband, whom he hates as the usurper of that title.

In the present of the book Sabbath is a battered sixty-four, still looking for the next woman, though dirty, ugly and suffering a grossly enlarged prostate. As with Henry Zuckerman in the first version of his biography in *The Counterlife*, Sabbath's fear of impotence is greater than his fear of death; he is fully and furiously aware that 'the prick does not come with a lifetime guarantee'. Borrowing his term from a lexicon he regards as contemptibly symptomatic of the present age of schlock, he turns the tables on politically correct feminism and alludes to his 'disempowered dick'.

Split from his wife and driving from his remote place of exile in New England to New York for the funeral of an old friend, a suicide, Sabbath relives the past. He contemplates the corpse, notes its utter lack of relation to life, and feels, against what has been, or seemed to be, the natural current of his feelings, that his time has come to die. But life, the life of the con man and the seducer, is not easily reduced to resignation and acceptance. Playing the devil in the apartment of another old friend, now hatefully rich and secure, he almost succeeds in seducing the man's wife, makes sordidly free with his daughter's underwear, terrorizes the Hispanic maid, and steals enough money to buy himself a grave plot in the ravaged Jewish cemetery where his family is buried.

The past, as he recalls it, includes the fine time he once had as a sailor, perpetually delighted with the whores of Latin America, and later as a man of the theatre turned puppeteer, using his nimble fingers, now arthritically distorted, to unbutton the blouse of a bold Barnard girl attracted to his pitch on Broadway and 116th Street. This deed gets him into trouble, avoidable but hilarious, with the police. Charged with disorderly conduct, he seems determined to achieve a conviction. 'I am disorderly conduct,' he proudly tells the judge – an accurate and truly Falstaffian claim. In the old New York days Sabbath had an actress wife, long since gone missing; he seems to think it possible that he murdered her, and on occasion claims to have done so, although he also searches frantically for her, as for so much else that has gone missing.

A second wife, despised and despising, is now intoxicated with the teachings and rituals of AA, and has also become a lesbian. She has a dangerous admiration for the woman in the news who cut off the penis of her violent, but at the appropriate moment sleeping, husband. Marital discussion of that case provides some horrifyingly funny pages (the wife is a convinced opponent of circumcision). Fear of a copycat amputation was one of Sabbath's reasons for leaving her; it might have seemed cogent to any man, but in view of Sabbath's penile obsessions it was especially strong for him. On the other hand, to leave her, the breadwinner, meant destitution and homelessness. For Sabbath had been fired from his job at the local college when one of his bouts of telephone sex with a woman student was taped and publicized. (The tape is here, in the true spirit of this outrageous book, transcribed in the grossest detail.)

A weakness of Sabbath's is that he is not wholly incapable of love, and in these, his seemingly terminal, moments the memory of it returns to plague him. He thinks a lot about his family, and above all of his adored elder brother, killed in the war. The immeasurable loss, from which he has never wholly recovered, also destroyed the happiness of his parents. 'This is human life,' says his mother, by way of comforting him. 'There is a great hurt that everyone has to endure.'

He is never quite free of his family bonds; after her death his mother haunts Sabbath, even when he is with Drenka. He wears and winds his dead brother's military-issue watch as if to do so constitutes a secularized act of ritual mourning. Love of a brother, as Morris Sabbath discovers like King David before him, can 'be not stranger but stronger even than the erotic'. Caught in such treacherous pieties, recalling with pain the 'rich times' when the brothers caught bluefish and were sometimes allowed to cook them, Sabbath seems drained of mockery and defiance, left with nothing but desperation. Yet except perhaps when thinking of his brother he is not sure that he is capable of not faking; even in what looks like an extremity of deprivation he is always, however faintly, asking himself whether he isn't acting: 'Despite the arthritis that disfigured his fingers, in his heart he was the puppeteer still, a lover and master of guile, artifice, and the unreal – this he hadn't torn out of himself. When that went, he *would* be dead.' To be genuinely himself he needs to fake.

The energy of this book is amazing. As Sabbath remarks, 'For a pure sense of being tumultuously alive, you can't beat the nasty side of existence.' Farcically tragic invention is matched by sheer colloquial vigour. Or the mood may change: Sabbath, now easily identified as just another panhandling bum, finds himself sitting in a subway train beside a young woman who can, for a moment, play Cordelia to his Lear. Of course this lyrical episode ends badly, ends farcically, but the point is made. Such scenes have a force and originality that strike me as extraordinary, as springing from some deeper source than that which supplied good, skilful books such as *The Professor of Desire* or the recent *Operation Shylock*; or perhaps any of Roth's books since, it must be said, *Portnoy's Complaint*.

Here is the aged Sabbath giving his views on adultery: 'A world without adultery is unthinkable. The brutal inhumanity of those against it. Don't you agree? The sheer fucking depravity of their views. The *madness*. There is no punishment too extreme for the crazy bastard who came up with the idea of fidelity.' And when he is told, by his generous but finally disgusted friend, that he is nothing but a battered relic of the Sixties, a pathetic, outmoded crank, sad, lost, isolated, he stands up unabashed for isolation, preferring it to the captivity of civilized life. Panhandling in the subway with his cardboard cup, he is again caught between truth and fake; in one sense that is where he belongs, in another he is still fooling around, faking. Finally dismissed as a 'filthy, sick son of a bitch', no longer plausible as a diabolic manifestation of unlimited life, he proclaims his just and implacable hatred of the denying world.

The end of the novel is complex and beautifully sustained: there is a great scene in the desecrated cemetery, where all noted as 'beloved' on their tombstones are dead and probably beloved no longer; and a perfect narrative of an interview with a hundred-year-old man remembered from youth. As we may suppose of his author, Sabbath has a certain reverence for extreme old age, perhaps because in spite of the casualties inevitably sustained it has at least delayed the usual defeat by death, which will have to be content with a points victory. But Sabbath encounters this old man in the course of a demented search for what is left of his brother, and he steals from the old man's house a bundle of his brother's belongings, which include a Purple Heart and a carefully rolled Stars and Stripes. There follows a last vivid memory of that brother, of the Jersey shore – a not unfamiliar locale in Roth, but here most passionately evoked – and of childhood love. He says goodbye to the memory of Drenka (encapsulated in a candid recollection of an undinist adventure), and even finds time to indulge in an extremely detailed fantasy of his wife masturbating.

Returning, however unwillingly, to her New England house – having nowhere else to go – he finds himself shut out, finally isolated. He makes his will, plans a last visit to Drenka's grave. But one last unwanted encounter with the forces of decency in the shape of Drenka's disgusted policeman son leaves him alive in spite of himself, and now full of hatred. We are at last invited to despise him, but that is a mere feint – novelists feint as well as puppeteers and con men – and instead we are left admiring the unextinguished energy of his contempt for the decent.

For all the anarchic force of its language there is nothing unruly about the structure of *Sabbath's Theater*; it is hardly news that Roth is a bold and skilful architect. Like his hero, he has illusionist skills, everywhere in evidence – a sort of puppeteer, a virtuoso of both dissimulation and impersonation. It is well known that he likes to set himself difficult technical problems: *Deception* is an example, a novel entirely in dialogue, finely exploiting its self-imposed constraints, and, although not in what one immediately recognizes as his palette, it gives a new colouring to certain of Roth's obsessive interests. He is fascinated by all the different possible ways of doing narrative, as well as by the relation of the told to the teller, the problem to the solver. Roth may well believe, or wish one to believe that he believes, that writers are, or ought to be, in certain respects, quite like Sabbath: from *Deception* we learn that the nature of the writer is 'exploration, fixation, isolation, venom, fetishism, austerity, levity, perplexity, childishness, *et cetera*. The nose in the seam of the undergarment – *that's* the writer's nature. I*m*purity . . .' The speaker here is condemning Lonoff, the austere, temperate, dignified author celebrated in *The Ghost Writer*. He is also impersonating his own author. It is almost redundant to point out that 'The terrible ambiguity of the "I"' is a topic that obsesses Roth. The provisional title of a biography of the alter ego Zuckerman is *Improvisations on a Self*. In Roth there is no question of the disappearance of the author; he is there, sometimes even under his own name. But he is there on his own terms, in charge; he doesn't despise Lonoff's control of affairs.

Other themes recur, whatever the narrative finesse; one is the distinctiveness of being an American Jew, so different from being Israeli, yet equally bound to a terrible past and to connoisseurship of the varieties of anti-Semitism. These preoccupations take many different narrative shapes, but the novelist's passion for strange, newfangled narratives is always in some respects a passion for his own narrative, his improvisations on himself. Roth likes to look back over his own work and consider, in its many transformations, the terrible ambiguity of the 'I'.

Sometimes he does so with that saving hilarity which can be a mask of tragedy. *Sabbath's Theater* is funny, but as a means to an end; it succeeds in the task Shakespeare set his young lords in *Love's Labour's Lost*, to move wild laughter in the face of death. Possibly another laugh might come from awareness of the pretentiousness of that intention; but all the same this book is undoubtedly, in the final analysis, about matters of life and death.

Even for Sabbath life cannot be one long bout with a matching carnality, a Drenka. He cannot quite exclude the other kinds of love; to do that is one of the few illusionist tricks he hasn't mastered. In normal circumstances he has a crafty double, supervising his tricks – so permanent a companion that he can't easily distinguish between the true and the fake. Happiness, among other things, is always likely to be whisked away as if by an omnipotent conjurer. In *The Professor of Desire* what seems like true contentment in love is shadowed by the sense that this is not what can last, not even what the happy man can make himself want to last; desertion of some sort will move in on happiness, as death on life. The trick is to use this intelligence as the propellant of a great kick at misery. If it has to be delivered by one whose opinions or improper prejudices, whose monstrous conduct, are disgusting, well, too bad. Others may make their way to the tomb measured and considerate; good for them, poor suckers. But theirs is not the only way: there is a diabolic alternative. Of course it will all end in despair, in hell – the hell of rejection by the *salauds* of respectability. But hell is energy, even if it has to be the energy of hatred, as if a passion for the body of a Drenka must be converted, by the action of time and disease and death, into a salutary loathing for the world that permits and institutionalizes horror – the horror of her cancer, the horror of the brother's death at twenty-two.

King Lear, with whom Sabbath advertises a certain affinity – each, in his way, a foolish and a fond old man – rages not against his own faults but against justice, as it is conceived by its exponents, the corrupt judge and the beadle with the lash – all covert lechers, all enemies of life, of a sexual freedom they secretly envy. It is this justice that Sabbath rages against; and so, with all his characteristic ironies and reservations, does the author of this splendidly wicked book.

Index